D0843367

Flavor and Soul

FLAVOR

and SOUL

*Italian America at
Its African American Edge*

John Gennari

The University of Chicago Press
Chicago and London

The University of Chicago Press, Chicago 60637
The University of Chicago Press, Ltd., London
© 2017 by The University of Chicago
Published 2017. Printed in the United States of America

26 25 24 23 22 21 20 19 18 17   1 2 3 4 5

ISBN-13: 978-0-226-42832-1 (cloth)
ISBN-13: 978-0-226-42846-8 (e-book)
DOI: 10.7208/chicago/9780226428468.001.0001

Library of Congress Cataloging-in-Publication Data
Names: Gennari, John, author.
Title: Flavor and soul :
Italian America at its African American edge / John Gennari.
Description: Chicago ; London : The University of Chicago Press,
2017. | Includes bibliographical references and index.
Identifiers: LCCN 2016029051 | ISBN 9780226428321
(cloth : alk. paper) | ISBN 9780226428468 (e-book)
Subjects: LCSH: Italian Americans—Ethnic identity. |
Italian Americans—Social life and customs. | African
Americans—Relations with Italian Americans. | Popular
culture—United States. | United States—Ethnic relations.
Classification: LCC E184.I8 G43 2017 | DDC 305.85/1073—dc23
LC record available at https://lccn.loc.gov/2016029051

♾ This paper meets the requirements of ANSI/NISO Z39.48-1992
(Permanence of Paper).

In memory of Remo Nicholas Gennari (1926–2011)
and Clara Maria Dal Cortivo Gennari (1928–2015)

and

In honor of Giulia Naima Bernard Gennari
and Isabella Pannonica Bernard Gennari

Contents

INTRODUCTION

"Who Put the Wop in Doo-Wop?"

There was something about the sight of those four Italians, decked out in city slicker clothes, snapping their fingers and acting like Negroes, that must not have set too well with the folks in the Midwest. We were kind of exotic, which meant foreign, and that, in turn, meant dangerous.
    DION DIMUCCI, on his appearance with Dion
    and the Belmonts on *American Bandstand* in 1958

My dream was to become Frank Sinatra.
    MARVIN GAYE

Negroes and Italians beat me and shaped me, and my allegiance is there.
    AMIRI BARAKA, "The Death of Horatio Alger"[1]

Three scenes to set the stage and establish the tone:

I

August 27, 1989. Bensonhurst, a predominantly Italian neighborhood in the southern part of Brooklyn. Four days earlier, a group of four African American teenagers from Bedford-Stuyvesant, a black neighborhood a few miles away, had come to look at a used car. A group of some thirty men, mostly Italian American, accosted them. In the chaos that ensued, a young man from the Italian posse shot and killed one of the young black men. On this day, a group of demonstrators meet at the site of the murder, Bay

Ridge Avenue at the corner of Twentieth Avenue, for a prayer service in honor of the victim, Yusuf Hawkins, followed by a protest march up Twentieth Avenue. A newspaper estimates that there are 100 marchers, 250 policemen, and 400 counterdemonstrators on hand. The latter, almost all Italians from the neighborhood, hurl racist slurs at the mostly black demonstrators. Many wave Italian and American flags. Some hoist watermelons as they spit out their taunts; these tend to be younger men who walk, talk, dance, and occupy public space in ways that combine an older mode of Italian American street toughness with newer, fresher stylizations drawn from hip-hop music and the wider field of black urban youth culture.

One of the demonstrators that day is an Italian American graduate student named Joseph Sciorra. A native of Brooklyn and a student of local Italian American culture (later the author of the essay whose title I have borrowed for this introduction), Sciorra has been deeply disappointed by what he regards as obtuse and defensive responses to the tragedy from Italian American politicians and community leaders. To show his solidarity with the demonstrators, Sciorra shows up with a homemade poster board sign that reads "Italians against Racism."

"My use of the plural was a simple expression of hope," Sciorra would later write. What he encounters in Bensonhurst that day does little to nourish that hope:

> My sign and my whiteness in the midst of the predominately black demonstration got the attention of the Italians lining the sidewalk. People pointed in my direction, laughing, cursing, spitting. Some clearly thought it was a ludicrous proposition: Italians against racism. Others were incensed. My cardboard placard called into question the popular notion that joined Italian American identity and racial hatred in some natural and essentialist union. I was a race traitor, an internal threat to the prevailing local rhetoric.[2]

FIGURE 1. Bensonhurst-born New Yorker Stephanie Romeo joined Joseph Sciorra on his "Italians against Racism" march. Later she did this painting, "March for Yusuf, Sunday, August 27, 1989." (Courtesy of Stephanie Romeo.)

II

November 14, 1998, the final day of a conference at Hofstra University called "Frank Sinatra: The Man, the Music, the Legend." Coming just months after Sinatra's death, the conference has generated unprecedented media buzz for an ostensibly academic gathering. Joining professors and graduate students among the thousands in attendance are musicians (Vic Damone, Milt Hinton, Joe Bushkin, Monty Alexander, Al Grey, Bucky Pizzarelli, Ervin Drake), writers (Gary Giddins, Will Friedwald, Nick Tosches), celebrities (former Los Angeles Dodgers manager Tommy Lasorda, comedian Alan King), media and music industry professionals from across the globe, and a legion of devout Sinatraphiles. After I deliver a paper about Sinatra's relationship with his formidable mother, I am greeted by a woman of my own mother's generation up from Philadelphia. After an exchange of pleasantries, she wraps me in a big hug and plants a kiss on each cheek.

Later in the conference I present a second paper, this one focused on hip-hop's appropriation of Sinatra as an icon of stylish, renegade masculinity, what black men call an OG (original gangster). I'm on a panel that includes a fellow scholar who talks about Sinatra's use of profane and aggressive language as a weapon of ethnic retribution and another who discusses sexual innuendo in "Nice 'n' Easy," "Witchcraft," and other Sinatra songs. The Philadelphia woman, all ears in the front row, is not happy. No sooner does the audience Q&A kick off than she stands up to speak with fierce righteousness about coming from a family and community that revere Sinatra as a great Italian on the order of Michelangelo and Leonardo da Vinci. "I did not drive all the way up here from Philadelphia," she says, seething, "to hear this great man disgraced with talk of"—now she points her finger at the defamers of the tribe seated on the dais—"swearing, sex, and . . . and . . . mobsters."

For our panel, the scene is not unprecedented or even surprising. We have attended many Italian American studies conferences whose mission is to counteract or, better, transcend Italian American stereotypes—conferences, alas, at which people routinely cry, break into song, kvetch about the food, read poems about their saintly or demonic mothers, and promise retribution for this or that *infamia*. More surprising and hopeful is the presence at this conference of at least a smattering of African Americans, fellow musicians and others, proud to pay tribute to a man they consider a stalwart friend of their people, an antiracist hero, and—not least—a superlative entertainer. A Detroit-based singer and pianist talks about Sinatra's fighting Jim Crow at hotels and nightclubs and applying special pressure on the Fontainebleau in Miami Beach to let her perform there in the early 1960s. Then comes her son, a journalist, to further lionize the Chairman of the Board and to proffer an intriguing defense of Sinatra's controversial 1981 performance at Sun City in apartheid South Africa. In 1987, at a Los Angeles NAACP event honoring Sinatra with its lifetime achievement award, protesters condemned Sinatra for that 1981 concert in South Africa. Here the journalist endorses the speech Sinatra gave that night condemning "the bigots who criticize me" and stating categorically, "Botha is a bum." The journalist goes even further, speculating that perhaps the *real* reason Sinatra went to South Africa was to work covertly to bring down South African president P. W. Botha and—yes—to spring Nelson Mandela from prison. Many in the Hofstra audience nod in agreement.[3]

III

A few months later, in the spring of 1999, I sit in a New York hotel lobby with the actor Giancarlo Esposito. Esposito is a mixed-race black Italian, the son of an African American opera singer from Alabama who spent part of her career in Italy. I've been fascinated by his range of performances as straight-up black characters (notably in Spike Lee's *School Daze*, *Do the Right Thing*, *Mo' Better Blues*, and *Malcolm X*), Latinos (notably as the drug lord Esteban in the 1994 movie *Fresh*, foreshadowing his award-winning portrayal of Gus Fring in the blockbuster cable series *Breaking Bad*), and, less often, black Italians. At the time we meet, he happens to be playing a black Italian character in the acclaimed NBC police drama *Homicide: Life on the Street*. FBI agent Mike Giardello, Esposito's character, is the prodigal son of Baltimore police lieutenant Al Giardello (Yaphet Kotto), affectionately known as G, an Afro-Sicilian who runs his detective squad like an Old World padrone and is fond of issuing sage pronouncements on what's wrong with America—such as "We Italians know that a proper red sauce has only tomatoes and garlic, not all these vegetables the Protestants are always throwing in there." I'm interviewing Esposito for a magazine profile. With me is my friend Ficre Ghebreyesus. Ficre, an Eritrean who emigrated from his country in the late 1970s, is a chef and restaurateur, a painter and photographer, and he is there to shoot pictures for the profile. Ficre moves deftly around Esposito and me in a silent dance, capturing beautiful

FIGURE 2. Actor Giancarlo Esposito during an interview with the author, New York City, May 1999. (Photograph by Ficre Ghebreyesus, Permission of Ficre Ghebreyesus Fine Arts.)

images of Esposito gesturing gracefully and talking animatedly about his life and work.

Esposito tells me the role he prizes as his "most Italian" was one he created for himself from whole cloth in the 1995 indie film *Blue in the Face*, improvising on the situations set up by writer Paul Auster and director Wayne Wang. The movie, like its better-known twin *Smoke*, is a hymn to what Auster calls "the People's Republic of Brooklyn," complete with statistics on the borough's polyglot ethnicity and documentary footage of local characters who reek of authenticity. Esposito's character, Tommy Finelli, is one of the regulars who hang out in Auggie's cigar store reading the racing form, copping a smoke, shooting the breeze.

Esposito's climactic riff comes when a black con artist (Malik Yoba) wanders into the store hawking fake Rolex watches. "I got the African price and the European price," he announces. Looking warily at Auggie (Harvey Keitel), he says, "I deal with the African first. Black people always first." He turns to Esposito, and the two start trading fours:

> **Esposito:** I'm not from Africa. My name is Tommy Finelli. That's my name.
>
> **Yoba:** What you doing hanging out in the neighborhood, man? How'd you get the name Finelli?
>
> **Esposito:** This *is* my neighborhood. I'm from Italy. My father's Italian, my mother's black.
>
> **Yoba:** You ain't no mulatto, you as black as me. Y'all want to be white, that's the problem.
>
> **Esposito:** How do you know what I am?

The improvisational format of *Blue in the Face* allowed Esposito to get up a costume from his own wardrobe of vintage clothes and to "think jazz." Esposito speaks of his friendships with jazz luminaries Dexter Gordon, Lee Konitz, Philly Joe Jones, and Russell Procope and lets on that he is studying jazz alto saxophone to "loosen up" from the classical piano he's played since childhood.

Sporting a porkpie hat and striking the easy hipster pose of a Count Basie sideman, Esposito takes his solo time in *Blue in the Face* to evoke a person and an experience that remain deeply etched in his memory. The name Tommy Finelli pays tribute to the man who sold Esposito his first house, one of those Italians whose lovingly tended backyards sing out to the neighborhood like a beautiful melody. "I remember feeling so at home on this little piece of land," Esposito recalls. "It was just a little seventy-five by one hundred foot lot, but every inch of it bore fruit. Cherry trees, a plum tree, a pear tree, an apple tree. You see, the Italians, they love working with their hands. They're about the earth, about nature, about sustaining themselves by themselves." As he talks, Esposito mimics the hand movements of a man working the soil, and the effect is just as expressive as when he demonstrates Thelonious

Monk's hand spread on the keyboard and Charlie Parker's fingering of the alto sax. For Esposito, arboriculture meets jazz craft in the laying on of hands.

After I finish the interview, Ficre—a jazz aficionado and expert gardener in addition to his many other interests and talents—takes up his own lively conversation with Esposito. The men speak in mellifluous Italian. Both retain the language from their childhoods, Esposito's as the son of a theater set designer from Naples, Ficre's as the subject of the colonial Italian education system in his native Eritrea.

Suddenly it hits me: here in this hotel lobby on the edge of Central Park, by virtue of my skin tone I am the only one in our group that most New Yorkers might perceive as Italian American. But in many respects I am the least Italian of the three of us.[4]

The Contact Zone

This is a book about the fascinating and complicated intersection between Italian America and African America, a space of hopeful encounter and wary suspicion, dangerous, sometimes violent collision, and magnificent, joyous collusion. It's a study of expressive ethnicity and raciality with a focus on the contact zone—the edge and the overlap—between Italian American and African American cultures. I come at this with a personal and professional history located right at that edge, deep within the overlap, firmly inside the contact zone.[5] In being so situated I hope to illuminate something important about these two cultures, but something even more important about the dynamics of their interculturality. Anthropologist Fredrik Barth defined ethnicity as a set of performances of difference and sameness enacted at the boundaries between groups, performances that both reflect and create interdependencies across the boundaries.[6] I suggest that performances at the boundary between Italian culture and black culture—the mutual and interdependent creation of an Italian cultural self and a black cultural self—have made an indelible mark on American

culture writ large. I also aim to show how expressive culture—
music, film and other media, sports, and food—can help us think
more deeply and in more subtle and nuanced ways about race and
ethnicity.

Although I began this project at a time when my scholarship
and teaching were primarily centered in African American history and culture, my vantage point here is that of an Italian American curious about my tribe's reckoning with its place and role in
the national racial system. I'm fascinated by the ways Italian
Americans have occupied a liminal and transactional space in the
ethnoracial order of the United States—at once white, near-white,
and dark ("the hottest of the white ethnics," Pellegrino D'Acierno
asserts, "white but temperamentally and erotically dark");[7] northern and southern; putative heirs to both Renaissance high culture
and the criminal underworld; colorfully emotional ghetto tribalists and assimilated suburban conformists; fashion and culinary
sophisticates and Jersey Shore guidos. Italian Americans, I argue,
have mediated US concepts of black and white, alien and citizen,
outsider and insider, high culture and low culture, masculine and
feminine, in ways that have decisively shaped American thinking
about race and ethnicity.

In recent decades, scholarship unpacking the interracial histories of American entertainment, labor, politics, and civil rights
activism has taught us a great deal about Irish blackface minstrels
and Irish/black Civil War draft riots; the intimate association between Jews and blacks from vaudeville to early rock and roll, the
1963 March on Washington, and the welfare rights movement;
cultural and political crossover between blacks, Asians, Native
Americans, and whites from colonial era American revolutionaries "playing Indian" to West Coast South Asian youths embracing blackness through hip-hop.[8] The black-Italian nexus has figured less prominently in accounts of US interracialism in spite of a
long history we might telescope by invoking a handful of examples:
nineteenth-century black opera star Thomas Bowers, known
as "the Colored Mario" because his voice sounded so much like
that of the Italian tenor Giovanni Mario; Sicilian American poet

Philip Lamantia, who pinned the roots of his surrealist aesthetic to the negritude movement in France, bebop jazz in New York and San Francisco, and a long forgotten (if ever known) Afrocentric, Egyptophilic wing of the Italian Renaissance; the great Brooklyn Dodgers catcher Roy Campanella ("little bell" in Italian), whose Sicilian father peddled vegetables in his native Philadelphia, one of the handful of black players who broke the color line in major league baseball in the 1940s; the Rat Pack, that alluring spectacle of outcast ethnic excess helmed in Las Vegas and Hollywood by Sinatra, Dean Martin (Dino Crocetti), and Sammy Davis Jr.; the tight Bronx/Harlem association between Dion DiMucci and Frankie Lymon, of Frankie Lymon and the Teenagers, raising that ever-pressing question, "Who put the wop in doo-wop?"; *Black Caesar* and other blaxploitation films of the early 1970s, with their stock formula of black gangsters vanquishing Italians for control of Harlem; "Franco's Italian Army," the group of Italian American fans of the NFL's Pittsburgh Steelers, cheering wildly for star Afro-Italian running back Franco Harris; LA hip-hop star Snoop Dogg titling one of his early CDs *The Doggfather* and deftly tossing off the line "And Lucky Luciano 'bout to sing soprano."[9]

It was the lynching of Italians in turn-of-the-century New Orleans that first moved W. E. B. Du Bois, the pioneering African American intellectual and civil rights leader, to "conceive the plight of other minority groups"; later he penned strong condemnations of the "Anglo-Saxon cult" that was lobbying to restrict the immigration of Italians and others, even as he was among the first to systematically theorize whiteness as a privilege that European immigrants learned to embrace in spite of—or because of—their own experiences of racial discrimination.[10] Black writer James Baldwin lived in a largely Italian neighborhood in Greenwich Village in the 1940s and '50s, one reason his novels *Giovanni's Room*, *Another Country*, and *If Beale Street Could Talk* feature important Italian and Italian American characters.[11] One night he found himself menaced by a white mob on a street close to the San Remo, a neighborhood restaurant where previously he'd been welcomed only when he showed up with the president of Harper and Row. The

FIGURE 3. In the 1970s, Pittsburgh Steelers star running back Franco Harris, born to an African American veteran of World War II and his Italian "war bride," served as symbolic commandant of "Franco's Italian Army," whose other members were Steelers fans from Pittsburgh's Italian American community. (Detre Library and Archives, Heinz History Center.)

owners now pulled him inside, closed the restaurant, and sheltered him until the danger subsided. "I was *in*, and anybody who messed with me was *out*," Baldwin later wrote. "I was no longer black for them and they had ceased to be white for me, for they sometimes introduced me to their families with every appearance of affection and pride and exhibited not the remotest interest in whatever my sexual proclivities chanced to be." Baldwin concluded: "They had fought me very hard to prevent this moment, but perhaps we were all much relieved to have gotten beyond the obscenity of color."[12]

Across the Hudson River in Newark, Amiri Baraka grew up among working-class Italians he later reckoned as suffering from a serious case of "it's supposed to be better than this for white people." In 1967, when riots broke out in the city and Baraka led a brigade of black revolutionaries in an assault on the city's power structure, his key target was Newark's Italian American leadership: Mayor Hugh Addonizio, ward boss and vigilante Anthony Imperiale, and the police captains who sanctioned the beatings of Baraka and other black activists. (In Newark, Baraka wrote, "Italian Power must be second only to that in the Vatican.") Still, Baraka championed Italian American cultural ethnicity as an important antidote to the stultifying force of whiteness, and he invoked Italian immigrant anarchists as an important part of the American left's usable past.[13]

Mindful of such cases, in this book I work against received notions of Italian Americans as either straight-up white or not quite white, and against both romantic and benighted assumptions about a black-Italian relationship that is uniformly and predictably either hospitable or hostile. By exploring how Italian American performance in the arts, sports, and foodways continually complicates and reconfigures racial boundaries, I show that the intersections and overlaps of Italian American and African American expressive culture constitute a distinctive space in the American imagination. This is so, I argue, because of common traditions of vocal and bodily performance marked by intensity of ear and eye and a penchant for extroverted, charismatic presentations of the self; a shared set of fluid gender dynamics that scrambles the schematic boundaries of the dominant culture (with matriarchs who nurture through fierce, antisentimental toughness and patriarchs given to passion and tenderness); a pragmatic approach to the difficulties and cruelties of life, which leads paradoxically to a heightened capacity for indulgence and enjoyment; and overlapping—sometimes competing and conflicting—claims to US histories of suffering and pleasure, oppression and power, exclusion and inclusion. These commonalities and affinities certainly are not limited to relations between Italian Americans and African Americans, nor do they categorize all (or any particular) instances of black-Italian contact. I'm writing about a particular kind of cultural overlap that fascinates me.

I've organized the book as a set of interlocking case studies. We begin with Frank Sinatra, the dominant icon of Italian America, but also a formidable figure in the interracial American imagination owing to his narrative as a racial/ethnic outsider who becomes the ultimate American insider. I first locate Sinatra in concise histories of Italian American immigration and American popular music, then consider at some length how his ethnic corner boy background, clannishness, cunning working of the system, gangster glamour, and (most of all) grandiosity of the self have resonated with black hip-hop celebrity performers and entrepreneurs. After narrating some of my personal family history in relation to Sinatra, I explore the intriguing relationship between Sinatra and his legendarily colorful mother. I map out a pattern in which Italian American and African American men have been marked as dangerous public enemies while Italian and black mothers have been sentimentalized as tough yet surpassingly nurturing figures crucial to the "mothering" of the entire nation. Chapter 2 enlarges and intensifies this metaphor of national mothering, arguing that the expressive cultures of black and Italian music and food, both born out of warping poverty, oppression, and dislocation, together have occupied roles of nurturance, material and spiritual feeding, and affirmation of body and soul for American society as a whole. In a series of fragments drawing on black and Italian cultural history, literature, television food shows, performance art, and cultural criticism, I explore the dialectics of pain and pleasure, suffering and joy, deprivation and abundance that have produced bounties of rhythm and melody, flavor and soulfulness intrinsic to the nation's spiritual and psychic health.

Chapter 3 considers African American film director Spike Lee's early "Italian American" films *Do the Right Thing* and *Jungle Fever* against the backdrop of the New Hollywood and the urban decline narrative of the 1980s and '90s. I argue that Lee's effort to define and market a black Brooklyn neighborhood ethos against the national image of inner-city ghetto danger and privation is best understood in dynamic relation to established Italian American narratives of family and neighborhood cohesion such as *The Godfather*, and to newer narratives of neighborhood and tribal decline and dislocation such as those generated by the Hawkins murder in Bensonhurst. I suggest that Lee, in spite of his problematic representations of both blackness and Italianness, captures something important about trajectories of black cultural renaissance and Italian American cultural exhaustion in the early 1990s. Chapter 4 makes the perhaps counterintuitive argument that the hypervisible and much discussed blackening of American basketball since the 1980s has been accompanied by—and to no small degree enabled by—the sport's equally important if far less recognized Italianization. My argument centers on big-time men's college basketball, where Italian American coaches, broadcasters, and marketers have operated both as mediators of black masculinity and as paragons of a style of charismatic ethnicity I call (borrowing from D'Acierno) *dagotude*. In these two chapters, as throughout the book, my central geographic focus is on the urban Northeast, especially New York City, New Jersey, Connecticut, and Pennsylvania.

In a concluding chapter, I review the history of the black-Italian cultural weave in the context of both US racial politics and the American intellectual history of race and ethnicity. I briefly consider the racial dynamics of the television series *The Sopranos*, by far the most powerful representation of Italian American life and culture in the first years of the twenty-first century. I end by spotlighting two people—the aforementioned Eritrean American artist Ficre Ghebreyesus and the writer Kym Ragusa, whose memoir about her experience as the daughter of an African American mother and an Italian American father has positioned her as a powerful black Italian voice in the US multiculturalism movement—to consider how expressive cultures of the eye, the ear, and the hand, as practiced in transnational and multiracial contexts, both enrich and complicate conventional models of US race and ethnicity.

Throughout this book I try to counteract the tendency to dismiss white ethnicity as *simply and always* a denial or avoidance of white privilege and a cover for politics against people of color, even as I recognize that it has certainly been that. I find it ironic that critical race studies, in spite of its celebration of difference and its stated intention of deconstructing Eurocentric binaries, persists in thinking and talking about a singular, reified whiteness. I propose that we try to think about race and ethnicity in ways that deepen our understanding of history *and* develop a future-oriented focus in which we engage dynamically and creatively in a continuing process of racial and ethnic reinvention.[14]

A Sensuous Scholarship

Although its core topics center the book in American popular culture since the 1960s, my discussions of music, food, and sport invoke histories of African and Italian people reaching back to the transatlantic slave trade and the "great wave" of southern and eastern European immigration. As befits my training in American studies, the underlying subtext of the book is the shape and tenor of US national culture—specifically, the ways black and Italian expressive cultural practices have enhanced the flavor and soul of the country. My attribution of flavor and soul to blacks and Italians is meant not to imply that other groups lack these qualities, but to underscore their heightened salience within common discourses of and about these particular groups. And if framing my discussion of blacks and Italians with concepts like soulfulness and soundfulness (a big one in the pages that follow) makes me a sinner in the church of antiessentialism, well so be it. Hailing as I do from a long line of anticlerical Italian Catholic sensualists, savory flavor and majestic sound are essential to me and hence also to this book.

I believe strongly that it is in literature, the arts, and what I am calling expressive culture that the most meaningful, searching, creative, and finally consequential molding of our racial and ethnic lives takes place. We must look carefully at the realms of cultural production and consumption, that is, to fully understand how the boundaries of the American ethnoracial social order come to be defined and experienced. It is here that narratives, symbols, and aesthetic forms give tangible shape, substance, and texture to the ways race and ethnicity are lived out at the level of desire, imagination, and feeling. This is not to deny the hugely determinative nature of political, economic, legalistic, and institutional processes and spaces or to suggest that life in the public sphere does not make itself felt at the level of the private, the internal, or the imaginative. One need only read Louise DeSalvo's stunning essay "Color: White/Complexion: Dark," recounting her immigrant Italian grandmother's dehumanizing experience at the hands of a US customs agent, to grasp how state policies and protocols figure preeminently in what is now commonly called the social construction of race.[15] But the upshot of such reading is to make one understand that the meaning and the feeling of a racial classification system (or a census, an application form, a passport, a health report, a school report card) may not be fully revealed by the methods of political science, sociology, or other social sciences. We need the insights of the writer and the artist along with the scholar and the cultural critic to help us decipher the literature and the art.

"[The] macrolevel language of generalizing science," Yiorgos Anagnostou avers, "cannot name the vagaries of identity formation—the notion of identity as becoming—including depths, ambiguities, and contradictions at the level of lived experience." This call for attention to vagary, depth, ambiguity, and contradiction is especially vital and timely when it comes to recent academic discourses and formations in the area of race and ethnic studies. Too often a knee-jerk, generalizing race language freighted with monolithic schemes of dominance/subordination and racism/antiracism gets in the way of what might be most illuminating and important in relations between people of color and white ethnics. I again defer to Anagnostou:

> One of the most potent contributions of critical studies of whiteness lies in establishing the historical participation of the peoples from Europe in the reproduction of U.S. racial hierarchies and their reward with privileges. But once this fact and its implications are acknowledged, one might ask, how about those "white ethnics" who supported interracial coalitions, fought to include the immigrant left in historiography, interrogated racism within their own

communities, engaged in activism for fair-housing policies and immigrant rights, or supported affirmative action policies?[16]

How about Joseph Sciorra bravely battling racism in Benson-hurst? Or Vito Marcantonio, the democratic socialist who while serving in the US Congress in the 1930s and '40s advocated for poor Italians and Puerto Ricans in his East Harlem district and fought vehemently for black civil rights? Or civil rights orga-nizer Viola Liuzzo, shot to death in Alabama in 1965 after help-ing Martin Luther King Jr., John Lewis, and other black leaders mobilize the epic marches from Selma to Montgomery? Or Sicil-ian American record producer Cosimo Matassa, who engineered the "New Orleans sound" of 1950s and '60s rhythm and blues and rock and roll in his work with Little Richard, Fats Domino, Big Joe Turner, Aaron Neville, and other local black musicians?

I have read with great interest the work of historians and soci-ologists who conceive of US ethnicity as a one-way, linear process of gradual assimilation to the political and cultural mainstream and who in following that logic have posited the emergence in post-1960s America of a largely or purely "symbolic ethnicity" or a "twilight of ethnicity."[17] In my own work as a professor in a race and ethnic studies program centered on people of color, my teach-ing and my university activism bluntly emphasize racial hierarchy and white privilege as defining features of American society and our own community. Still, neither the literature on the declining significance of ethnicity nor the critical race studies dogma helps me to behold and decipher the nuances and complexities of the three scenarios with which I opened this introduction.

For that I turn to—and aim with this book to augment and amplify—a body of scholarship that has emerged in recent years at the crossroads between American studies, history, ethnic studies, and cultural studies. I feel a special indebtedness to the work of Gerald Early, Thomas Ferraro, and Pellegrino D'Acierno, each of whom engages American culture with intellectual dex-terity, aesthetic discernment, and an unmistakable personal signature; to Robert Orsi, Joseph Sciorra, and Simone Cinotto for their agile and brilliantly illuminating interdisciplinary approaches to Italian American culture; to Jennifer Guglielmo and Salvatore Salerno for their groundbreaking edited volume *Are Italians White? How Race Is Made in America* (2003); to Laura Cook Kenna, Fred Gardaphé, and George De Stefano for their powerful insights into Italian American masculinity; and to David Roediger, Matthew Frye Jacobson, George Lipsitz, and Grace Hale for seminal, paradigm-shifting work in the history of US whiteness that is rich and multilayered in ways that "whiteness studies," as it came to be known, sometimes is not. All have helped me develop my framework for thinking about the dynamics of US race and ethnicity and the particular shape and rhythm of the black-Italian cultural weave.[18]

In a period when the academic humanities commonly are seen as a preserve of theory-besotted obscurantism—a slanted perception based on wanton cherry-picking of the evidence—I seek a tone that is warm, openhearted, and true to the spirit of what Thomas Ferraro simply but perfectly names *feeling Italian*. This entails more reference to my personal experience than perhaps anybody but my mother would want to read. I can only say that, in the interest of at least the appearance of scholarly gravity, I tried hard to cut down on the book's I-ness, but in doing so found myself unable to deliver the particular argument, analysis, or—most of all—*feeling* I was going for. The black Italian world I live in is one in which people are deeply attuned to what they hear, see, touch, taste, and feel. What seems to me most appropriate for representing and interpreting that world is something Paul Stoller calls "sensuous scholarship," the kind of scholarship in which it is possible for Stoller's fellow anthropologist Thomas Belmonte to write of his Italian father: "I can still see [his] hands. Even in old age, they are as powerful as a champion boxer's but capable of the finest precision. . . . The creases of his hands are still stained with black engine grease. His palm may not tell you his future, but from its lines you can read the story of his life. He labored."[19] I too hail from a family steeped in traditions of handwork and blue-collar labor, with a father, a welder, who worked with fire and metals and a mother, a seamstress, who worked with needle and fabric. As a result, I cannot help but find bracing, transforming inspiration in the work of Carlo Rotella, especially his book *Good with Their Hands: Boxers, Bluesmen, and Other Characters from the Rust Belt* (2002), a work of serious cultural analysis whose every beautifully crafted sentence carries the imprint of his Sicilian paternal grandmother's thimble and the melodious ring of his Catalan maternal grandfather's violin.[20]

Like many working-class Italian American households, mine was one where privacy was hard to come by and loud voices constantly ricocheted off the walls, conditions that made for a loving family life but worked against a reading habit. "Shut up, Johnny's trying to read!" my mother would yell at the top of her ample lungs, adding another sonic layer to the cacophony of television, radio, sewing machine, electric mixer, and boisterous relatives. Perhaps this experience predisposed me to a heightened interest in the sociality of sound and to the use of a scholarly tool James Clifford calls "the ethnographic ear."[21] I am interested in sound worlds, or audible spaces, that include but also exceed the boundaries of music. "How can you not talk about identity when talking about music?" Josh Kun asks in *Audiotopia: Music, Race, and America* (2005). Kun's approach to music is a powerful way to think about sound more generally, especially in his emphasis on the practice of listening as key to subjectivity.

> When you hear it, music makes you immediately conscious of your identity because something outside of you is entering your body— alien sounds emitted from strangers you sometimes cannot see that enter, via vibration and frequency, the very bones and tissue of your being. All musical listening—(*all* listening, I insist)—is a form of confrontation, or encounter, of the meeting of worlds and meanings, when identity is made self-aware and is, therefore, menaced through its own interrogation.[22]

Kun suggests that when we listen with critical depth, music proves to be "one of our most valuable sites for witnessing the performance of racial and ethnic difference against the grain of national citizenships that work to silence and erase those differences."[23] I will go even further and suggest that only through an acute attention to the larger auditory realm, including but not limited to music, can we register the nuances of difference, sameness, affiliation, and disaffiliation indispensable to a full reckoning with issues of cultural identity and power both between *and* within racial and ethnic groups.

We live at a time in American history when a heightened awareness of police violence against African Americans coexists with a semiofficial ethos of multiculturalism under which many of us regularly participate in dinners, festivals, and other enjoyable events designed to "celebrate our differences." *Race* carries connotations of heaviness and intractability; it is thought of as a problem we need to solve, a serious conversation we need to have. *Ethnicity* signifies pleasurable cultural immersion, renewal, discovery, feel-good heritage activity like international travel, language and cooking classes, authentic wedding music and religious rituals, and arts appreciation. There's a commonly held notion of a clean distinction between race, an identity held to be rooted in either biology or sociopolitical construction, and ethnicity, an identity or a resource assumed to be grounded in culture. In practice, this distinction and these definitions prove difficult to maintain logically and coherently—especially in a book like this, where cultural notions of both blackness and Italianness cross over between people ostensibly situated on either side of a US race line, and where both blacks and Italians engage in discourses of belonging rooted in metaphors of blood (*Blood of My Blood* is the name Richard Gambino gave to his founding work of Italian American studies; *Bloods* is the name Wallace Terry gave to his oral history of black Vietnam War veterans, borrowing the term black men of that generation used to refer to each other).[24] But even if we agreed to use *race* and *ethnicity* loosely or interchangeably—or, better, to use them with an acute awareness of their own historical and political constructedness—we would still be left with most scholars, intellectuals, artists, and social activists emphasizing the painful wounds of our racial/ethnic history and most heritage entrepreneurs, corporate advertisers, politicians, and school principals spotlighting the positive, heartwarming, uplifting nature of our glorious diversity.

Writer and editor Bill Tonelli asserts, with no small ethnocentric bravado but also with the sanction of professional opinion polling, that Italians are the most envied of all American ethnic groups. To the extent that such envy exists, we can assume it hinges largely on amiable stereotypes of abundant food and a warm, convivial family life. Tonelli's explanation does not exclude these notions, but it puts them in a larger context. "To be Italian was the most fun you could have and still be white," he recalled of his own youth in Philadelphia in the 1950s and '60s. "That you could be passionate, you could be loud, you could be maybe a little dangerous, you could definitely have some anti-authority traits as a group and as a culture." But there was a line you didn't want to cross: the race line. "You don't want to take it too far. You don't want to be Puerto Rican, you don't want to be black, you don't want to be poor, you don't want to be underclass, you don't want to be part of some permanent despised minority. But as an Italian, you somehow bridge that. You're seen as being passionate, loud, flamboyant, but also one of the descendants of the race that essentially built civilization."[25]

There is so much to unpack here that I will barely even try—at least for now. In many respects this whole book is simultaneously an elaboration and a repudiation of what Tonelli is saying here, with his blithe assumptions about what it means to be white and nonwhite and about what qualifies as civilization. But if we recognize the transitional spaces, the liminal areas where Tonelli is situating post—World War II urban Italian Americans—the edges between inside and outside, conformity and transgression, respectability and stigma, polite culture and freewheeling sociality—we must acknowledge his keen insight into the ways Italian Americans have defined exactly where the race line is drawn in American culture. Implicit in Tonelli's banter is that Italians at one time *were* an underclass and a despised minority, then they were not, and this had everything to do with their whiteness; then they became an envied ethnic group, and this had everything to do with their colorful resistance to whiteness's cultural norms.

A familiar argument about nineteenth-century white minstrels holds that by performing in blackface, then removing the face paint, they highlighted their whiteness by making it clear that their performances of blackness (flamboyance, passion, bodily appetite, the kind of expressive freedom that was attributed to the most unfree people in the nation) were just that—masked performances, not the reality of their actual, civilized selves. But what if the mask *is* the real self, or the self—like Dion and the Belmonts "decked out in city slicker clothes, snapping their fingers and acting like Negroes," or Marvin Gaye dreaming of becoming Frank Sinatra—one really wants to be? Perhaps the reason blacks and Italians have been drawn to each other, both as intimates and as antagonists, is because of a similar propensity for the kind of everyday performance that yields a forthright engagement with the real, the nitty-gritty, the unvarnished fundamentals of life. It is here, in the region of performed reality—in the space where, as Pellegrino D'Acierno puts it, blacks and Italians "use the world of everyday practices" to enact "a work of total art"[26]—where pain and pleasure are constant companions, the mournful and the festive spill into each other, and the glandular and lowdown are kith and kin to the fine and exalted.

This, pure and simple, is the region of the blues, the great art form of the American South. The great theorist of the blues is a black Italophile from Alabama named Albert Murray. For the moment, he gets the last word:

> Long before there were southerners in the U.S.A., there were southerners in Italy, and it meant a certain climate, a certain hospitality, a certain musicality in the language, and sometimes even a certain kind of violence and tendency to vendetta. In the more learned

circles, the European vision of the Italian southerner is much like that of anyone who understands the American South. The feeling is that of an easeful relationship to culture and a spontaneity that says, deep down, the point of learning to cook all this food, and talk this way, and wear these fine clothes, is to have a good goddamn time, man.[27]

ONE

Top Wop

Italian Hot, Italian Cool

Frank Sinatra was born in Hoboken, New Jersey, in 1915, six years before the murder convictions—twelve years before the executions—of Nicola Sacco and Bartolomeo Vanzetti. Sacco and Vanzetti, a shoemaker and a fishmonger, Italian-born anarchists who believed fervently in a coming revolution on behalf of exploited workers, had been tried for the murders of a guard and paymaster at a factory in Braintree, Massachusetts. The 1921 trial and the long interval before their executions in 1927 took place in an atmosphere of intense hostility toward immigrants, especially those who held radical political views—this being the moment of the Russian Revolution and, in the United States, of a countervailing Red Scare. In 1924 a new federal law, the Johnson-Reed Act, imposed severe restrictions on US immigration, helping slow to a trickle the historic "great wave" in which, from 1880 to 1924, four million Italians, including Frank Sinatra's parents and many of their Hoboken neighbors, left Italy for America.[1]

The vast majority of these immigrants were fleeing the grinding poverty (*la miseria*) of Sicily and the Italian South (*mezzogiorno*). Many had worked on large landed estates (*latifundia*) under conditions the African American former slaves Frederick Douglass and Booker T. Washington appraised as more brutal than those found on the plantations of the American South. In fact, after the Civil War ended in 1865, it was largely Italian immigrant laborers, especially Sicilians, who replaced freed black slaves on sugar and cotton plantations in Louisiana, Mississippi, and eastern Texas. Many of these Italian immigrants found themselves subject to Jim Crow segregation laws and customs recently enacted by former slaveholders in an effort to preserve and augment white supremacy behind a rigorously maintained color line. In New Orleans, after the murder of a popular police chief in 1890, the acquittal of nineteen Italian men accused of the killing triggered an act of brutal mob vengeance in which eleven of the acquitted men were lynched and left hanging from lampposts and trees on Canal Street.

In the North, where segregation prevailed in a less fully entrenched and legally institutionalized mode, Italian immigrants were—in historian Thomas Guglielmo's crisp phrase—"white on arrival." This did not guarantee anything even remotely approaching meaningful freedom and economic security. "If the southern Italian peasant once had imagined that America's streets were paved with gold," Maria Laurino writes, "soon he learned, as the old story goes, that one, they weren't paved, and two, he was expected to pave them." Italians predominated in the backbreaking labor that produced much of the infrastructure (subway systems, streets, water and electrical lines, bridges and tunnels, residential, civic, and commercial buildings) of the newly modernizing cities of the Northeast and Midwest. In 1911, at the Triangle Shirtwaist Factory in lower Manhattan, 146 employees, most of them young Italian and Jewish immigrant girls, were killed in a fire that destroyed the building; many of the factory's seamstresses and tailors, trapped inside because the owners kept the doors locked to prevent the workers from taking breaks, leaped to their deaths from the upper floors.[2]

These events underscored the acute vulnerability and precarious existence of men and women who were not only poor and physically abused, but also subject to a racial discourse that portrayed them as dark-skinned, intellectually inferior, oversexed primitives with a predisposition toward violence and criminality. This racist discourse originated in the work of northern

Italian anthropologists and other intellectuals during the period of Italian unification, part of an effort to resist the national citizenship of southern Italians (derogated as "Africans" in much of this literature) deemed unworthy of affiliation with the glorious cultural histories of Rome, Florence, Bologna, Siena, Venice, and other northern urban centers. As American WASPs increasingly came to equate true whiteness with Anglo and northern European culture—"Nordic" was the term that circulated popularly in the 1920s—they swiftly adopted northern Italian racism for their own purposes.[3] Throughout the first decades of the twentieth century, American newspapers, magazines, and other organs of popular culture brimmed with caricatures of Italian "dagos," "wops," "spaghetti benders," and mafiosi. In the popular imagination, if an Italian man was not a knife wielding rogue, he was a physically robust but simple-minded ditchdigger or some other downtrodden worker. In a cartoon of the period captioned "A Wop," a husky bootblack with animalistic features services a thin white dandy wearing a bowler hat and a cravat and sporting a fancy cigarette holder. The caption uses dialect to further racialize the "wop": "A pound of spaghett' and a red-a-bandan' / A stilet' and corduroy suit / Add gurlic wat' make for him stronga da mus' / And a talent for black-a da boot!"[4]

In the American popular imagination, an Italian man was a bootblack, a ditchdigger, a dago, a wop, a stiletto-wielding bandit. Or a lover like Rudolph Valentino, whose film roles as a fantasy Mediterranean lover made him Hollywood's first male sex symbol. Or a singer—like Enrico Caruso, the product of a Naples slum, who became a household name, a global media celebrity, the first international pop star of the twentieth century. Italian men, like black men, were feared, reviled, denigrated, and subjected to ritual violence; they were also, like Bert Williams, Buddy Bolden, Louis Armstrong, and other black entertainers, progenitors of a new and exciting modern culture, a culture of physical expressiveness, fleshly desire, motion, and emotion that changed American middle-class culture by overturning the country's Puritan and Victorian mores. In 1920s New York, middle-class Anglo slummers went to Harlem for the racy cabaret culture; white bohemians settled in Greenwich Village, meanwhile, where their rebellion against Victorian asceticism included their intimacy with Italian immigrants, who were seen as the most exotic of the European ethnic groups: dark-haired, olive-skinned descendants of a Mediterranean culture steeped in mystery and sensuality.[5]

In 1904 Caruso made the first million-selling record in history, "Vesti la giubba," the tenor aria from Leoncavallo's *Pagliacci*, for the Victor Talking Machine Company. Photographs of his fleshy visage appeared in newspapers and magazines the world over alongside articles detailing his fastidious attention to dress and his insatiable appetite for the foods of Naples, his native city. During a time of sharpening cultural hierarchy, Caruso was a force of Whitmanesque cultural democracy, a bridge between the elite and the popular, as comfortable onstage in an ornate concert hall as chatting and backslapping with his fans on city streets.[6] In a culture rife with anti-immigrant fear and prejudice, Caruso's amiable, generous spirit contradicted widespread stereotypes of southern Italians as sullen and antisocial. Caruso instead became an exemplar of other, relatively benign Anglo/Nordic notions of Italians (and of blacks and other "darker" peoples): the Italian as innately musical, physically emotive, sensual, primitive in the sense of retaining a healthy animal vitality against modernity's bloodless rationalism. Asked what made a great singer, Caruso quipped, "A big chest, a big mouth, ninety percent memory, ten percent intelligence, lots of hard work, and something in the heart."[7] It was said that Caruso sang from his heart: his voice, the image suggests, was a blood-pumping artery. A thrilling belter whose records brought the impassioned verismo style of Italian opera to the masses, Caruso consolidated a shift in popular taste for opera away from a Germanic text-centered approach to an emphasis on the spectacle of vocal display. Voice and performance became more important than text, sound more important than sense. This aesthetic shift was perfectly in tune with the conditions of an early twentieth-century American popular culture whose burgeoning mass audience consisted of immigrant working classes speaking in a multitude of tongues but often remaining illiterate in their native and adopted languages. Caruso's phonogenic voice, the vocal blood he pumped through the acoustic technology of early recording, became a universal sound of desire and longing.

Caruso's trademark was the soaring crescendo, the dramatization of intense emotion, the feeling of passionate love, and even more, of love's betrayal and loss. In this the famous tenor gave the world something fundamental to the tradition of *canzone napoletana*, something that became a cliché of Italianness writ large: the Italian as acutely sensitive, hyperbolically emotional in matters of the heart. With male singers this entailed a masculine affect quite distinct from the Anglo-Victorian model of stoical, stiff upper lip restraint. In "Core 'ngrato" ("Ungrateful Heart"), recorded by Caruso in 1911, the singer addresses the lover who has spurned him, pleading for recognition of his pain and suffering ("Traitor, you don't know how much I love you / Traitor, you don't know how much you hurt me"). The male protagonist in this drama of amorous rupture assumes the more conventionally feminine, abject position—not just spurned but forgotten—while the female is figured as heartless, bereft of sentiment, able to carelessly move on ("You've taken my life, and it's over, and you don't think about it anymore").

Pellegrino D'Acierno writes of Neapolitan song as a "music of *passione*" (the Italian equivalent of "soul") and exacerbated *melancolía* (the Italian equivalent of "the blues").[8] We find a similarly explicit analogy between African American and southern Italian music in some of the responses to the film *Passione* (2010), John Turturro's ode to the music and people of Naples. "The music in *Passione*," wrote *New York Times* film critic A. O. Scott, "combines sensual suavity with raw emotion, mixes heartbreak with ecstasy, acknowledges the hard realities of poverty and injustice and soars above them. I suspect that if artists like Marvin Gaye, Otis Redding or Aretha Franklin were to see this film, they would recognize their own art within it."[9] Songs of yearning, of fleshly pleasure, of love and love lost, bilateral aggression and derision, betrayal and revenge; songs that speak frankly about the intrigue and anguish of personal intimacy—this is the domain of the blues, soul, and Neapolitan music alike. The art in each of these idioms is a ritual of confrontation and catharsis, a sharing of feelings so deep they exceed the capacity of verbal language—hence the power of this music even among listeners who may not understand the lyrics. The Neapolitan term of art is *la comunicativa*, an act of communication that is contagiously expressive.[10]

The history of Afro-Italian intersection in popular music from jazz to doo-wop, soul to hip-hop, is a deep and fascinating one rooted in analogous and sometimes shared vernacular cultural practices of orality and aurality, sounding and listening. A voluminous scholarly literature on African American music, religion, literature, social history, and even politics has taught us to recognize spaces of sounding and listening such as family social events, Baptist and Pentecostal church services, street corners, and barbershops as a central—some would say defining—feature of black vernacular culture.[11] Italian American culture has a similar claim to soundfulness not simply as a valued ethnic trait and badge of communal solidarity, but as a foundational dimension of group discourse and sociality. Much as in African American culture, the canonical spaces of Italian American life are fundamentally audible and aural spaces. Dinner tables, kitchens, delis, cafés, pizzerias, social clubs, barbershops, schoolyards, candy stores, street corners, front stoops—what Joseph Sciorra calls "a beguiling realm" of "landmarks on the mythic topography of the Italian imaginary," all of them scaled adaptations of the Italian piazza—are spaces where Italian Americans literally create themselves as a social body through practices of sounding and listening.[12] What makes this acoustic terrain so vivid and richly layered is the performativity that marks it. D'Acierno describes Italians and Italian Americans as a people with a feeling for scenes and spectacle: not just a deep appreciation for the visual, musical, and performing arts, but a disposition to dramatize and aestheticize interpersonal and public encounters, to make the everyday world a "work of total art."[13]

In the first decades of the twentieth century, the music of

southern Italy circulated in a Mediterranean/Atlantic orbit connecting the peninsula and its islands to Africa, the Middle East, the Caribbean, and both South and North America. Naples and Palermo were cultural crossroads where European, African, and Arab music had intermixed for centuries; the migrants who passed through these port cities on their way to the New World participated in the intercultural synthesis that produced jazz, the tango, the rumba, and other new song forms and dance styles that in turn traveled from New Orleans, Buenos Aries, Havana, and other cities back across the Atlantic. The growing phonograph record and music publishing industries commercialized this process and quickened its cultural impact. "Core 'ngrato" was composed and recorded in New York, then returned to Italy to enter the *canzone napoletana* canon and serve over the next century as a symbol of authentic *italianità*.[14] In New Orleans a teenager named Louis Armstrong went to work in Henry Matranga's honky-tonk; there, among Sicilians and blacks, he first heard Caruso on record. This helps account for the operatic bravura of Armstrong's trumpet style, his red-hot high-register pyrotechnics, and his cagey habit of sneaking opera sound bites into his solos (the "*Rigoletto* break" in his 1927 recording "New Orleans Stomp," the quotation of "Vesti la giubba" in his 1930 and 1932 recordings of "Tiger Rag").[15] Armstrong knew a lot of opera aside from his Caruso favorites, but it was from Caruso above all, Ben Ratliff provocatively suggests, that Armstrong absorbed the "long tones and flowing annunciatory statements" that the trumpeter used "to change the jerky, staccato nature of early jazz."[16]

In New Orleans, Sicilian open-air *festa* bands, funeral corteges, and Catholic saint's day processions joined US military bands, wagon advertisements, Mardi Gras revelers, and African American "second line" parades to make that city's street soundscape the most polyphonic and polyrhythmic in the Western Hemisphere. The Jim Crow color line that had taken hold in New Orleans in the 1890s flew in the face of the city's long history of racial mixing, but musicians of all backgrounds continued to listen to and learn from each other. As Bruce Boyd Raeburn has observed, "Perceptions that Sicilians, Jews, Creoles, and light-skinned African-Americans inhabited the penumbra between whiteness and blackness sometimes allowed them to manipulate racial boundaries to their own advantage, swinging in both directions."[17] Raeburn has coined the phrase "bel canto meets the funk" to characterize the New Orleans–based synthesis of an Italian vocal aesthetic of melodic beauty with a black vernacular emphasis on earthy, sensual vitality. This joining of lyricism and rhythmic groove—characteristic of the *alto basso* dynamics of Italian culture writ large—would become an essential feature of jazz, rhythm and blues, doo-wop, and soul.

The most famous jazz musician to hail from New Orleans's "Little Palermo" neighborhood was Louis Prima, a fiery trumpeter, flamboyant singer, and dynamic showman.[18] Like his idol Louis Armstrong, Prima embraced his role as an entertainer with an infectious joy and an intuitive gift for humor. Ethnicity is a concept with many meanings (heritage, culture, identity, and more), but in the context of American entertainment it is perhaps best understood as an act, a performance, and very often a performance meant to induce laughter. Prima worked at the intersection of music, comedy, and theater, in the expressive territory of minstrelsy and vaudeville where Irish, Italians, blacks, Jews, and other "ethnics" built the nation's formidable tradition of popular live entertainment. A key part of Prima's repertoire was material that drew on Italian folk music and riffed on Italian American nomenclature, slang, and accent. With songs like "Angelina" ("the waitress at the pizzeria"), "Please No Squeeza da Banana," "Felicia No Capicia," and "Baciagaloop," Prima helped Italian Americans laugh and sing during hard times and, through the wide commercial appeal of this material, hear and see themselves represented in the nation's multiethnic popular culture.[19] Like the Brooklyn-born Italian American vaudevillian Jimmy Durante—"the Great Schnozzola," an ample-nosed, gravel-voiced, language-butchering wisecracker who started as a ragtime pianist with the Original New Orleans Jazz Band, one of the first New York-based bands to identify with the new music—Prima was largely ignored by critics and historians bent on canonizing jazz as a high art.

With a gift for shtick matched by a savvy business sense, Prima responded to the postwar collapse of the big band swing economy and the advent of bebop by pioneering a stage act for Las Vegas, a desert outpost soon to become an unlikely mecca of gambling and entertainment. Sharing the spotlight with female sidekick singer Keely Smith (his wife during this period) and the Witnesses, an instrumental combo featuring saxophonist Sam Butera, a fellow New Orleans Sicilian, the now middle-aged Prima jumped and jived with manic exuberance to a 6/8 tarantella-inflected shuffle rhythm.[20]

Louis Prima's "hot" affect (fervent, animated, carnal) moved diverse audiences in a fully urbanized, post—World War II America; the urban culture it invoked was the World War I era of clamorous streets, crowded living spaces, and sweaty work, and of ecstatic liberation pursued in clamorous, crowded, and sweaty speakeasies and dance halls. The Witnesses' 6/8 shuffle captured both the joyous pulse of Italian wedding dancing and the rolling rhythms of industrial work (shoveling coal, laying railroad track) by laborers reared in an agricultural economy who became the builders of the infrastructure of American modernity. Yoked to the Witnesses' boisterous swing groove, Prima's hotness inhered in his ability to excite others through his own high-affect frenzy. In this fashion Prima, like Louis Armstrong, translated into American vernacular the kind of intense feeling that Caruso expressed in his naturalistic, verismo vocalizing.

In jazz history, "hot" refers to the small-group, collectively improvised, syncopated music that originated in New Orleans and Chicago and served as the soundtrack for the bouncy, frolicsome spirit of Roaring Twenties youth culture. In the 1930s, "sweet" emerged as a style distinct from "hot" in its use of written charts, a sumptuous instrumental blend woven from the sonority of string instruments (violins, harp), a patina of smooth polish, and a decorous air suitable for the high-toned hotel ballrooms where the music was played for polite social dancing. Big band swing grew out of this bipolar paradigm: most bands advertised their sound as hot or sweet, while the very best bands, like those led by Duke Ellington and Benny Goodman, devised a brilliant synthesis of both styles. Meanwhile these bandleaders and other of the most compelling, original swing performers, notably Lester Young and Billie Holiday from the Count Basie band, chafed at the minstrelsy-tinged dynamics of the music business, with its image of the musician as a happy-go-lucky servant-entertainer rather than a serious and challenging artist. A new performance persona and cultural style arrived with this change in attitude, a change that coincided with World War II–era demands for racial equality. Called "cool" (even when the music itself burned hot, as with bebop's blistering tempos and mercurial chord changes), it was defined by an ineffable charisma, an air of mystery, a relaxed intensity, an ability to "create excitement without showing excitement."[21]

The Italian term for this quality is *la sprezzatura*: making hard work look easy, affecting nonchalance even while conveying deep passion; answering the mandate, as the old Italian adage goes, to "never let them see you sweat."[22] Not surprisingly, jazz's shift from the sweating brow of the fervent entertainer to the furrowed brow of the contemplative artist included a number of Italian American jazz musicians of distinction, including Lennie Tristano, William Russo, Buddy (Boniface) DeFranco, Tony Scott (Anthony Joseph Sciacca), Jimmy Giuffre, Pete and Conte Candoli, Frank Rosolino, Joe Morello, and Scott LaFaro.[23] Like jazz, mid-twentieth-century Italian American popular music registered changes in temperament and attitude driven by evolving social, cultural, and political aspirations. From the 1940s to the 1960s, while many second-generation Italian Americans realized their American dream in the security of owning automobiles and homes, Italian American popular singers (Sinatra, Perry Como, Dean Martin, Tony Bennett, Mario Lanza, Vic Damone, Jerry Vale, Joni James, Connie Francis, Bobby Darin) virtually defined the way America dreamed about love and romance. If they did so in a way that sublimated their immigrant, working-class origins, they still delivered style, soul, sensuality, and even an edge of danger to the anodyne mainstream culture of the Organization Man and the suburban happy homemaker. Paralleling what Robert Farris Thompson has theorized as a core African aesthetic of "high-affect juxtaposition," the best of Italian American song and performance commingled and fused Italian hot and Italian cool—Italians being, in D'Acierno's words, "the hottest of the white ethnics," white but "temperamentally and erotically dark."[24] On stage, record, radio, and television, the voices and the personae of Italian Americans tantalized America and the world with their powerfully affecting juxtapositions of hot and cool, hard and easy, happy and sad, cocksure and vulnerable, tough and tender.

The generation of American popular singers before Sinatra had invented a new vocal approach, "crooning" as it was called, in which the microphone served as a kind of electronic ear connected to every listener. Whereas the great male opera singers were usually tenors, crooning found its ideal in the baritone voice, with its lower register closer to the sound of everyday speech. The leading crooner, Bing Crosby, would emerge as the unrivaled king of Depression-era pop and one of the singular figures in twentieth-century American culture, if for no other reason that that Sinatra, Perry Como, Dean Martin, and every other midcentury popular singer embraced him as a model. An Irishman from the Northwest, Crosby became a paragon of Middle American whiteness, an insouciant, pipe-smoking lounger, as casual in dress and demeanor as in his buttercream vocal delivery.

Henry Pleasants, a classically trained singer who wrote standard reference works on the history of singing from the dawn of opera down to Elvis Presley and Aretha Franklin, has said that as a young music critic in the 1930s he and his fellow longhairs found Crosby's voice "saccharine, lugubrious, callow, maudlin, musically slovenly, lacking in vocal virility and incisiveness, short of range—in brief, just something tasteless for schoolgirls to become excited about." Still, with Crosby the art of singing had not quite reached its nadir. "Then came the young Sinatra," Pleasants continued, "and our worst fears seem to have been realized." Pleasants recalled this bout of critical dyspepsia by way of explaining his transformation from a classical music snob to an evangelist for the excellence, even technical superiority, of singers like Crosby, Sinatra, Billy Eckstine, and Elvis Presley. Once his epiphany occurred, Pleasants would hear in these singers "a wonderfully relaxed, intimate vocal communication, a feeling for rhythm, phrase and line rarely matched by classical singers, and a smooth, often lively, almost always pleasing vocal tone."[25] In Sinatra, Pleasants and other critics would come to realize, we find an extraordinary synthesis of the classical and the popular, the European and the American: a restoration of the bel canto ("beautiful song") principles of eighteenth-century Italian opera (well-rounded tone, eloquence of phrase and cadence, purity of intonation) combined with the air of casual ease introduced by the radio crooners.

Sinatra began singing for tips in a neighborhood saloon when he was eight years old. His break into show business came in 1935 when a local singing group he'd recently joined, the Hoboken Four, won first prize on the *Major Bowes Amateur Hour*, garnering a contract for stage and radio appearances across the country. From 1939 to the mid-1940s, first as a featured vocalist in the swing bands of Harry James and Tommy Dorsey and then as a solo artist, Sinatra perfected a style of singing romantic ballads that attracted a massive audience of avid teenage girls that the astonished press dubbed bobby-soxers. By the end of the 1940s, Sinatra had also established himself in Hollywood, costarring with Gene Kelly in the popular musicals *Anchors Aweigh* (1945), *Take Me Out to the Ball Game* (1949), and *On the Town* (1949).

Sinatra spoke openly about his reverence for Crosby, even as he rivaled and eventually eclipsed his idol in critical and popular acclaim. He was also indebted to Tommy Dorsey, not just a shrewd bandleader but also a superb trombonist whose breath control technique Sinatra studied and turned to his own account in honing his ability to sustain long, legato-phrased vocal lines. Yet the most powerful influences on Sinatra's specific style were the

black American jazz singer Billie Holiday, whom he heard on Fifty-
Second Street in the early 1930s, and the black British cabaret
chanteuse Mabel Mercer, whose performances in Upper East Side
Manhattan supper clubs he frequented in the late 1940s. Combining the careful phrasing he learned from Holiday and, later, the
sensitivity to nuances of lyric and narrative modeled by Mercer,
at his best Sinatra delivered deeply moving, intimately personalized interpretations of the most beautiful, sophisticated material
in the canon of American popular song.

Sinatra preferred to sing from what became known as the Great
American Songbook: Cole Porter's "Night and Day," "What Is This
Thing Called Love," and "I've Got You under My Skin"; Jerome
Kern and Ira Gershwin's "Long Ago and Far Away"; Kern and Oscar
Hammerstein's "The Song Is You"; Kern and Dorothy Fields's "The
Way You Look Tonight"; Harry Warren's (Salvatore Antonio Gua-
ragna's) "I Only Have Eyes for You"; Frank Loesser's "Luck Be a
Lady"; Richard Rodgers and Lorenz Hart's "The Lady Is a Tramp";
Jimmy Van Heusen and Sammy Kahn's "All the Way"; "Come Fly
with Me," "(Love Is) the Tender Trap," and many, many more. Such
songs constitute an American literature on the vicissitudes of romance, a canon studied and essayed by virtually every important
modern popular singer (including such rock icons as Bob Dylan,
Paul McCartney, Linda Ronstadt, and Rod Stewart) and absorbed
into the popular consciousness as a common cultural inheritance.
And yet such songs will always be known as Sinatra's songs, so singular and memorable were his performances of them.

This identification has less to do with the particular grain of
Sinatra's high baritone than with the distinctive persona he constructed with his voice, combined with the way, as actor as much as
musician, he dramatized shared emotion and made listeners feel
he was singing directly to them. The Sinatra croon of the 1940s
was the sound of a tender, precarious love perfectly attuned to the
collective heartache of a nation of young women whose brothers,
boyfriends, and husbands were off fighting the war. In the early
1950s, following a devastating downturn marked by a hemorrhag-

ing of his vocal cords and an ill-fated foray into early television, Sinatra's career rebounded with an Oscar-winning portrayal of an Italian American GI in the movie *From Here to Eternity* (1953). Over the next decade and a half, the rejuvenated singer would record a remarkable series of albums for Capitol and Reprise with top-drawer arrangements by Billy May (*Come Fly with Me*), Nelson Riddle (*Songs for Young Lovers, In the Wee Small Hours, Nice 'n' Easy*), Gordon Jenkins (*September of My Years*), and Quincy Jones (*Sinatra at the Sands*), reinvigorating swing music and heralding a new style of sophisticated, adult-oriented popular entertainment.

The young Sinatra, the skinny songbird of the Paramount Theater, sang primarily to women while embodying characteristics (emotionality, frailty) socially coded as feminine. The fully ripened Sinatra—the saloon singer, the free-spirited swinging bachelor, the icon of urbane cool, the self-described "eighteen-karat manic depressive" with "an over-acute capacity for sadness as well as elation"[26]—sang primarily to men with a combination of brassy ebullience and fragile tenderness that captured the tensions and ambivalence of an American masculinity both exalted and traumatized by the war and the period of official national happiness that followed. Sinatra's courtly árt put popular music and jazz in conversation. Tackling the same universal subject as the blues, the darkness of amorous loss and erotic dependency, Sinatra's art created its own sensibility of urban loneliness and existential mystery.

Henry Pleasants, John Rockwell, Will Friedwald, Gary Giddins, and several other exceptional music critics have written beautifully about Sinatra as the consummate popular singer. The Sinatra who interests me here is that and something more: a complex cultural icon, a personal touchstone, and in particular the exemplar of a fascinating and complicated ethnic masculinity that continues to draw serious attention across the race line.

Original G

In a 1995 issue of *Vibe*, the slick photo magazine devoted to hip-hop music, style, and politics, one of the most hotly debated questions in 1990s rap aficionado circles—"Who is the original gangsta?"—was settled once and for all. The final word came from Bonz Malone, known to *Vibe* readers as a redoubtable arbiter of street authenticity. Malone's OG, interestingly, was not one of the usual suspects—not Ice-T, Ice Cube, Tupac Shakur or Schoolly D; not Suge Knight; not even Snoop Dogg. No, the dopest, phattest, most uncompromising voice of hip-hop authenticity turns out to be . . . Frank Sinatra. "Way before [gangsta rap] there was already a king on the hill," Malone enthused, "a G with the kind of class that makes a person untouchable. . . . No matter where he showed up throughout the country, [Sinatra] would do anything to blow up the spot—always looking for a lamppost so his big band could G off." In Malone's hagiography, Sinatra's music is inseparable from his image, both setting the standard for stylish virility. "His tough Jersey accent redefined the American language, plus he used his voice—not a gun—and made the girlies stick out them tits like it was a hold up! Mind you, this was in the '40s when girls wasn't giving up the coochie."[27]

So keen was Malone's infatuation, so awed was he by Sinatra's facade of mastery, that he was overcome by racial envy. "I've always wanted to be Italian," he said ruefully, "but [I'll have to settle] for being black and cool." Malone was being playfully hyperbolic, but his sentiment resonates with a distinct tradition of interethnic identification. One finds the black-Italian crossover fantasy, for instance, lurking in the imagination of no less an icon of black male cool than Marvin Gaye. "My dream was to become Frank Sinatra," Gaye said. "I loved his phrasing. . . . He grew into a fabulous jazz singer and I used to fantasize about having a lifestyle like his—carrying on in Hollywood and becoming a movie star. Every woman in America wanted to go to bed with Frank Sinatra. He was the king I longed to be. My greatest dream was to satisfy as many women as Sinatra."[28]

Such fantasies of Sinatra as the ultimate player—or playa, in hip-hop slang—go back to the iconic swinging bachelor period of the late 1950s. Writing in the jazz magazine *Metronome* in 1957, Bill Coss hailed Sinatra as "the most fantastic symbol of American maleness yet discovered," a man who "looks at women as if he didn't care what they thought and lives as if the world and its women were pretty much built for him."[29] Looking back, alas, there's something curiously strained about this image of Sinatra as the paragon of no strings attached, übermale sovereignty and freedom. Coss's breathless hype came just a few short years after Sinatra suffered near-suicidal despair at losing Ava Gardner, the love of his life. And 1957 was the same year Sinatra recorded his finest version of "I'm a Fool to Want You," revisiting the pathos of that famously vexed relationship.

Pictured in his rakish fedora on some of the Capitol album covers of this period—I'm thinking especially of *Songs for Swingin' Lovers* (1956) and *Come Fly with Me* (1957)—Sinatra was the free-spirited swinging bachelor, all crisp confidence and insouciant swagger. But in many of his film roles of the period, Sinatra's physique is so pathetically frail that his trademark fedora seems like nothing so much as the protective armor of a man racked with insecurity. "In appearance Frank Sinatra lacks almost everything you'd expect of a movie star," *Woman's Home Companion* sniffed. "His ears stick out. He has a scar on his neck. He is far from handsome in the conventional sense. And he doesn't have the build of a Burt Lancaster or Rock Hudson."[30] Gardner and others let it be known that Sinatra's genital endowment more than compensated for such visible flaws. But the phallus can take you only so far. If we look closely at a movie like *The Tender Trap* (1955), we find a story curiously out of sync with the sexual fantasies of Coss and many other men. On the surface, Sinatra's character, theatrical agent Charlie Reader, fully embodies the image of the playboy swinger. But throughout the film Charlie envies his closest friend's marriage as he finds himself used as a plaything by a series of single career women who are the true swingers of the story.[31]

In truth, the allure of Sinatra's masculinity—what mesmerized Bill Coss and Marvin Gaye back in the day and still bewitches hip-hop admirers today—was never about sex itself so much as the sexiness of power, especially the brand of power that attaches to the outsider who becomes an insider, the demonized outcast who carves out his own imperial dominion. This is especially true of New York–area "East Coast" rap musicians and entrepreneurs who dominated the airwaves starting in the 1990s. Witness Jay Z (Shawn Corey Carter), product of a Bedford-Stuyvesant housing project, proclaiming himself "the new Sinatra" in his 2009 hit "Empire State of Mind."[32] Behold Puff Daddy (Sean Combs), the rapper, producer, and urban style entrepreneur, dubbing himself "the black Sinatra."[33] What resonates for these black entertainer/businessmen, as it has for many white ethnics, is not just the mythical story of Sinatra's rise from a humble, ethnically suspect background to the top of the heap; it's also the "air of stylish menace" he maintained once he got there.[34] That aura was crucial to his crafting an image of masculine sovereignty and grandiosity, a big-man front no doubt partly a matter of ego projection, but equally a matter of ego defense against the forces of emasculation and conformism visited on ethnic men perceived as dangerous to the dominant white majority.

In fact, Sinatra's childhood was far less hardscrabble than myth portrayed it. Young Frankie sang for tips in a Hoboken saloon where his Sicilian father Marty quietly tended bar and his Genoese mother Dolly noisily worked as a neighborhood ward heeler and pampered her son with fine clothes. Sinatra's experience of anti-Italian bigotry on his path from Hoboken to the big time inspired his starring role in the short film *The House I Live In* (1945), a wartime propaganda vehicle promoting racial tolerance. This was the public Citizen Sinatra, the liberal do-gooder who delivered earnest speeches on juvenile delinquency in urban high schools. The private Sinatra was a far messier, more conflicted man. The re-

FIGURE 4. Frank Sinatra, well known for his close relationships with a number of notable African American entertainers and athletes, here poses in a late 1940s photograph with his friend heavyweight boxing champion Joe Louis, the "Brown Bomber." (Archive Photos/Getty Images.)

ceiving end of a racist taunt proved an excellent occasion to flaunt the over-the-top pugnacity Frank inherited less from Marty, a former boxer, than from Dolly, a legendary hailstorm of a woman. Dolly's son carried her combativeness to the Hoboken schoolyards and far beyond. "Sometimes with me, it was a case of if-you-got-the-name-you-might-as-well-have-the-game," Sinatra reflected to writer Pete Hamill. "You think I'm just some wop wise guy off the street? All right. I'll *be* a wop guy off the street and break your fucking head."[35]

Hamill parlays such testimony into what D'Acierno calls the canonical "wound of ethnicity" reading of Sinatra.[36] The wound registered for Sinatra at the level of language—of words, of naming. "I grew up for a few years thinking I was just another American kid," Sinatra told Hamill. "Then I discovered at—what? five? six?—I discovered I was a dago. A wop. A guinea. You know, like I didn't have a fucking *name*. That's why years later, when Harry [James] wanted to change my name [to Frankie Satin], I said no way, baby. The name is Sinatra. Frank fucking Sinatra."[37] This wound was common property of the black, Jewish, and Italian members of the Rat Pack, whose verbal rituals, D'Acierno writes, "constantly played out the game of the improper name, essentially as a way of depriving these pejoratives of their stigmatizing force and also as a way of expressing tribal connection."[38] Not unlike today's hip-hoppers spinning variations on the n-word to detoxify poisonous language and repurpose it to their own ends, the Sinatra who helmed the multiethnic bachelors' club floating between Las Vegas, Hollywood, and Palm Springs called himself the Top Wop.

The Top Wop was also known as the Chairman of the Board. The frisson of those two monikers conjoined—the man who rises to the top but remains proud of his denigrated tribe of origin— precisely captures what the hip-hop celebrity entrepreneurs find inspirational in Sinatra. Sinatra was a mogul who ran his own record label (he founded Reprise the same year Kennedy was elected), produced his own films, and controlled majority shares in casinos and racetracks. As a political broker cut from the same Democratic cloth as his mother, he triangulated the White House, Hollywood, and the urban ethnic wards. And yet the Frank Sinatra whose fan base was so wildly enthusiastic that he redefined what it meant to be a popular artist, the Frank Sinatra who championed FDR and helped put JFK in the White House, spent a good part of his life under a cloud of suspicion made tangible in the form of congressional investigations and FBI surveillance so extensive it produced a dossier running to 1,275 pages.[39] In a time of rabid Cold War paranoia, red-baiting smears of Sinatra as a closet Communist, coupled with constant innuendo about the Top Wop's presumed mob connections, urged the public to consider that the swinging bachelor might secretly be doing the dark work of sinister conspiratorial organizations.

"Dark" is the key word here: even as Sinatra triumphantly bestrode the national political stage, to Italians and non-Italians alike he remained essentially and unalterably *ethnic*. This is something to ponder. A supercompressed but widely believed story of Italian America goes like this: An oppressed and criminalized lower-class ethnic minority proves its American loyalty during World War II, parlays postwar prosperity into blue-collar security, then rides the baby boom wave to middle-class white suburbia. This brisk account of the incorporation of Ellis Island immigrants into the mainstream flow of American life—of colorfully emotional, racially inscrutable ghetto tribalists and "enemy aliens" turning into de-ethnicized conformists—is a simplistic caricature, of course, open to challenge both in its general thrust and in its particulars. One thing it fails to recognize is that strong ethnicity has always been a potent form of American countercultural identity, precisely *because* official, state-sanctioned codes of proper and loyal Americanism, from the Progressive Era on, have attempted to weaken, if not summarily erase, ethnic identification.

"The Italian-American man has usually signified nothing but trouble in American culture," writes Fred Gardaphé. "From the sweaty workers in the Boston Common who frightened Henry James to the exotic Rudolph Valentino's sensuous strides across the silver screen into the hearts of American women, from the cocky strut of dapper gangsters across television screens to the gold-chained disco dude played by John Travolta," Gardaphé continues, "the Italian-American man has been called on whenever a breach of status quo civility needed to be displayed, especially through the body."[40] Beginning in the 1920s, the gangster figure widely circulated in newspapers, newsreels, and movies was perceived as a "public enemy" not just because of his violent criminal behavior, but also because of his defiance of the Protestant work ethic, his flouting of deep-seated puritanical strictures against public displays of bodily appetite, pleasure, and extravagance. In his dandified dress, his luxury cars, and his gaudy nouveau riche taste, the gangster breached Anglo-Protestant norms of restraint, abstinence, and delayed gratification.[41]

Rocco Marinaccio and Laura Cook Kenna have offered especially astute insights into the ways Sinatra and the Rat Pack thumbed their noses at Cold War–era ideals of assimilation, honest work, virtue, civility, and conformity. In Marinaccio's reading, the Rat Pack stage show was a spectacle in which gifted, exceptionally hardworking entertainers played out, at a symbolic level, their refusal to work. Their "abandonment of sobriety and structure," their "ceaseless ad-libbing, gleeful fluffing of dialogue, musical numbers that went nowhere, and terrible jokes" undermined standards of professional performance and deportment in a way that mocked and scorned dominant Anglo expectations and requirements for properly assimilated, dutiful ethnic subjects.[42] Kenna portrays the Las Vegas scene where the Pack originated their Sands Hotel stage show as a tableau brimming with "alluring, ethnicized excess," a spectacle of "conspicuous abundance." Sinatra anchored the spectacle with displays of personal indulgence embodying "a fantasy of going from humble roots to making it big, an American dream that wasn't centered just on hard work." Kenna has devised a term that perfectly captures what made (and continues to make) the Top Wop a figure of allure and envy: *gangster glamour*. Regardless of the true nature of Sinatra's relationship with the underworld, the possibility that he might be "mobbed up"—coupled with the open secret of organized crime's investments in Vegas casinos—was enough to give the Rat Pack a seductive whiff of illicitness. Sinatra possessed and distributed gangster glamour because he was not a real gangster yet often acted like one (particularly in his extravagant spending) and still was able to maintain public relationships with people like the president of the United States.[43]

Sinatra understood the power of the Mafia's mystique, a power that both defamed and exalted Italian masculinity. "Something about the Mob got—and still gets—to everyone," Sinatra biographer James Kaplan writes. As we have seen with the whole cycle of gangster media running from *The Godfather* through *The Sopranos*, "the American fascination with gangsters stems from the unpleasant fact that they have razored away the troublesome complexities of life by sheer brutal acts of will." Sinatra, for his part, "sometimes fantasized that his celebrity had accomplished the same end."[44]

Sinatra was not alone in generating this fantasy, but he became its singular symbol, for reasons Simone Cinotto has deftly parsed:

> The Italian American singers, actors, and comedians that dominated American popular entertainment in the 1950s and early 60s possessed a defiant, uncompromisingly blasé approach, a charming outcast identity, a characteristically plebeian cunning, and a certain dose of clannishness, which coalesced in their attitude about *working the system*—i.e. getting the most from the dominant economic/cultural complex in terms of material rewards and recognition, while resisting being absorbed into its foreign values and codes of behavior. If Dean Martin, Connie Francis, Louis Prima, and Frankie Valli all embodied such cultural traits to a certain degree, it [took] the immensely popular Frank Sinatra to represent them all, and demonstrate the dramatic fungibility of this distinctive Italian American style.[45]

The "fungibility of this distinctive Italian American style" was such that Sinatra was able to impose it on all the social circles and spaces he entered. In *Frank: The Voice* (2010), Kaplan makes much of the famous incident from 1947 in which Sinatra was photographed in Havana cavorting with Lucky Luciano and Joe Fischetti, while Robert Ruark's Scripps-Howard syndicated columns reported on his partying with Meyer Lansky, Vito Genovese, Frank Costello, and other Mob leaders. According to Kaplan, Sinatra was in Cuba for a vital personal reason: "to be accepted by those mostly Italian men of honor" and thereby to "reclaim his

Italianness."[46] This implies, of course, that Sinatra somehow had lost his Italianness, or that the only way or the best way for him to be a real Italian was to hang out with made men. I'll resist the temptation to go antidefamation on Kaplan and simply suggest that elsewhere in his book, in his rich descriptions of Sinatra at work in recording studios, concert halls, and movie lots or at play in bars and restaurants, he often unwittingly captures Sinatra at his most idiomatically *ethnic*. Sinatra's "distinctive Italian American style" inhered in a style of living that carried over into the way he made songs and pictures; it wasn't something he turned off and on or ever lost and reclaimed.

Italian Americans perceived Sinatra's Italianness in a variety of ways, and what we know of tribal fellow feeling comes mainly in the form of anecdotal family lore. But at least one notable exception from the world of scholarship looms large. In the late 1950s, sociologist Herbert Gans conducted an ethnographic study of Italians in Boston's West End that led to his 1962 classic *The Urban Villagers: Group and Class in the Life of Italian-Americans*. In the course of his research, Gans found it striking that his subjects, who usually were brazenly cynical about big shots, made an exception for the Top Wop:

> Sinatra is liked first because he is an Italian who is proud of his lowly origin, not so much because of his ethnic background per se—although it is not disparaged—but because he is willing to admit and defend it. . . . He has become rich and famous, but he has not deserted the peer group that gave him his start. Nor has he adopted the ways of the outside world. Still a rebellious individual, he does not hesitate to use either his tongue or his fists. . . . Also he shows his scorn for those aspects of the outside world that do not please him, and does not try to maintain appearances required by middle-class notions of respectability.[47]

Gans's emphasis here was less on Sinatra's working the system than on his striking a pose of prideful, chip on the shoulder disdain for that system's condescension toward him and his people.

This is the figure D'Acierno has in mind when he observes, "Of all American performers, Sinatra has been the one most involved in the aggressive performance of the grandiose self." Sinatra, writes D'Acierno, "has waged a steady agon with the press and other intruders to reterritorialize his preserve." In so doing, Sinatra's grandiose self becomes—here D'Acierno adopts the vocabulary of Erving Goffman—a "confrontational self" and a "territorial self."[48] The territory being defended is that zone of self-sovereignty we know as the primal space of Italian masculinity that goes by the venerable name *rispetto*. For certain Italian American men—and for certain African American and Latino men too, and for men of all ethnicities who mimic this pose that has become commonplace in American culture—the demonstration of mutual *respect* is the very essence of masculinity, while the specter of *disrespect* looms as an ever-present danger of emasculation. In this sense, we must recognize in Sinatra's gangster glamour something intrinsic to the total image of his ethnicized masculinity, something operational in all his purposeful breaches of "middle-class notions of respectability."

In the annals of 1990s gangsta rap, the projection and defense of the grandiose, confrontational, territorial self sometimes cranked up to a level of violence far more lethal than Sinatra's penchant for profanity and fisticuffs. As the body count rose—Tupac, Biggie, and others—it sometimes became hard to remember the origins of hip-hop in the schoolyards, playgrounds, and streetscapes of New York City neighborhoods as a form of adolescent *play*. From rap emceeing's links to West Indian boasting and toasting and the African American tradition of "playing the dozens" to break dancing's stylized combat postures, hip-hop grew out of everyday recreational practices in which neighborhood b-boys and b-girls reveled in competitive display of the grandiose self. Thomas Ferraro describes Sinatra's working method as coming from a "boys on the corner" ethos in which "showmanship and spectatorship, competition and camaraderie" create an environment for performances of stylized masculinity both playful and exacting.[49] Sinatra's grandiose self would have been unimaginable had he surrounded himself with chumps; his grandiosity hinged on being part of a posse of deft performers richly skilled in verbal, physical, and sartorial self-presentation.

The Sinatra who was an icon of New Frontier–era men's fashion—the Sinatra of the snap-brim hat, the oxford-gray suit, and the wing tip shoes that, as Gay Talese memorably quipped, seemed to be shined even on the bottom of the soles[50]—was also the Sinatra who stylishly mediated the interracial spaces of jazz, entertainment, sports, and liberal politics, moving lithely among Count Basie and his sidemen, boxer Sugar Ray Robinson and his entourage, Harry Belafonte and the civil rights leadership. This was the same Sinatra, alas, who was fond of giving his male friends diamond-studded gold cigarette lighters with obscene inscriptions. As an Italian American with strong antiracist commitments, I've always boasted about Sinatra as a noble crusader who insisted on the desegregation of the hotels where he performed and could always be counted on to host a fund-raiser for the civil rights cause. But this is not the reason hip-hop–era black men like Bonz Malone and Sean Combs revere Sinatra. A number of white liberal men far outperformed Sinatra in the struggle for racial equality. Should we be surprised that Puff Daddy has not chosen to fashion himself after the white Justice Department lawyers who risked their lives registering blacks to vote in Mississippi? When P Diddy calls himself "the black Sinatra," the territory he's claiming is not the moral space of political righteousness; it's the imperial space of grandiose manhood.

We come closer to understanding Sinatra's racial liberalism if we think about it not just as a deep and genuine repugnance for social injustice but also as a matter of personal loyalty and largesse, as something that nourished his self-image as a Sicilian padrone. This is the point Edward Santurri makes when he likens Sinatra's relationship with Sammy Davis Jr. to the relationship between a lord and his vassal. There was something "ambiguous [and] troublesome about Sinatra's egalitarianism," Santurri argues, something that owed less to his experience as an outsider to power and privilege, more to his instinctive sense of "Mediterranean noblesse oblige with its various patterns of deference and subordination."[51] This is a game effort to demythologize Sinatra's racial liberalism, a helpful corrective to his overblown image as a Hollywood Thaddeus Stevens. Still, there is something to be said— and said without cynicism—for the Sinatra who *secretly* covered hospital bills and other living expenses for several famous but financially strapped African American athletes and musicians.[52] So I say, let's give Sinatra his due as a civil rights celebrity and as a generous friend whose noblesse oblige crossed the race line at a time when such personal gestures were exceptional. But let's not pretend that when Sammy Davis Jr. called Frank Sinatra a "very great man" Davis didn't understand that this was what he was *expected* to say. And let's not pretend that among his hip-hop idolaters Sinatra's mythic status hinges on what he did to advance the careers of Davis and other black entertainers as much as it reveals their awe for the Top Wop as a playboy lord who commanded deference and *respect*.

My Empire State of Mind

In the neighborhood where I grew up in Lenox, a small town in the Berkshire Hills of western Massachusetts, my mother's Sinatra records, like my soul and funk records, produced an out-of-place, shake-it-up sound. It was a sound marking not just ethnic and racial difference but a more sweeping set of clashing histories and cultural geographies. Here in one of New England's most storied and stalwartly Protestant old money towns, a town that in the summer becomes a center of the European classical music world (at Tanglewood), *this* sound—the swaggering, sexy, flavorful, soulful sound that marks both Sinatra and, say, James Brown in distinctly different but (for me at least) intimately related ways—was edgy and urgent, definitely not local. It simply was not the sound of my town. It was the sound of "the city."

"The city" was shorthand for New York City and its geocultural sphere, of which New Jersey (or simply Jersey) was tacitly assumed to be an integral, flavorful part. People who live in New Jersey, and for that matter in the outer boroughs of New York City itself, reserve "the city" for the island of Manhattan, with its dense street grid, soaring skyline, nonstop hustle and bustle, and an allure of transgression that clings to the edges and overlaps connecting some of the wealthiest and poorest neighborhoods in the country. My Jersey relatives use "going into the city" for their short trip across the Hudson River to Manhattan. Their three-hour drive up to the Berkshires, on the other hand, is called "going up to the country." For country yokels up in the Berkshires, meanwhile, "going down to the city" meant going anywhere within commuting distance of Manhattan. For me it meant going anywhere within broadcasting range of New York City–based radio stations. It meant getting somewhere in Westchester County, spinning the car radio dial, and landing on the Jackson Five, the Commodores, Kool and the Gang, the Spinners, the Ohio Players, Earth, Wind and Fire. Back home this music was scattered throughout Top 40 playlists moderated by an anodyne announcer and interrupted by local advertisements redolent of the mundane acoustics of provincial small-town life. Here, riding down the Taconic Parkway, this music was woven into a seamless sonic whole by DJ jive and super-loud commercial spots sizzling and popping with the electricity of "the city."

I'd be lying if I said I was hoping to hear Frank Sinatra on these family car trips, or on other trips down through New Jersey to Philadelphia, even as I'd later take to calling this swath of the Northeast the Sinatra Belt. Sinatra's was the adult, living room music I'd become accustomed to overhearing, not the music I was choosing to listen to in basement and attic rec rooms, alone or with friends, siblings, and cousins. In western Massachusetts, among my father's siblings, who had grown up on a farm in the north of Italy, the sound of Sinatra was not the ubiquitous, singular, and ritually charged thing it was in New Jersey with my mother's family. In the homes of my Massachusetts aunts and uncles in the early 1970s, Sinatra's voice more often than not was a trebly television sound commingled with other celebrity voices of the time, vestigial voices from the Rat Pack glory years creaking out one last hurrah on the banal network variety shows. This was not the majestic voice of the 1950s Capitol masterpieces or the 1960s hits "It Was a Very Good Year" and "Summer Wind"; it was the sound of a glib and uncomfortable conversationalist, a nervous, even neurotic, man trying too hard to be funny—comedy being a genre of entertainment that Sinatra, perhaps the greatest entertainer of his time, had very little talent for.

More familiar and appreciated in this setting, in fact, was the voice of Sinatra's sidekick Dean Martin. Martin emanated a warm, easy humor that eluded Sinatra. Martin could be winningly self-effacing and poignantly resigned in a way that was difficult for Sinatra. And Martin was sentimental in a way Sinatra chose not to be: he sang Italian love songs in his native tongue, songs like "Arrivederci Roma" and "Non Dimenticar" and "O Sole Mio." And even when Martin crooned a song like "Everybody Loves Somebody" in English, he sounded like someone who had grown up in an Italian-speaking household, something Sinatra worked assiduously to hide.

In my mother's New Jersey, by contrast, Sinatra was in every respect a state-sanctioned compulsory experience. The state government in question was a tribal operation helmed by my mother's younger brother, Uncle Abby, a beefy, convivial Italian Falstaff with an unmatched appetite for life. Everesto (named after Mount Everest in honor of his off-the-scales birth weight) "Abby" Dal Cortivo was a hardworking Bergen County construction business owner (builder, in fact, of one of Dolly Sinatra's houses), a devoted hunter, mythical eater, and jocund raconteur. He was also an inveterate ham performer who would buy specialty records with the vocal track cut out so he could sing over the top of the band in a home-friendly version of karaoke. His husky, glandular voice meant the best performances were his imitations of King Pleasure ("There I go / There I go / There I go / Therrrre I go . . ."), Barry White ("Girl, I don't know, I don't know, I don't know why / I can't get enough of your love babe"), or other of his favorite thick-waisted, Mack Daddy singers. But his true passion, his fanatical

FIGURE 5. Everesto "Abby" Dal Cortivo and Celeste "Bunny" Dal Cortivo, the author's maternal uncle and aunt, in 1973, dancing (very likely to Frank Sinatra) in their Leonia, New Jersey, home. (Author's private collection.)

passion, was Sinatra, whom he first saw and heard as a young kid tagging along with my bobby-soxer mother to the Paramount The-ater in Times Square. At the Paramount, he planted himself right in front of the stage, staring up at his crooning idol in rapt awe.

Aside from a curatorial display of classic Capitol LP covers and regular rounds of hagiographic storytelling, Uncle Abby and Aunt Bunny's house was no reverent shrine to Sinatra. There were no earnest listening sessions, no nerdy discussions of discographical minutiae, or anything hinting at the cultish elitism I would later encounter in certain corners of the jazz world. Instead of a that rarefied atmosphere, there was something more mysterious and magical: a convincing sense, at least in my mind, of Sinatra's pal-pable presence, a sense that his voice, his face, even his body were right there with the bodies of my parents, my aunts and uncles, and their friends. It was a sense of Sinatra's tangible intimacy with the scene my uncle had created, a sense of his corporeal participation in the intensely communal cultural space engendered by his music and his persona—a space of song and dance, laughter, intoxication, and fleshly appetite. A sense, that is, of Sinatra's charismatic immanence, in the vocabulary of folk Catholic–inflected ritual, as I now understand it to have been.

At the time, all this seemed like nothing more elevated than the older generation of the family getting their groove on. And for all the fugitive allure of cigarette smoke and the smell of men's aftershave and women's perfume wafting through the living room and kitchen, *our* cultural space (mine, my siblings', and my cousins') was downstairs in the fake wood–paneled, linoleum-floored rec room with the pool table, the bowling trophies, the rococo tchotchkes, and the hi-fi stereo with a stack of 45s. Upstairs and downstairs overlapped on a few voices and tunes, notably Frankie Valli singing "Can't Take My Eyes off You." Abby was a contemporary of Valli (born Francesco Castelluccio) and the two moved in some of the same New Jersey circles: Abby's first wife, Annette, knew Valli and the other Italian men in his band, the Four Seasons, growing up in Newark and Belleville. Valli was working the same emotional territory as Sinatra, but he was doing it through musical textures and grooves shaped by doo-wop, Motown, middle-of-the-road pop, and (later) disco rather than through the swing aesthetic that Sinatra continued to hone in his 1960s collaborations with Count Basie and Quincy Jones. In "Can't Take My Eyes off You," when the soaring brass section bridge carries Valli into the chorus ("I love you baby / and if it's quite all right / I need you baby / to warm the lonely nights . . ."), his beseeching voice conjures surging dramas of deep feeling and desire that hit me then in the same way the elegant crescendos in Sinatra and Basie's version of "Fly Me to the Moon" hit me now. Forty years on, both songs take me back to the smell of that cigarette smoke laced with aftershave and perfume.

Still, this wasn't *my* music in the same way that, downstairs with the 45s on the hi-fi, the opening bars of the Rolling Stones' "Honky Tonk Woman," with the cowbell riff and the crackling backbeat and the affect of illicit desire, felt like my music, or at least felt like the feeling I wanted from music. I felt this feeling, too, in another staple of these basement sessions, the Rascals, the New Jersey–based band for which the term "blue-eyed soul" had been invented a decade earlier. Eddie Brigati's erotically imploring voice on "I Ain't Gonna Eat Out My Heart Anymore" ("the sexiest record I ever heard," said Stevie Van Zandt); Felix Cavaliere's soulful pleading and sweet elation on "I've Been Lonely Too Long" and "Groovin'" ("life could be ecstasy / you and me endlessly")—here was a combination of swagger and tenderness, warm desire and cool aplomb I'd only later fully appreciate in Sinatra. And here it came wrapped in the velvety gospel overtones of Cavaliere's Hammond B-3 organ, the zest and sinew of Gene Cornish's guitar, and the tattooed precision of Dino Danelli's superb rock/swing drum groove: a sonic arrangement that at the time felt much hipper and more relevant than the ones Nelson Riddle, Billy May, and Quincy Jones had crafted for Sinatra.

"To sound that black, they had to be Italian," Stevie Van Zandt said in his induction speech when the Rascals entered the Rock and Roll Hall of Fame in 1997.[33] It took me years to discover that the Rascals *were* Italian, and several years more to appreciate their deep engagement with black music (and their equally deep commitment to the civil rights movement) while recording at Atlantic Records under the same producers as Ray Charles and Aretha Franklin. To me their vocals simply sounded like the local tribal idiom coming off the tongues of my older cousins Lisa and Richie Annunziato and their friends. And the Rascals' grooves personified the contraband vibe I associated with the sexy, tanned men and women I saw on Jersey Shore boardwalks just as I was hitting puberty.

In my small-town New England cosmology, the Jersey Shore was very much part of "the city," and not just because it was well within range of New York radio. The Jersey Shore in the heat of summer was nothing less than a cauldron of ethnicity, an outdoor virtual disco floor (when it wasn't an actual outdoor disco floor) of loudness and flamboyant, over the top self-dramatization. Our yearly vacation there was as much a performance of extended family bonding as was the Sinatra experience up north in Bergen County. And for that reason it still puzzles me somewhat that the musical sound of the Jersey Shore in these years, the sound of Bruce Springsteen and the E Street Band, did not move me as much as the Rascals or Frankie Valli did. As best I can now fathom it, there was something about Springsteen's mid-1970s sound and persona I found to be *too* New Jersey—or, to be more precise, too New Jersey in a way that didn't seem to invoke a deep emotional connection to New York City. Not in the way Sinatra always made Hoboken seem like a structure of feeling saturated with a longing for Manhattan. Not in the way the Rascals channeled the black feeling of the Atlantic Records studio.[54]

It was around this time I first became enthralled with the soul- and jazz—inflected rock/pop group Steely Dan, especially the voice of singer/keyboardist Donald Fagen. Here was yet another New Jersey voice tinged with the feeling and fantasy of "the city." Coming of age just a few bus stops from my cousins, Fagen was so transfixed by New York radio that he would later conceive a solo record, *The Nightfly* (1982), based on the figure of an all-night DJ inspired by Mort Fega on WEVD ("the cool uncle you always wished you had"), Jean Shepherd on WOR, and a couple of others who filled the early 1960s greater New York metropolitan airwaves with jazz, R&B, and comic patter.[55] Fagen was a Jewish hipster who channeled black soul with a sly, sardonic irony that felt original and authentic in a way that acknowledged but also diverged from both British Invasion rock and American blue-eyed soul. It was only years later that I would appreciate Springsteen for the supreme populist rock poet he is. Fagen and his collaborator Walter Becker hit me right away as literary, intellectual, and hip in a way that meshed with my teenage pretensions and aspirations.

It is the function, indeed the defining purpose, of any hip sensibility to be disdainful toward the unhip. There was nothing quite so unhip in my world circa 1976 as a leisure-suited Frank Sinatra covering Neil Diamond's "Sweet Caroline"—except maybe Sinatra singing his own late-career anthems "My Way" and "New York, New York." This is to admit that there is quite a bit of revisionism in the Sinatra I now romanticize—if not the Sinatra I invoke as a touchstone of ethnic familism, then certainly the Sinatra I (and many others) idealize as an icon of cool and as an exemplary racial liberal. Some of Sinatra's post-1970 unhipness can be chalked up to age: how hip, after all, should we expect a man in his fifties to be? Well, in Sinatra's case, pretty damn hip, especially if we put in evidence his late 1960s collaborations with Antonio Carlos Jobim. In those recordings we hear Sinatra tapping the erotic languor of Brazilian bossa nova, finding the ideal space for his aging voice to sound insouciant, cosmopolitan, and perhaps more deeply cool than ever. This is my favorite Sinatra music, and to my ears the last great music he made. What followed over the next three decades, under this or that "Ol' Blue Eyes Is Back" legacy banner, was not without its occasional nostalgic pleasure. But the general situation became a straining for relevance, a trying too hard vibe (like the vain stabs at humor) at odds with the grace and charisma of Chairman of the Board regal hipness.

In his politics, too, Sinatra disappointed me (and my parents) with what seemed like a betrayal of the noble liberal ideals he once personified. Sinatraphiles generally explain Sinatra's Republican conversion not as the predictable by-product of prosperity and aging, or even as a rightward ideological shift, but rather as payback for slights and betrayals he suffered from Democratic Party insiders (especially the Kennedys) throughout the 1960s.[56] The explanation hinges on a Sinatra scriptural cliché, the sacrosanct belief that the great man lived by a moral code anchored in an expectation of unconditional and reciprocal personal loyalty. Gay Talese diagnosed this as "the Sicilian in Sinatra": "He permits his friends, if they wish to remain that, no easy Anglo-Saxon outs. But if they remain loyal, then there is nothing Sinatra will not do in turn—fabulous gifts, personal kindnesses, encouragement when they're down, adulation when they're up."[57] In 1970, Steve Allen published an open letter pleading with Sinatra to call off his campaign of "Sicilian vengeance" and come back to the Democrats.[58]

We might question the explanatory power of such ethnic typecasting, especially if we think of Sinatra in this period as a Hollywood/Palm Springs celebrity potentate whose wealth and power had elevated him far above the tribal warfare of the ethnic wards. But this was a historical moment when the salience of race and ethnicity was escalating across all sectors of American life. In this historical context, Frank Sinatra and James Brown were more than just kindred figures in my personal music canon; they were symbols of pride and consciousness amid the intense ethnic and racial turbulence of 1970s America. Brown was the much stronger figure in this regard—less a symbol of African American racial pride, in fact, than a primary force in its creation. Brown's lyrics articulated black nationalist politics, and the groove and grammar of his music expressed African American vernacular cultural traits and attitudes in ways that had no parallel in Italian American popular music. There was nothing in Sinatra's music during this period that said "Say it loud, I'm Italian and I'm proud." Sinatra became an honorary figure for Italian American ethnic pride ideologues and ethnic heritage entrepreneurs, but he did not engage directly with Italian American communities or Italian American youth in the same way James Brown engaged with black neighborhoods and black youth in an effort to build an African American economic and cultural infrastructure. Sinatra and Brown linked up during this period, figuratively speaking, in both siding with Richard Nixon over George McGovern in the 1972 presidential election. But such head-scratching political maneuvering bespoke no deeper alliance. While Sinatra never turned his back on his black friends and fans or lost their respect, his general disdain for the 1960s counterculture and its legacy put him out of touch with any of the black empowerment initiatives of the 1970s.

Still, in spite of his nagging political contradictions, and notwithstanding how the melodramatic excess of "New York, New York" infringed on my poignant adolescent romance with the city, Sinatra most certainly reached me in the 1970s in my New England WASP enclave, and he reached me even more deeply in my relatives' multiethnic suburban New Jersey neighborhoods. My feeling for Sinatra was less about politics than something much more basic and far more enduring: it was my baptism and confirmation as the son of my New Jersey mother. This is another way of saying it was my awakening to my identity as an Italian American.

This awakening was primarily acoustic: it was the difference between the lingering Italian accents of my father's brothers and sisters and the brassy, high-affect New York—area American accents of my maternal relatives, a difference that commingled in my ear with the sonic dissonance between small-town radio and big-city radio. This awakening also registered at the level of bodily presence and personality. Uncle Abby was the kind of guy who showed his affection by wrapping you in a headlock and squeezing you within an inch of your life. His highest praise for another man was to say he was "strong as a bull"—something he said often about his own father, my *nonno*, and also about my father, as if to confirm that my mother had chosen a spouse who'd passed muster with the men of the family. My father's considerable strength, physical and otherwise, was evident to everyone who knew him. But nobody ever said my father was *tough*. Nobody who knew him could ever imagine my father settling a score with his fists, something you wouldn't say about my mother and her side of the family. Unlike my New Jersey relatives, my father's default mode of interpersonal relations was not bilateral verbal aggression. Through my mother, what I came to associate with New Jersey Italian Americanness is that the biggest-hearted, most fun-loving, generous-spirited people express their love and affection through exactly the same confrontational means by which they express wariness and hostility. Perhaps this is what Bruce Springsteen meant when he said of Sinatra: "Every song seemed to have as its postscript, 'And if you don't like it, here's a punch in the kisser.'"[59]

This is exactly the way my Uncle Abby was tough. But even he wasn't as tough as my mother.

Song for the Mothers

A dramatically different Sinatra image than the one romanticized by macho rappers and other idolaters has long circulated on the New York/Las Vegas/Hollywood grapevine. Nick Tosches, in his biography of Dean Martin, claims that Sinatra remained enthralled by Dino because he, not the Top Wop, had more cachet with the "racket guys"; that it was Dino who mastered the nuances of *menefreghismo*, the "I don't give a fuck" pose of willed nonchalance. Sinatra, said Tosches, always "seemed to be killing himself over one broad or another," always "seemed to be dispatching others to do his dirty work," and was viewed in New York and Vegas mob circles as a "half-mozzarella" whose *mammissimo* relationship with his mother raised questions about his manliness.[60] For a man who fancied himself an *uomo di rispetto*, a man of respect, such innuendo cut deep.

The tag of *mammissimo*, Italian slang that translates roughly as "mama's boy," might have been a heavy liability for the man who, as Gay Talese and others observed, relished his role as the *uomo di rispetto* and the padrone, the honored and feared boss known for going out of his way to redress a wrong or settle a score.[61] But then we're not talking about just any mama: we're talking about Dolly Sinatra, the *real* original gangsta, by all accounts the toughest guy ever to come out of Hoboken.

In Sinatra biographies, it's commonplace to locate the source of Frank's combativeness and cunning (not to mention his courage and loyalty and humanity) in the example set by Dolly, a blizzard of a woman who not only operated as a political fixer (in Talese's memorable phrase, "a kind of Catherine de Medici of Hoboken's Third Ward"),[62] but also as a Prohibition–era saloon keeper, a midwife, and—most notoriously—an abortionist. The Tina Sinatra-produced TV biography, *Sinatra: The Authorized Movie*, features a stirring performance by Olympia Dukakis, whose Dolly is always smacking the young Frankie but also hot-wiring her son with passion and ambition. Dukakis's performance makes a strong case for the tough-love school of immigrant bootstrap parenting; she makes us wonder how different mid-twentieth-century American child-rearing practices might have been if Dr. Spock had been raised by an old-school Italian mother. When Dukakis's Dolly checks her son's self-pitying "I'm a nobody" lament with a feral grab of the ear and a rousing "You *are* somebody, you're Frankie Sinatra," you feel a charge of maternal heart and soul you know is going to carry the young singer to the top.[63]

Not surprisingly, the unauthorized biographies have a different take. Donald Clarke, in *All or Nothing at All* (1997), begrudgingly credits Dolly with instilling in her son a feeling for the underdog that ignited a liberal passion for social justice. But since Clarke otherwise characterizes Dolly as "a small-time gangster who never did anything for anybody unless it was going to bring a payoff," even this small tribute rings hollow.[64] Kitty Kelley's pathography *His Way* (1986) makes the case that Frank's way was actually Dolly's way, and her way was long on selfishness and mendacity. Looming over the book's opening scenes as a hulking ogress, Dolly Sinatra needs less than fifty pages to scramble her son's psycho sexual wiring by dressing him up as a girl; force him to turn to his grandmother's kitchen to stave off emaciation and debilitating latch-key loneliness; terrorize his pregnant girlfriend into a miscarriage; mortify and embarrass him with her ubiquitous abortionist's black bag; disguise her lack of true affection by spoiling him with fancy clothes and lavish walking-around money; and finally, totally emasculate his father, Marty, portrayed as a gentle, asthmatic man bowled over by his wife. Kelley gasps at the sheer gall of this protean character—Dolly, who knew not only all the Italian dialects but also the salty language of cigar-chomping Irish pols; who cross-dressed as an Irish bloke to defy gender restrictions and attend her husband's boxing matches when he fought under the name Marty O'Brien; who moved the family out of Hoboken's Little Italy into a more respectable neighborhood only to deck the place out with gaudy "guinea" furniture.[65]

John Lahr, in *Sinatra: The Artist and the Man* (1997), describes Dolly as "a typical *balabusta* [who] controlled the Sinatra household and had a stevedore's heart and mouth"; she called Sinatra's sidekick Jilly Rizzo (and many others) "fuckface," reserving for her granddaughter Tina the more endearing nickname "Little Shit."[66] Of all the biographers, Lahr offers the most provocative theory about Dolly's influence on Frank's life and art. Arguing that Sinatra "embraced and bullied the world as his mother had embraced and bullied him," Lahr adopts Pete Hamill's belief that Sinatra's relationship with his mother prefigured his entire tortured romantic history. "I married the same woman every time," Sinatra told Hamill, leading Hamill to speculate, "That's Ava [Gardner]. That's all the women. He had this mother who punished and hugged him, and they were all part of the same thing."[67] Lahr ventures even further in his paradoxical twist on the mama's boy theme, arguing that, as a singer, Sinatra turned to his audiences for the affection he craved but never received from his mother. "The stillness, attention, and unequivocal adoration that were never there in Dolly," Lahr writes, "were undeniable in the rapt enthusiasm of his listeners." Shirley MacLaine, in her memoir *My Lucky Stars* (1996), goes even further, intriguingly describing Sinatra's relationship with his audiences as a kind of displaced oedipal fantasy. "His survival was his mother audience," she writes. "He needed her to love him, appreciate him, acknowledge him, and never betray his trust. So he would cajole, manipulate, caress, admonish, scold, and love her unconditionally until there was no difference between him and her. He and she had become one."[68]

Though psychoanalytic explanations generally leave me with more questions than answers, I must admit I find something tantalizing in these conjectures about Dolly Sinatra's hold on Frank. But I feel even more strongly that Dolly Sinatra continues to elude understanding, specifically in the way she confounds and resists sanctioned codes of mothering. The strange combination of fascination and disgust with which Dolly Sinatra has been represented fits squarely into larger discourses of mother bashing that pervade American culture. When we consider popular American stereotypes of the welfare mother, the teen mother, and the postfeminist career woman who spends less time with her children than stay-at-home mothers, we see a consistent and recurrent public desire to stigmatize those who fail to live up to sentimentalized ideals of the good mother.[69]

I would argue that a cultural presumption of "good" mothering in the Italian American family has been created by the popular media's hypersentimentalizing of an ideal Italian mother who serves symbolically as *everyone's* mother. Who but the most hardhearted among us, after all, didn't laugh and feel a little safer when Danny Aiello's *Moonstruck* (1998) character Johnny Cammareri, who has scotched his marriage plans to go back to Sicily to be with his dying mother, returns to Brooklyn and announces, with just the right touch of operatic schmaltz, that she had miraculously risen from her deathbed and "started cooking for everybody."[70] The Italian slang term for this kind of figure is *mammissima*. In an e-mail exchange, I asked a cousin of mine in Italy for her understanding of this term. She wrote back: "'Mammissima' is like a big mammy, in the sense of the heart, the mother of all children, the one that always has bread and jam for all—you know, '*mammissima mia*' with a big kiss!"

I found it significant that she used the spelling m-a-m-m-y. Here in the United States that word packs plenty of mythological punch, of course, albeit in relation to African American rather than Italian American motherhood—that is, the black mammy of an untold number of southern white boys' dreams. But if we keep our eyes open, we see Italian American analogues to such commodified black mammy figures as the famous Aunt Jemima (who, as I'll discuss in the next chapter, herself has a little-known Italian American background): recall the ample-bosomed, plump-armed pizza maker Mama Celeste, and the next time you buy your Italian-seasoned bread crumbs, check out that *simpatica* woman smiling from the top of the Contadina container. Like the black mammy, these are mythical mammy figures whose power resides in their availability to all of us. We are invited to symbolically feed at their breasts and tug at their housecoats. They are the mothers of all mothers.

Historically, the dutiful, self-sacrificing black mammy of romantic lore was presumed to love her white family and its children every bit as much as her own. Indeed, the black mother lost her sentimental glow as soon as the focus shifted to her relationship with her own children. In the wake of the 1965 Moynihan

Report, it became respectable even for liberals to blame black "matriarchy"—the pseudoanthropological term for putatively dominant and overnurturing black mothers—for all alleged social dysfunction in the black community.[71] In the 1990s, while public debates about welfare continued to demonize black mothers, mainstream media presentations of the black mother nevertheless offered fugitive flickers of sentimental imagery. A notable example was basketball. For television network broadcasts of NBA and big-time men's college games, producers commonly assigned one cameraman to track players' parents in the stands, capturing reactions to their sons' performances at key points in the game. Black players were linked solely to their mothers far more often than white players. Frequently the camera on the black mother's face came with a human-interest backstory underlining her heroic struggle to shield her children from the ravages of inner-city poverty and violence. Similarly, this was the period when the NBA's clever marketers started to fetishize Mother's Day, turning that Sunday's game broadcast into a spectacle that intermingled new jack machismo on the court with old-school mother worship in the pre- and postgame player interviews. When Reebok resolved to cut into Nike's share of the lucrative basketball shoe market, the strategy was to craft a series of advertisements showing the mothers of black NBA stars at home proudly watching their sons on television.[72]

These were positive if hackneyed media images of proud, strong, soulful black women. All the same, in the mainstream US collective imagination, it's hard to compete with the Italian mother for sentimental appeal, especially in the world of tough guys. Former New York senator Alfonse D'Amato and his handlers understood this in 1980, when they used his mother, Antoinette, in a media campaign centered on her cookbook *Recipes for the Forgotten Middle Class*.[73] The strategy was brilliant and by many accounts it was crucial to D'Amato's upset victory over Jacob Javits. The son may be a vulgar machine politician, the subtext seemed to be, but how untrustworthy can he really be with an old-fashioned Italian mother in his camp? Witness, along similar lines, the canonizing of Martin Scorsese's mother, Catherine. In a pungent cameo as the mother of Joe Pesci's demonic character in *Goodfellas*, she provides the late-night, spontaneously whipped up snack for the wiseguys who stop by on their way to bury a body. Not the most flattering context, to be sure, but the juxtaposition of mobster savagery with maternal humanity comes off as extremely funny—because we know that Scorsese is toying with the stereotype of the Italian mother who is always available to tend to the basic needs of her son, and of *all* sons.[74] Thanks to Catherine Scorsese's posthumously published cookbook, *Italianamerican* (1996), we now have access to her pasta sauce recipe—and a fine one it is. In a *New York Times* story covering a testimonial dinner in her honor, a number of her son's film-world associates gushed over Catherine's outsized nurturing qualities. "If you could bottle her and spread it around the world," said Nicholas Pileggi, "there would be no need for social workers."[75]

Given such powerful assumptions about the humanizing compassion of the Italian mother, no one should have been surprised by the scornful invective many Italian Americans (especially Italian American men) directed at David Chase, creator of *The Sopranos*, for giving birth to Livia Soprano, one of the most unloving, manipulative, passive-aggressive, and malevolent matriarchs imaginable. "Everybody thought Dad was the ruthless one, but I gotta hand it to you, Ma," Tony Soprano says to his mother. "If you'd been born after these feminists, you'd have been the real gangster." Livia proves it by putting out a hit on her son. Regina Barreca has argued that Livia is the literal embodiment of a "smothering maternal presence" well known in "two-family houses throughout the tri-state area."[76] Barreca is talking about the dark underbelly of Italian American matriarchy, but this territory is not ethnically exclusive. When we imagine a mother who is *too* nurturing, a mother who is overprotective and smothering and neurosis producing, usually we're thinking about the stereotypical *Jewish* mother. Although a Jewish friend of mine says that the only Jewish mothers he knows are Italian, I see Dolly Sinatra as an example of an Italian American mother who couldn't possibly be confused with the eternally suffering, guilt-mongering, son-eating Jewish mothers we know from Woody Allen films and Philip Roth novels.

Dan Greenburg, who dramatized his plight as a recovering Jewish son in the satirical training manual *How to Be a Jewish Mother*, offered the following as an illustration of Jewish maternal weltschmerz:

> "Ma! Ma!" [says the young Jewish boy running home to his mother].
>
> "What's the commotion?"
>
> "The bad boys ran off with my hat."
>
> "The bad boys ran off with your hat? You should be glad they didn't also cut your throat."[77]

When I imagine Frankie and Dolly Sinatra in this vignette, I find myself changing the last line to something like:

> "The bad boys ran off with your hat? Let's find the son of a bitch bastards and slit their throats."

I jest, of course, but only to celebrate the spirit of an Italian mother who sabotaged hackneyed images of ethnic warmth and projected her spirit far beyond the confines of the flowered housecoat of domesticity. As Barbara Grizzuti Harrison put it in a sharp rejoinder to Kitty Kelley's Sinatra bashing: "In Italian-American families, tough, noisy women are often the rule," and "it is almost impossible for an outsider to locate the source of power in those families—the whole canny point being to deceive the outside world."[78] In her own exaggerated way, Dolly Sinatra typifies the pattern of Italian American mothers who serve not merely as the expressive core and emotional center of the family, but as—in Richard Gambino's apt metaphor—powerful ministers of internal affairs.[79] Of course Dolly Sinatra *also* reigned over half of Hudson County as a powerful minister of *external* affairs, and in this, as in much else, she brazenly scrambled traditional gender codes.

Did she also, as the tough guy in the Sinatra household, consign her son Frank to a lifelong crisis of masculinity? We've been encouraged to think so by one of the most powerful myth-making machines in the history of American popular culture, Mario Puzo's *The Godfather*. In both the 1969 novel and the 1972 movie directed by Francis Ford Coppola from the screenplay cowritten by Puzo and Coppola, the Sinatra-like character Johnny Fontane, a bobby-soxer-beloved Italian crooner, is caricatured as a weak, womanly figure desperately in need of Don Vito Corleone's protection and patronage. "You can start by acting like a man. LIKE A MAN!," the Don fulminates when Fontane seeks counsel for his woman problems. Puzo coyly avoided confirming the Fontane/Sinatra connection in press interviews and in his 1972 book *The Godfather Papers and Other Confessions*. Folklore has it, however, that Sinatra, with his combination of arrogance and fragility, couldn't imagine that Puzo would *not* model his character on him, or that the characterization would not be meant to impugn his masculinity. According to a story originated by Puzo, when the two men crossed paths in a Los Angeles restaurant, Sinatra screamed insults at Puzo and threatened to beat him up.[80]

Like Sinatra's highly publicized assault on Hollywood gossip columnist Lee Mortimer in 1947—Mortimer was an ardent purveyor of innuendo tying Sinatra to both the Mafia and the Communist Party—this was the kind of event that bolstered Sinatra's reputation for a "Sicilian temper." But shouldn't we ask, How virile and menacing, really, is a guy who makes public scenes out of bullying *writers*? "Macrophallus and all," James Kaplan reasons, "Frank was a little guy (not a single record exists of his ever having prevailed in a real fight), and secretly he knew he was an artist, with an exquisite sensibility. How could such a person be a man among men? Even grunting, illiterate Marty—boilermaker, athlete, fireman—was that."[81] By this line of thinking, Sinatra never got over his working-class father's questioning his manhood for pursuing a singing career over a manual trade and for divorcing Nancy, his loyal Italian wife and the mother of his children. Sinatra's longtime butler, George Jacobs, was surprised early in his tenure to discover that Sinatra frequented his ex-wife's house and that there "Mr. S was like a little boy who had just gotten out of camp coming home for a home-cooked dinner. . . . Big Nancy was so maternal to Frank, she seemed like his mother rather than his [ex] wife."[82] Jacobs took instruction from Nancy on how to cook for Frank. And so it was that in the privacy of his own home, long after his divorces and the years of his storied playboy escapades, Sinatra's "mammy" was his African American butler, George Jacobs.[83]

To compensate for his shaky purchase on Old World ideals of manhood, and to camouflage the softer, more sensitive, feminine sensibility that marked aspects of both his music and his personal life, the argument goes, Sinatra turned to the exclusively male milieus of gangsters, boxers, and saloon goombahs. This was the world Mario Puzo brought famously to life in his mythic fiction. But Puzo also knew about strong Italian mothers, and he was insistent about locating the source of his inspiration there.

Puzo wrote about his own mother's greeting him at the front door wielding a policeman's billy club and deputizing his oldest sister to smack young Mario upside the head with an empty milk bottle should he dare to come home with a bad report card. This was a woman who hailed from the generation of illiterate southern Italian peasants who clustered in tenements on the mean streets of American cities, willing their children to a better life. She was a stone-cold pragmatist, a master of working the system: poorest of the poor, yet somehow able, in the depths of the Depression, to provision her table with "the finest imported olive oil, the best Italian cheeses."[84] She'd been bred in a culture in which, as Luigi Barzini concisely put it, "men run the country, but women run the men."[85] Puzo fictionalized his Hell's Kitchen childhood in his 1964 novel *The Fortunate Pilgrim*. In that book, a classic of Italian American literature, Puzo channels his mother through his lead character, Lucia Santa, a classic patriarchal matriarch who governs her fatherless Tenth Avenue tenement household with a finely calibrated regimen of brutality and compassion, callousness and generosity.[86] Lucia Santa is perhaps the most powerful, resonant fictional characterization of an Italian American mother in American literature. Still, Puzo's more powerful tribute to his own mother came through his much more famous character, Don Vito Corleone, the Godfather. "Whenever the Godfather opened his mouth, in my own mind I heard the voice of my mother," Puzo said. "I heard her wisdom, her ruthlessness, and her unconquerable love for her family and for life itself, qualities not valued in women at the time. The Don's courage and loyalty came from her; his humanity came from her."[87] In Don Corleone, Puzo created a matriarchal patriarch for the ages.

What we know from Mario Puzo's autobiographical writings is that in his kind of patriarchy strong men need strong women. This was no consolation to feminists who saw *The Godfather* as a reactionary, even misogynist response to women's liberation—a not unfair reading of a novel that depicts a world in which men are beset by problems posed by liberated women and the Corleone ethos consigns all the women in the family to roles of deference and obedience. Yet the idea that the Corleone family is an old-fashioned patriarchy is so transparent, so overwhelmingly obvious, that it threatens to hide more complex and subtle aspects of *The Godfather*'s gender dynamics. And it may hide what the book can help us understand about Frank Sinatra. Perhaps it is the Don himself, not Johnny Fontane, who most productively opens up our thinking about Sinatra. Perhaps the Don's gender dimorphism—what Fred Gardaphé calls "the female core of Don Corleone's masculinity"—might help us make sense of Sinatra's shimmy between padrone and *mammissimo*. Perhaps, that is, the maternal soul of Vito Corleone's patriarchy can point us to the female core of Sinatra's masculinity.

Some of our shrewdest Sinatra interpreters hear this clearly in the music. Philip Furia has called attention to the "lyrical drag" element of the classic 1950s Sinatra recordings—that many of the songs Sinatra made his own in the swinging bachelor period were Broadway show tunes from the 1920s and 1930s written for women characters.[88] There has never been any question that Sinatra's early-career crooning was heard as a feminized sound. To his detractors, such as Henry Pleasants before his come to the Voice epiphany, that croon was the sound of a weak, hysterical mama's boy; to his admirers it was the sound of a rare artistic mastery, an ability to express love, loss, longing, pain, and desire while avoiding any hint of cloying sentimentality or abject self-pity.

Sinatra was the rare popular singer who was respected, even revered, by jazz musicians, not only because of his commitment to civil rights or his social ease in crossing the color line. Jazz has a long history of antisentimentalism that goes hand in hand with its anticommercial artistic ideology, an ideology that turns on gendered patterns of thinking. Throughout its history, notions of jazz's authenticity and purity have been advanced through denigration of a purportedly feminized realm of mass culture said to be tainted by the banalities and melodramatic excesses of popular song. Even during periods of glory, some of Sinatra's less glorious Columbia and Capitol records struck many jazz-minded listeners as the kind of trifling and trivial ditties that only trifling and trivial young women could find appealing. The case made for Sinatra's greatness, when he was great, was like the case for Billie Holiday's greatness: both singers were said to overcome the banality of weak, treacly material and, when presented with stronger lyrical material, to achieve a kind of austere dramatic intensity that elevated and refined feelings and emotions rather than surrendered to them.

If Frank Sinatra and Billie Holiday could sing romantic ballads, achieve massive popular success, and still be cool or hip by jazz standards, it was because they were heard to be accessing feelings and emotions we think of as feminine but doing so through techniques of style we think of as masculine. They brooded over the idea of emotional intimacy without being *overly* emotional. They reflected and ruminated on the pleasures and costs of romance without being *merely* romantic. Theirs was what Lauren Berlant calls a "mass mediated sense of intimacy" in which powerful sentiment and deep feeling served as the occasion for lofty, contemplative private soliloquy.[89]

I will confess to being as beholden as anyone to the gendered presuppositions behind these musical interpretations. Much of the male jazz instrumental music and soul music I find most moving is what we might call the sound of sentimental masculinity: Miles Davis's version of "My Funny Valentine," Eddie Brigati of the Rascals singing "How Can I Be Sure," Otis Redding singing "Try a Little Tenderness." The Sinatra I revere is the one whose juxtaposition of ebullience and tenderness—even neediness—captured the anxieties lurking beneath the urbane skinny-black-tie machismo of the Rat Pack years. This is the Sinatra whose power as a performer owed much to his gift for dramatizing his insecurities and vulnerabilities so compellingly as to suggest that his tough-guy front was the biggest performance of all.

In the wake of gangsta rap, the tough-guy front has become not just an all too familiar trope, but very often an unyielding, non-negotiable criterion for the only street-certified brand of masculinity, so-called hard masculinity. In a certain corner of the hip-hop world, and among the wannabes who strain to attach themselves to it, any hint of vulnerability about women is thought to reveal a softness that violates an unbending code of manhood. That some of hip-hop's most powerful male celebrities and entrepreneurs who live by this code would emulate Sinatra's playboy élan, his gangster glamour, and his working the system pluckiness speaks to undeniable affinities and continuities between African American and Italian American masculinity. But these are not Sinatra's true heirs. That honor must be reserved for tough, hard-living men's men who are so confident of their masculinity they are unafraid to face up to the power of women; men who are unafraid, indeed, of the female energy at the core of their own manhood. These men, Sinatra's true heirs, are the men who embrace the femininity at the heart of their musical art and their soul, the men who sing the song of their mothers.

TWO

Everybody Eats

A Prelude in Six Courses

I

Cultural critic Greg Tate has popularized an expression that speaks bluntly to the issue of unrecognized, uncompensated historical and cultural debts owed to African Americans. The phrase "everything but the burden"—the title Tate gave one of his books—comes from a poem written by Tate's mother, Florence. "Mom once wrote a poem [called 'Everything but the Burden']," Tate explains,

> to decry the long-standing, ongoing, and unarrested theft of African American cultural properties by thieving, flavorless white folk. A jeremiad against the ways Our music, Our fashion, Our hairstyles, Our dances, Our anatomical traits, Our bodies, Our soul, continue to be considered ever ripe for the plucking and the biting by the same crafty devils who brought you the African slave trade and the Middle Passage.[1]

This is tasty cultural nationalism catnip of the sort that has been crucial to post-1960s black consciousness in a way that Italian Americans can only envy. For the frank reality is that Italian Americans never have mounted political or cultural programs on the order of the black arts movement and the black power movement. Perhaps that is why Italian Americans are not accustomed to thinking about the huge American appetite for pizza, pasta,

gelato, and espresso as mass larceny by the flavorless, gastronomically challenged people who executed Sacco and Vanzetti and
worked others of our kinfolk to slower deaths.

I say this, and saying it gives me a bracing jolt of righteous
ethnic pride, but then I wonder if there is any honest moral claim
for thinking this way. Perhaps the very concept of cultural property
(food, music, fashion, language) is a self-defeating trap. Perhaps
when we insist on thinking of something as ours and ours alone,
there is no way not to perpetually suffer the feeling that someone
is trying to steal that thing from us. Perhaps any abundance worth
having *must* originate in deprivation—the bountiful glory of blues,
jazz, soul, and hip-hop comes, after all, from the music's origins in
the harsh agricultural work, migrations, and urban struggles black
men and women endured to feed their families—and perhaps any
abundance worth having is best enjoyed through sharing it. Perhaps culture itself, at its essence, is *both* love and theft.

II

A tavola si sta sempre in allegria. Recently I encountered this old
Italian adage ("At the table one is always happy") in the introduction to Michele Scicolone's *1,000 Italian Recipes*.[2] It's a sentiment
that resonates throughout the Italian food and cooking mania that
has seized the imagination of the American bourgeoisie over the
past couple of decades, shifting foodie notions of the gastronomic
good life from Julia Child's Francophilia to the Mediterranean
ideal. Marvelous cookbooks like Scicolone's, Marcella Hazan's *Es-
sentials of Classic Italian Cooking*, and Lynne Rosetto Kasper's
The Splendid Table give us not just recipes but a code for living
well, organizing our lives around fresh ingredients and daily rituals of culinary transubstantiation. The Slow Food movement, Italian in origin but now global in impact and a badge of righteous hipness in ecosustainability epicenters like Berkeley and Burlington,
propagates a farm-to-table ethos at once good for the planet and
good for the soul.

Television cooking shows abound with a range of Italian personalities ranging from hot to cool, charismatic and sexy to ma-

ternal and sentimental. Mario Batali dances to tarantella bumper music while chopping onions, spinning anecdotes about his travels in the old country and singing the praises of the old copper kettles essential for making polenta. Giada De Laurentiis, a fetching Mediterranean beauty with Sophia Loren élan and plunging neckline, gushes orgasmically when she goes for the money shot first taste of her finished dishes. Michael Chiarello glides around his fabulous California wine country kitchen with all the insouciance of a West Coast jazzman, anointing this plate with a drop of extra virgin olive oil, that one with a shaving of Parmigiano Reggiano. Lidia Bastianich tenderly feeds her granddaughter from a steaming pot of hearty minestrone; together they sing an Italian folk song.

We know these sweet and savory images are confections, advertising clichés stoking consumerist fantasies. Yet we are happy to wink at the manipulation and distortion —the unsexy prep work edited out of the cooking shows, the airy cookbook rhetoric of perfection, even the elitist leanings of Slow Food's authenticity fetish— because we want to believe, no matter the vexed and grubby reality, that, finally, "at the table one is always happy." It makes us happy to believe in the ideal of the happy table, the table as a space of family communion, storytelling and singing and laughter, nurture and love, memory and redemption. I speak here in particular of Italian Americans, who wear as a badge of ethnic pride their reputation as nonpareil masters of the domestic kitchen and table—and talk endlessly, sometimes wearyingly, about this reputation. Perhaps they enjoy the envy they sense from de-ethnicized or never-ethnicized Americans, or perhaps they themselves feel envy when they see these same values strongly expressed in the Asian, African, and Latin American immigrant cultures of more recent vintage.

These matters are deeply personal and become more intensely so during times of family crisis. In 2011, when my father was in the last weeks of a terminal heart illness, I gathered with my mother, my wife and children, my brother and sister and their families at my parents' kitchen table to tell stories. In this space of food preparation and ceremony, most of the stories were about—as they had always been about—procuring, cooking, and eating food. There were stories about my father's boyhood on a farm in Marola, a small village close to Vicenza, in the Veneto region: stories about milking cows and butchering pigs, about making cheese and salami. There were stories about my father's garden at our home in western Massachusetts: its bounty of herbs, vegetables, beans, aromatics, and lettuces; its beauty (a marvel of weedless Palladian elegance); its almost sacred status as a site of heroic labor. Hunting stories. Wine-making stories. Stories about foraging for mushrooms and blueberries in the Berkshire woods. Stories about recipes: the risotto with chicken gizzards, a dish my mother inherited from my father's mother. Stories about the stories ("You remember the time Uncle Abby told the one about . . .").

My mother, old and frail herself, legally blind from macular degeneration, pressed on with her cooking, feeling her way around the kitchen by muscle memory, sound, scent, and instinct. When the hospice nurse said my father's heart numbers had worsened, that the end was near, my mother still held out hope. "He's still eating well," she assured us. "He still wants to come to the table."

It makes me happy (or at least less sad) to believe that my father, in his last weeks and days, was taking pleasure from my mother's cooking and fondly remembering the good times at the table: the risotto with gizzards, the laughter, the stories.

III

The African American singer and bandleader Cab Calloway's mid-1940s recording of "Everybody Eats When They Come to My House" is high-spirited and very funny. The humor comes from Calloway's skills as a swing vaudevillian, which hinged in no small part on his interest in the ethnic communities surrounding him in New York City. Smokey Joe and Minnie the Moocher, the hepcat characters in Calloway's pop-surrealist fantasies, are always running off to Chinatown to procure substances. Calloway's scat singing and hi-de-ho antics bespoke a playful curiosity that carried over into a fascination with Yiddish and Italian slang. This is apparent in the rhyme scheme in "Everybody Eats," which features such antic lines as "Pastafazoola, Tallulah," "Oh, do have a knish, Nishia," "Here's cacciatore, Dorie," and "Taste the baloney, Tony." Calloway's contemporary, singer and guitarist Slim Gaillard, developed his own hipster language, "vout," which similarly looked to ethnic food for some of its stream of consciousness material. Gaillard and his partner Slam Stewart introduced the world to "Matzo Balls-ereenie." He changed the opening line of "Bei Mir Bist Du Schoen" to "bei mir bist du spaghetti."[3]

"Everybody Eats When They Come to My House" is one of those songs that played as big a role in the popular culture of future decades as it did in its own time. In this respect it is very much like "Jump, Jive, an' Wail," the song written and first recorded by Louis Prima in 1956, then rediscovered in the 1990s. The LP the song first appeared on, Prima's *The Wildest*, was featured—the LP album cover was even pictured—in the 1996 movie *Big Night*. Then in 1998, when the Gap clothing company used "Jump, Jive, an' Wail" in a television commercial for its khaki pants, that song (Prima's original and the Brian Seltzer Orchestra's cover) helped spark the "swing revival" that found high school and college students taking up partner dancing for the first time in decades.[4]

"Everybody Eats" and *The Wildest* spotlight Calloway and Prima as two bandleaders who easily made the transition—indeed, with Louis Jordan they helped forge the transition—between pre–World War II big band swing and postwar jump swing, R&B, and early rock and roll. While bebop and other postwar progressive idioms transformed jazz into a more serious and intellectual music, these bandleaders continued to think of themselves as good-time entertainers serving up uncomplicated but extremely flavorful music to audiences hungry to have their most basic appetites fulfilled.

In *Big Night*, two Italian immigrant brothers try to save their near-bankrupt New Jersey Shore trattoria by hosting a huge dinner for Louis Prima. In the kitchen, the brothers lovingly craft signature dishes from the old country. Out front in the restaurant, a band of wine-merry revelers preen, flirt, gossip, quarrel, and conspire. They dance exuberantly to Rosemary Clooney's "Mambo Italiano." At last they're called to the table for a sumptuous multi-course feast, a gustatory opera. The performance opens with a risotto artfully painted in the colors of the Italian flag. It intensi-fies with the dramatic presentation of the timpano, a baked pasta dish from a sacred family recipe. A soaring crescendo comes when a roast pig, its mouth stuffed with a juicy fig, rolls out on its own cart. By the time the grappa is served, romances have blossomed and fizzled; vendettas have been hatched; dreams and sorrows have marinated into bittersweet melody. In short, life has been lived to the fullest.

The twist in *Big Night* is that Louis Prima does not show up at the restaurant that night. His absence is deeply felt—not just as a plot point of the film, but because his presence would help us recall more keenly the intimate association between jazz and food, food experiences, and food spaces. Well into the twentieth century, on the streets of New Orleans, Charleston, Baltimore, Philadelphia, Chicago, New York, Newark, and other cities with large populations of blacks, Italians, and other ethnic groups, the air was filled with the cries and songs of vendors selling fruit, vegetables, fish, and other foods. On his 1958 LP *Porgy and Bess*, Miles Davis's haunting and sweetly evocative trumpet lines on the songs "Fisherman, Strawberry and Devil Crab" and "Here Come de Honey Man" capture the vendor cries that composer George Gershwin heard on the streets of Charleston. In 1962 Herbie Han-cock wrote "Watermelon Man" thinking of the men hawking the fruit on the Chicago streets of his youth; the tune's groove mimics the rhythm of the vendor's movement through the streets, while its simple riff melody invokes the five-syllable phrase voiced by neigh-borhood folks calling out "watermelon man." Off the streets, jazz and blues have always been played in spaces of victuals and liba-tion, from the cheap saloons memorialized in Louis Armstrong's "Gut Bucket Blues" to refined "jazz supper clubs" like Jazz Stan-dard, Birdland, Café Carlyle, Smoke, and Iridium in contempo-rary New York City. One of the most famous pieces of jazz folklore is the story Charlie Parker told about how he came upon the idea of using substitute chord changes in crafting his saxophone solos. He was "working over 'Cherokee'" and discovered that by "using the higher intervals of a chord as a melody line and backing them with appropriately related changes," he could finally "play the thing I'd been hearing." "I came alive," said Parker. So, the legend goes, did the new style of jazz called bebop. Parker's epiphany occurred not, as the elevated language might suggest, in a music conservatory, but in a jam session in the kitchen at Dan Wall's Chili House in Harlem.[5]

IV

In December 2008 I collaborated with the Italian American writer and performance artist Annie Lanzillotto on a piece we called "Frittatagoraphobia." Lanzillotto coined that word to describe the condition that afflicts her mother and many other Italian American women who grew up during the Depression: a morbid fear of leaving home without a frittata in the pocketbook. The piece unveiled a new performance genre we call the *jazz lazzo*. In the commedia dell'arte, the *lazzi* are gags or short comic scenes added into the play for color and pacing. Ours ran longer than a traditional lazzo, and as it developed during our rehearsals it took on something of the flavor of the comic kitchen sketches in *I Love Lucy*. For bumper music, we used a recording of Cab Calloway's "Everybody Eats When They Come to My House," making the piece a *jazz lazzo*. It opens with the two of us in a kitchen, singing and cutting up to a recording of the song and ends with my using an array of cooking implements to drum along with the song's final choruses. We performed the piece in a professional television kitchen studio in Greenwich Village, video-streamed live into an adjoining dining room where sixty or so New York City food enthusiasts were on hand to celebrate the publication of the book *Gastropolis: Food and New York City*. Our performance drew on stories Lanzillotto tells in the essay she contributed to the book, "Cosa Mangia Oggi" (What to eat today).[6]

In Lanzillotto's extensive and varied oeuvre of poems, essays, plays, and site-specific artworks, a recurring theme has been Italian American food spaces (kitchens, the table, restaurants, delis, markets) as sites of ethnoculturally coded expressive performance.[7] As a skilled urban ethnographer, Lanzillotto recognizes the New York City ethnic neighborhood street as a space where food and sound are mutually expressive. Lanzillotto has recorded food street cries in her travels throughout the Mediterranean and the Middle East and has studied their history in New York City. She has long been fascinated by the fact that in 1939, as part of a campaign to clean up and modernize New York City for that year's World's Fair, Fiorello La Guardia, New York's Italian American mayor, pushed through a ban on mobile vegetable peddlers, fishmongers, and other food purveyors and their calls, decreeing that henceforth fresh food would be sold only in markets like the Arthur Avenue Retail Market in the Italian neighborhood in the Bronx. In the late 1990s, when Lanzillotto received a grant to mount a set of site-specific performances at what remained of the Arthur Avenue market, one of her ideas was to create an acoustic environment for the market redolent of the old ethnic neighborhood before the La Guardia decree. This was no contrived postmodern avant-garde gesture: Lanzillotto was drawing on the historical meaning of the market as a space—think of the ancient agora and the Renaissance fair—where commerce and art, food provisioning and theater, singing and butchering, all were part of the same public discourse. She hired a professional opera singer, soprano Deborah Kartel, to sing arias in the market. In what emerged as an uproariously funny social drama, Kartel kept getting upstaged by a neighborhood "La Senora" who literally shoved her aside to sing her own old favorites. This sonic spectacle meshed with the entire fabric of the market, the voices braiding with the vegetables, fruit, aromatics, cooking oils, meats, and offal. Here the voice of the performing self was inseparable from the processes of transubstantiation (the killing, butchering, cooking, eating) that nourish the body and, indeed, create the social body, the culture.[8]

Let's think more deeply about the voice as a foundation of body and culture. In his much cited but seldom read essay "The Grain of the Voice," top-dog semiotician Roland Barthes bites the leg of

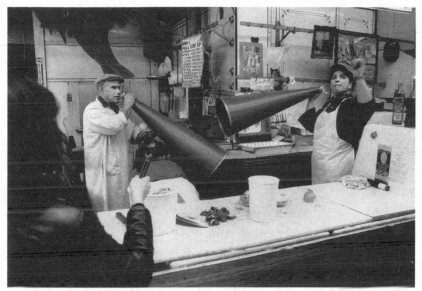

FIGURE 6. Butcher Mario Ribaudo, *left*, proprietor of Mario's Meat Specialties, and writer and performance artist Annie Lanzillotto, *right*, in 1996 during a "food art" performance at the Arthur Avenue Retail Market in the Bronx, New York. (Courtesy of photographer Andrew Perret.)

what he calls "the normal practice of music criticism," summing up that trade as the largely facile and trivial production of interchangeable adjectives: this music is *this*, this execution is *that*. Barthes wants to talk about music as something more than expression, representation, even communication; he wants to go deep into the materiality of music, into the sound particles as such, into the (if you will) *grain* of the thing. And he arrives at this simple but arresting corporeal image: "The 'grain' is the body of the voice as it sings, the hand as it writes, the limb as it performs."[9]

In her writing as in her performance art, the grain of Annie Lanzillotto's voice is . . . well, if I'm going to follow Barthes here I can't very well serve up a string of descriptive adjectives, even if I work hard to make them seem original. I have to deal with the body—the cavities, muscles, and membranes—of her speaking voice, not to mention the tendons and cartilage of the hands and limbs she writes and performs with: Lanzillotto's artistic voice, that is, in total. Barthes himself favored Russian cantorial singing, the church bass he heard coming "from deep down in the Slavonic language, as though a single skin lined the inner flesh of the music." Barthes said of the cantor's voice that it is best understood not as personal or original; it is, rather, "the materiality of the body speaking its mother tongue." Ralph Ellison was probing something similar when he wrote about the gospel matriarch Mahalia Jackson, describing the particular timbre of her voice as constitutive of the entire African American social body. Our voices, Ellison suggested, while distinctly ours, do not originate with us.[10]

The grain of Annie Lanzillotto's voice in her essay "Cosa Mangia Oggi" is the Italian soil, and the soil of Italian gardens everywhere, "breast-feeding [us] straight from the earth." It's the fibrous texture and toothsome virtue of bitter greens you learn to love the way you learn another language. It's the sinew and snap of the muscles you apply to labor-intensive vegetables like broccoli rabe. It's the dough Lanzillotto stretches the way she stretches the essay, the crust of the bread, the ridge of the rigatoni soaking up the sauce. It's the garlic—the garlic you never pay for, Lanzillotto says, because "some things in life you should never pay money for"— stuffed in ears for earaches, wrapped around the neck for swollen glands, dissolved in the blood to fast-track pork fat through the aorta. We feel and taste the grain in Lanzillotto's voice, and that grain is our mystical body, our holy sacrament. For someone of my age and disposition, someone who lives for art and ritual and thin-crust pizza but who came into Catholicism when all it offered was an Irish priest in a poncho singing bad folk music, Lanzillotto's verbal theology of the streets is my church, my communion, my immanence and transcendence. She gives me the Word and the Body.

In our *jazz lazzo*, our words and bodies, conjoined with those of wry trickster Cab Calloway, delivered stories about Lanzillotto's mother carrying a pocketbook frittata around New York City. She carries it on the bus and subway going to work, out on the town with friends, after a museum visit with her children in an Upper East Side restaurant so expensive they split a sandwich four ways and supplement it with the frittata. As Lanzillotto tells the stories and we improvise asides, we cook a frittata from scratch. We crack eggs, sauté leftover potatoes and asparagus with onions, and execute Lanzillotto's mother's "avant-garde" technique of flipping the frittata over on a plate, then returning it to the skillet for a double-sided finish. As the performance winds down, I drum on my kitchen percussion kit along with Calloway's band as Lanzillotto throws the fresh frittata into a handbag and delivers it, along with some crusty loaves of bread, to the hungry diners next door.[11]

V

In 2014 the African American visual artist Kara Walker mounted an in situ installation featuring an enormous sculpture of a black woman working in a canefield. The woman is crouched in a posture of acute sexual vulnerability, yet at the same time full of the self-possession and sovereign repose of a Buddhist icon or a monumental Egyptian sphinx. Heralded by the *Times* as "one of the most substantial works of art to hit New York in years," it sat in the cavernous sugar shed of the old Domino factory in Brooklyn, drawing hundreds of thousands of visitors over a three-month period.[12] Visitors inhaled the pungent aroma of burnt sugar and molasses still glazing the factory's colossal walls. Some solemnly contemplated the enormousness of Walker's concept, its evocation of the intertwined histories of the transatlantic slave trade, plantation labor, and food history; others snapped selfies against the backdrop of the sculpted woman's breasts and vulva. The sculpture was made from thirty tons of refined white sugar molded onto vast blocks of polystyrene foam. Walker titled the piece "A Subtlety, or The Marvelous Sugar Baby" after the elaborate dinner table centerpieces made of spun sugar ("subtleties") in aristocratic medieval households. Later, in early nineteenth-century France, Marie-Antoine Carême, a founder of the grandiose style of French cooking called *grande cuisine* and one of the first internationally renowned celebrity chefs, first gained fame in Paris by constructing ornate table centerpieces modeled on temples, ruins, and other structures Carême studied in architectural history books.

These centerpieces were made from sugar, marzipan, nougat, pastry, and even candy. Thus was European cuisine turned into a high art using one of the foods that drove the African slave trade.

The installation serves as a kind of diptych with a piece of performance art mounted by Walker in collaboration with the jazz pianist Jason Moran at the Whitney Museum in New York City. For the 2012 Whitney Biennial, Moran and his wife Alicia Hall Moran curated a set of performances called "Bleed," a title that invokes the bleeding together of art worlds and political discourses as well as the bonding of African American people through family bloodlines and shared memories of a history soaked in blood. The event featured a wide variety of sound, image, and dance-based fare interspersed with short talks by scholars, journalists, and artists. Alicia Hall Moran sang a version of Beyoncé's "Run the World (Girls)" accompanied by Japanese taiko drummers, a relatively conventional performance compared with the one in which she talked about her life as an artist while receiving acupuncture. Kara Walker joined Jason Moran's group for a performance called "Improvisation with Mutually Assured Destruction." While the band played along with a recording of the Rolling Stones' "Brown Sugar," Walker projected images of Mick Jagger alongside the song lyrics, coupled with words and phrases of her own that intensified the song's demonic aura of slave rape and heroin. Here Walker was a performance artist using the stage name Karaoke Walkrrr, singing in a deliberately grating voice while her laptop spit out words like "crawl," "beg," "grovel," "slit," "blood," and others connecting Mick Jagger's libido to the history of sugar, plantation slavery, and the subjection of the black female body.[13]

VI

Camille Paglia has written evocatively of "the Italian way of death," a kind of residual paganism in which "the primitive harshness of agricultural life, where food, water, shelter, and sex are crucial to survival" carries over into Italian American attitudes toward dying and dead bodies and their attendant rituals. "Italians," Paglia suggests in a cultural generalization that seems both atavistically tribal and utterly true, "recognize both the inevitability of death and its unique grisly signature, which seem fascinating to us in a way that strikes other people as morbid or insensitive." Paglia illustrates her point with a ghoulish description of the scene in *The Godfather* where young Michael Corleone shoots a rival mobster and a police captain in the head while they eat at an Italian restaurant. The dying men's blood spills all over the table and blends with the wine and the meat juices, creating a grisly, carnal vignette of food and human viscera.[14]

In death as in life, the body is an expression of the food and drink it consumes. Food and drink are themselves expressions of animal and plant bodies in various states of ripeness, transfiguration, and decomposition. Catholic liturgy provides a ritual space of symbolic transference between blood and wine, bread and flesh, but in the archaic pre-Christian worldview where Paglia locates the origin of Italian attitudes toward death, the human body completes the cycle of fertility, destruction, and rebirth not through divine mediation but rather through the mundane physical processes of nature itself.

The cover of Louise DeSalvo's memoir, *Crazy in the Kitchen: Food, Feuds, and Forgiveness in an Italian American Family* (2004), features a beguilingly unsettling image: a hand clutches a hearty, dense loaf of bread while a knife, facing upward, slices through the loaf's center. It's the knife that unsettles—the blunt edge, the force, and, most of all, the dangerous upward thrust of the blade toward the body of the person holding it. What sort of person cuts a loaf of bread this way?[15]

Bread. No food is more central to the life and identity of the ethnic tribe or to the exchange and interaction between ethnic tribes. Across cultures, no food has more practical significance or more symbolic, ceremonial, and religious meaning. No food is more deeply expressive of the relation between the land, the elements, agriculture, and culture—the intercourse of grain, water, and fire. No food is more tightly linked to the rhythms of deprivation and abundance. No food better signifies both the grim struggle for subsistence and the indulgence of plenty.

The knife. Stiletto, switchblade, serrated bread knife. No object was more intrinsic to the character assassination of Italian American immigrants in the late nineteenth and early twentieth centuries, or to the air of hip street toughness flaunted by certain Italian American teenage men in the 1950s, or to the kitchen tables of bread-loving Italian American families of all generations.

DeSalvo's grandmother, a desperately poor peasant from Puglia who became an old-school gothic *nonna* decked out in black shawl, rosary beads, and an air of perpetual mourning and suffering, looked to the young Louise like death itself, death incarnate. Still, an awesome life-affirming power manifested itself in her handcrafted, thick-crusted, coarse-crumbed breads, breads that she dipped in wine and the hearty soups and stews she made from scratch with her homegrown vegetables. Louise remembers her grandmother's tenderly swaddling the bread in a blanket, as if "putting a child to sleep."[16] And she remembers the solemn ritual when her grandmother cut the bread:

> My grandmother would bend over the bread that she had made, turn it right side up, and make the sign of the cross over it and kiss her fingertips, weeping. My grandmother would weep because to her the bread was sacred and to her the only way to cut the bread was to pull the knife through the bread toward your heart. And perhaps she was weeping, too, for all that she had lost, for all that she never had, and for all that she didn't have. For the insufferable life she was forced to live.[17]

This is rich sentimental territory DeSalvo is moving us through, and in the hands of a timid writer such sentiment could run to the trite and the generic. But DeSalvo is a fierce writer drawn to bluntness, literalness, and violence. She will thus tell us more about that knife:

> The knife that my grandmother uses to cut the bread is not a bread knife, not a serrated knife like every well-equipped American

kitchen now has. The knife that my grandmother uses to cut the bread is a butcher knife, the kind of knife that figures in nightmares, in movies like *Psycho*. The same knife, incidentally, that my father will use when I am a teenager, when he threatens to kill me.[18]

The invisible line between safety and danger, the intertwining of life and death—these are defining themes of both gothic horror and the immigrant experience. DeSalvo's grandmother forages for dandelions and other wild greens growing among the neighborhood's fugitive grasses; her grandfather kills pigeons with a slingshot and rocks. Her grandparents, in short, "won't eat anything that doesn't come in the home alive." Such kitchen primitivism preys on young Louise's active mind: "I am curious about, horrified by, how my grandparents wring birds' necks, pluck their feathers . . . kill fish by plunging a knife between their eyes." This leads to even more macabre imaginings: she begins "to wonder when life becomes non-life," begins "to think about death," begins "to have nightmares in which I, too, am dressed for the cooking."[19]

Later in the memoir, DeSalvo visits the New Jersey cemetery where her grandparents and sister are "all crammed into death . . . like we were all crammed in life in our tiny tenement apartments." She has an epiphany "about how we all die and how the dead outnumber the living and how the trees outside my house will be there after I'm dead." And it occurs to her that "you shouldn't bring flowers to people's graves, you should bring food to the dead, that you should bring them the kinds of meals they like to eat in life, that you should feed the dead, that you should have little picnics on their graves."[20] In this striking image linking barbarous sensuality with sentimentality and nurturance, DeSalvo conjures the deepest possible bond with her family, a bond rooted in a timeless, hungerless present, a never-ending banquet table transcending the contingencies of history and geography.

The message is simple: In an Italian family, people need to be fed—even if they happen to be dead and buried.

Greasing the Skillet

Italians, as I say, like to think of themselves as the most food-centered of people, an attitude that runs hand in hand with their sense of themselves as the most family-oriented. But are we really a uniquely or exceptionally food- and family-centered culture, or is it just that we *talk about* food and family more than most people? And is our food talk really any better or more meaningful than that of other ethnic groups? Eric Weiner says he was born into a family of "gastronomical Jews" whose sense of divine presence began and ended in the kitchen. "If we could eat it then it was Jewish and, by extension, had something to do with God," he writes. "As far as I was concerned, God resided not in Heaven in the Great Void but in the Frigidaire, somewhere between the cream cheese and the salad dressing. We believed in an edible deity, and that was about the extent of our spiritual life."[21] This sounds very familiar. Substitute anticlerical, saints- and Madonna-focused Italian Catholicism for Weiner's cultural Judaism, replace the cream cheese and salad dressing with salami and wheels of Asiago cheese, and you have my family in a nutshell.

Italian American popular music includes a smattering of songs with food themes or promiscuous references to food, such as Louis Prima's "Banana Split for My Baby" and Dean Martin's "That's

FIGURE 7. (*opposite*) German emigré painter, jazz musician, and gourmand Leo Meiersdorff (1934–94) developed a unique visual art combining jazz and culinary figures in a vivacious expressionist style. In the 1960s and '70s, Meiersdorff's work graced album covers for the Blue Note, Concord, and Chiaroscuro record labels as well as serving as background for several jazz-themed television specials. During a decade-long residence in New Orleans, Meiersdorff became a habitué of the city's jazz clubs and restaurants and a confidant of musicians, chefs, waiters, hoteliers, and bartenders. His original artwork has been displayed at Commander's Palace, K-Paul's, the Fairmount Hotel, and other iconic Crescent City establishments, while plagiarists continue to hawk cheap knock-offs of his style to the French Quarter tourist trade. One of many of Meiersdorff's works that capture the New Orleans music/food nexus is this 1979 painting "Cooking with Jazz." (© 1979 Leo Meiersdorff. Image used with permission by the Leo Meiersdorff Estate.)

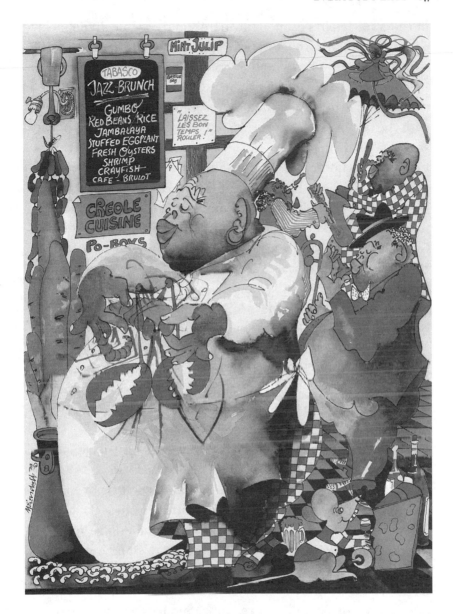

Amore" ("When the moon hits your eye like a big pizza pie . . ."). But one rarely hears Italian American music itself, as a body of expression, discussed in food metaphors—not in the way we have become accustomed to hearing New Orleans jazz described as a big pot of gumbo or Memphis soul as a savory stew. With the exception of the piquant Latin music that goes by the name salsa, no music tradition has been so intimately and organically connected with food as the African American one. In addition to the Louis Armstrong, Miles Davis, and Herbie Hancock food-themed tunes I mentioned above, consider this sampling of blues, jazz, R&B, and calypso song titles (identified here not with the songwriters but with the performers best known in connection with them): Armstrong's "Struttin' with Some Barbecue," Bessie Smith's "Gimme a Pigfoot and a Bottle of Beer," Lil Johnson's "You'll Never Miss Your Jelly," Jelly Roll Morton's "Big Fat Ham," Fats Waller's "Shortnin' Bread," "Rump Steak Serenade," and "All That Meat and No Potatoes," Louis Jordan's "Saturday Night Fish Fry," "Boogie Woogie Blue Plate," and "Beans and Cornbread," King Porter's "Chitlin' Ball," Memphis Minnie's "Keep on Eatin'" and "Good Biscuits," King Curtis's "Memphis Soul Stew," Ernie Andrews's "Pork Chops and Mustard Greens," Guitar Slim's "Cooking Big Woman," Booker T. and the MGs' "Green Onions" and "Red Beans and Rice," Junior Walker's "Home Cookin'," James Brown's "Mashed Potato, USA" and "Mother Popcorn," Ray Charles's "Stringbean," Harry Belafonte's "Banana Boat Song" and "Coconut Woman," Dizzy Gillespie's "Salt Peanuts," Olu Dara's "Okra," Charles Mingus's "Eat the Chicken," and Lou Donaldson's "Gravy Train."

Food metaphors marinate the insider language spoken by performers and audiences across these black music idioms. A soloist who is "cooking" or "greasing the skillet" is getting deep inside the groove of the music and drawing out its richest flavors. One recent night I was with a group of friends at the Village Vanguard, the famous New York jazz club, listening to Bandwagon, Jason Moran's trio. The band, as they say, was really cooking. One of my friends, a pianist himself, a scholar of black music, and a reliable practitioner of the call-and-response mode of mutual participation characteristic of the black music tradition, led our amen corner by calling out phrases like "You're giving us the chicken fat" and "I smell the fatback" when the music hit its ecstatic peaks. This language invoked the tight association between food and music that we've taken for granted since the late 1960s, when the homology between soul food and soul music anchored a whole

ethos of soul—a concept all the more deeply felt for being indefin-
able—driving the era's ascendant black cultural nationalism.[22] But
it also tapped into a much longer history of association between
black music, food, and animals dating back to slavery. Proscrip-
tions against slaves' use of drums, combined with the slaves' in-
genuity, led to stripped chicken bones and hambones becoming
makeshift percussion instruments; "hambone" was the name
given to the percussive slapping and patting of arms, legs, chest,
and cheeks that originated many of the rhythm patterns for slave
songs and dances. Throughout the nineteenth century and well
into the twentieth, white minstrels in blackface and later black
minstrels evoked plantation slave quarter scenes full of songs and
humor abounding with animal references. Dances carried names
like the turkey trot, the pigeon wing, the fishtail, and the bunny
hug. Notoriously, commercial marketers assigned the whole field
of black music the label "coon songs"—accompanying dances were
called "coon steps"—to conjure the hunting and eating of raccoons
by poor rural blacks.[23] Many early New Orleans jazz performances
evoked agricultural scenarios and sounds, notably the tailgate
trombone's mimicry of barnyard animal flatulence. Later, even
so exalted a modern jazz sophisticate as Charlie Parker remained
stubbornly connected to this past: in spite of Ralph Ellison's in-
sistence that Parker's nickname "Yardbird" (later shortened to
"Bird") had nothing to do with real barnyards or even the "randy
roosters and operatic hens" of animated cartoons, the legend persisted that Parker was tagged with the nickname because once,
when he was traveling with Jay McShann's band, the band car ran
over a chicken in the road, and Parker insisted on retrieving the
bird so it could be cooked for dinner.[24] Associations between African Americans, chickens, and black music being what they are,
we should also note the 1960s-era R&B dance the funky chicken,
along with Rufus Thomas's hit record "Do the Funky Chicken."

These associations are rooted in what Paglia calls "the primitive harshness of agricultural life," a primal connection to the raw
physical elements of life that persisted among people who moved
from plantations and farms to fast-growing American cities in

both the African American Great Migration and the southern and eastern European "great wave" of immigration. In the collision between peasant worldviews and urban modernization wrought by these epic migrations, a frankness about bodily appetites found expression in new modes of cultural expression, especially music and dance. This is the context in which best to understand the promiscuous metaphorical intercourse between food and sex that famously occurs in the blues—as when Lil Johnson, in "You'll Never Miss Your Jelly," plaintively appeals to her "sweet man": "If you don't like my sweet potato, what make you dig so deep / Dig my potato field, three, four times a week." Or when Ethel Waters, Alberta Hunter, and other blues women called for their lovers, in "My Handy Man," to "grease my griddle," "churn my butter," and "cream my wheat." Songs rife with food/sex double entendres, like Memphis Minnie's "You Stole My Cake," Blind Boy Fuller's "I Want Some of Your Pie," and Nina Simone's "Sugar in My Bowl," constitute their own distinct subgenre of black performance.

When he was still known as LeRoi Jones, the African American poet, essayist, and jazz critic Amiri Baraka expressed ambivalence about the style of late 1950s/early 1960s music that was being marketed as "soul jazz." Ever the avant-garde modernist, Baraka distrusted what he regarded as the crass commercialism of the music, finding its efforts to popularize jazz's gospel and blues roots intriguing but ultimately facile.[25] Years later, in 1997, a similar high modernist attitude crept into Baraka's derisive dismissal of "the chitlin circuit," the lowbrow traveling black theater productions that continued their bookings in black neighborhoods like Baraka's in Newark, as nothing more than latter-day crude minstrelsy.[26] In sharp contrast, in a 1962 essay titled "Soul Food," Baraka waxed enthusiastic about chitterlings, pork chops, neckbones, maws, knuckles, grits, hoppin' john, hush puppies, hoecake, okra, watermelon, fried chicken, sweet potato pie, and collard greens.[27] For Baraka, it seemed, righteous down-home eating could access authentic black soul in a way "soul jazz" could not. This was several years before "soul food" took hold as the name for politically correct authentic black cuisine during the black cultural nationalist period, and several decades before famous Harlem chef Sylvia Woods launched a line of canned soul food products; a chain of "chitlin drive-throughs" opened in Atlanta; and new age vegetarian soul cafés appeared in Washington, DC, New York, and other cities with sizable populations of upwardly mobile, health-conscious black professionals.[28] These latest developments might be said to bear out the suspicions of Eldridge Cleaver, the Black Panther party's minister of information, that soul food was nothing more than an au courant form of black bourgeois slumming. "Now that they have the price of a steak, here they come prattling about Soul Food," Cleaver wrote in his prison manifesto *Soul on Ice* (1968). "The people in the ghetto want steaks. *Beef steaks*. I wish I had the power to see to it that the bourgeoisie really *did* have to make it on Soul Food."[29]

Putting aside fried chicken and watermelon (hard as that is for a cross-racial slummer like myself) or (with no difficulty at all) tofu pepper steak, the fundamental basis of soul food is the pig or, to get right down to it, the pig's intestines: the chitterlings, chit lins for short. Getting right down to it—*down* to it—is the point: you can't get any lower, any closer to nature, the rawest, smelliest, *funkiest* part of nature, than the hog bowel. The bowel is the space, as Doris Witt puts it in *Black Hunger: Food and the Politics of U.S. Identity* (1999), which "transgresses the boundaries between food and excrement, phallus and anus, origin and decay." Chitterlings, as such, pack a great deal of symbolic sexual significance. Witt points to the famous scene in Ralph Ellison's *Invisible Man* when the narrator, a student at a southern black college who despises the school's leader, Dr. Bledsoe, seeing him as a white-loving Uncle Tom, fantasizes about exposing Bledsoe as an imposter. In the fantasy, the Invisible Man comes upon Bledsoe "in the crowded lobby of Men's House" as Bledsoe "suddenly whip[s] out a foot or two of chitterlings, raw, uncleaned and dripping sticky circles on the floor as I shake them in his face, shouting: 'Bledsoe, you're a shameless chitterling eater! . . . You're a sneaking chitterling lover!'"[30] Witt reads the scene as being as much a sexual "outing" as a racial one: "to put it in the crude terms implicit in the Invisible Man's accusation," Bledsoe is being exposed not only "as a nigger but [also] a faggot."[31] In a way that intriguingly complicates Baraka's identification with soul food, Witt argues not only for an association between hog bowels and polymorphous sexuality, but also for an association between "the discourses of soul associated with the filth of black self-hood generally with femininity and specifically with lower-class black maternity."[32] Getting right down to it, you can't get any closer to nature, the rawest, *funkiest* part of nature, than the womb. Therein lies the primordium of soul in all its funky glory.

In the relentlessly body-centered discourses of both food and music, chicken grease, fatback, and other slick lubricants signify pushing forward into life, delivery into the world of our beholding and our hearing the most vitally alive, desired and desiring, needed and needing, bodies and sounds. If soul—or before it the roundly disavowed but nevertheless intimately related term primitivism—means anything coherent, it is this: primal vitality, passionate aliveness. In 1948 Angelo Pellegrini, an Italian immigrant to the United States, published *The Unprejudiced Palate: Classic Thoughts on Food and the Good Life*, a proto–Slow Food treatise that preached the virtues of garden-to-table Italian eating and, with astonishing prescience, warned of the dangers of an increasingly industrialized, standardized, *soulless* American food culture. Pellegrini explained the virtues of tripe (cow stomach), sweetbreads (calf pancreas), kidneys, brains, heart, and liver ("pork liver, so little used, is more rich in the essential vitamins than that of beef or calf") as a matter of their essential, primitive aliveness. "Why, then, are these vital organs of the animal not generally eaten?" he asked. "One reason, certainly, is precisely that they are *vital*. They are associated with urine, blood, excrement, and the gastric functions of the animal. The average American clutches his hot dog and turns from them in horror."[33] Pellegrini was ahead of his time in his food-centered critique of American mass culture, anticipating the jeremiads about America's loss of soul that were to come in the 1950s from intellectuals like David Riesman, William Whyte, John Kenneth Galbraith, Dwight Mc-

Donald, and Norman Mailer, and in 1963 from Amiri Baraka (then LeRoi Jones) in his *Blues People*. There Baraka, in his own blistering critique of a flavorless American middle class, translated these notions of vitality and soul into the metaphorical domain of smell. "The adjective *funky*," he wrote, "which once meant to many Negroes merely a stink (usually associated with sex)," has been made into "a valuable characteristic of 'Negro-ness.' And 'Negro-ness,' by the fifties, for many Negroes (and whites) was the only strength left to American culture."[34] Smell, of course, is exactly what Pellegrini was talking about when he said Americans are afraid of the vitality of organ meats. Put Pellegrini together with Baraka, and you arrive at this formulation: such savor as America can claim comes from the real smell of soulful ethnic eating coupled with the metaphorical "funky" smell of black music.

Mammy, Mamma, Mario

In both African American and Italian American culture, the food/music nexus marks a space of intersecting freedom and servitude: an unembarrassed pleasure in one's own bodily appetites and a catering to the bodily appetites of others. The larger historical dynamic, central to the evolution of American capitalism, is the same one we will see later in the realm of sport: laboring bodies, bodies drawn from social groups firmly entrenched in the nation's agricultural and industrial production economies, themselves become objects of consumption and spectacle in the interlocking spheres of catering and entertainment. The paradigmatic example is Aunt Jemima, the mammy figure who has adorned the packaging of Quaker Oats pancake mixes and syrup for over a century. Though the precise details of Aunt Jemima's origins and evolution remain shrouded in corporate bureaucratic obfuscation, as Doris Witt shows, her very existence and her endurance testify to the "servant problems" of the American middle class deep into the twentieth century. Put simply, how could white Americans continue to feel an aura of devotional nurturance in the kitchen when food culture and eating practices were being industrialized and standardized by modern capitalist technologies? The shrewd answer Quaker Oats came up with was to harness the romantic iconography of plantation slavery. By invoking the deeply sentimental figure of the slave mammy, the company hid their large-batch industrial factory processes behind the image of the caring, solicitous, endlessly dutiful family servant.[35]

The history of Aunt Jemima includes a black-Italian twist now seldom recalled. Tess Gardella, the vaudeville actress most famous as Queenie in the 1927 production of *Showboat*, well known also for her rendition of "Carolina Mammy," performed in blackface in a number of productions under the stage name Aunt Jemima. Vaudeville historian Anthony Slide, writing in 1994, said, "Today Aunt Jemima is a familiar name on pancake syrup, but fifty years ago Aunt Jemima meant a plump, jovial Italian woman in blackface, whose real name was Tess Gardella." Slide conjectured that "the secret of [Gardella's] success lay in her being the black mammy of the Ethel Waters type in *A Member of the Wedding*, in whose arms everyone wanted to be held and loved. Aunt Jemima represented warmth and joy, and the fact that she was really white doubtless helped to win over those with racial antagonisms." As Witt notes, while Slide's view of Gardella as "really white" ignored the ambiguities of Italian racial status in the early twentieth century, the passage of time did not diminish the difficulty of perceiving Gardella's race through phenotypic observation. In 1974, in *The Black Book*, an African American history "scrapbook" compiled under the editorial supervision of Toni Morrison, the caption to a photograph of Gardella reads, "Lois (sic) Gardella, the original Aunt Jemima, 1933."[36]

From sheet music covers to food advertising and labeling (Aunt Jemima, Uncle Ben's Rice, Cream of Wheat's use of Rastus, a demeaning caricature of black male servitude, as product mascot), visual imagery connected to food and music served as a conspicuous location for black and Italian racial stereotypes. The racist depiction of African Americans in popular culture has been well documented in recent decades, notably in the documentary film

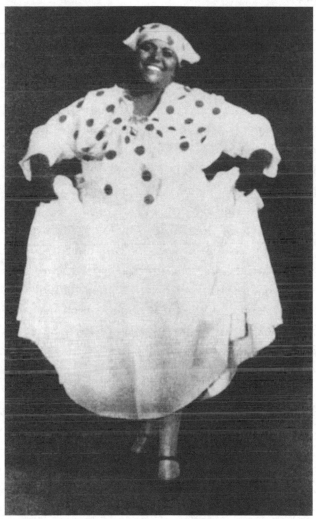

FIGURE 8. Italian American actor and singer Tess Gardella, from Wilkes-Barre, Pennsylvania, often was billed as "Aunt Jemima" in her vaudeville-era stage and screen appearances. In 1938, for example, the Vitaphone studio credited her as "Tess Gardella (Aunt Jemima)" in the two-reel musical short *A Swing Opera*. Here she appears in a publicity photograph for the 1927 stage premiere of *Showboat*, in which she played the "black" character Queenie.

Ethnic Notions (1986), now a staple in college courses.[37] Patricia Turner, in *Ceramic Uncles and Celluloid Mammies: Black Images and Their Influence on Culture* (2002), details how American kitchens became virtual museums of racist representation as minstrel images came to adorn not just food packaging but all manner of household bric-a-brac, containers, cookbooks, wall hangings, salt and pepper shakers, hand towels, pot holders, and grocery list reminders. Italian caricatures tended to be less racially charged while conveying (as the black imagery was intended to do) an aura of warmth, happiness, comfort, satisfaction, and abundance.[38] The Chef Boyardee line of canned pasta products, started by Italian immigrant Hector Boiardi in the 1920s, features the image of a dignified, mature, European-looking chef in his toque and whites. John Mariani, in *How Italian Food Conquered the World* (2011), notes that starting in the late 1940s, when pizza began its ascent toward becoming the most popular food in America, pizzeria takeout boxes were "usually imprinted with a roly-poly, mustachioed Italian *pizzaiolo* tweaking his cheek and saying 'Hot and Fresh!' or 'You've Tried All the Rest, Now Try the Best!'"[39] One of the first theme restaurants in the United States, Mamma Leone's, in New York's theater district, had as its own theatrical theme a fantasy of Italian mother-centered abundance and happiness. Heavily patronized by entertainers, stagehands, and legions of Times Square tourists, Mamma Leone's was a baroque spectacle complete with nude statues of Venus, cavernous dining halls, and waiters singing in endearing broken English. There was also food. "You sat down with your family," Mariani writes, and you were "presented with big baskets of Italian bread and a huge wedge of cheese. Platters of celery and olives followed, then garlic bread, massive portions of lasagna, gnocchi, meatballs and macaroni, pork chops, filets, veal steaming with marinara sauce and melted cheese, and fried calamari."[40]

In what Mariani describes as "the rise in status of Italian food from a low-class, coarse ethnic food to the most recognizable, stylish, and influential cuisine in the world," the culinary sensibility and aesthetic of a Mamma Leone's, or of the ubiquitous Italian American pizzerias and red sauce spaghetti-and-chianti joints dotting the American landscape, came to be derided, looked down on, or condescendingly sentimentalized by a number of American food writers, not to mention Italian American cookbook writers and celebrity chefs.[41] Joseph Sciorra regards Italian American food as its own authentic regional Italian cuisine, just like Tuscan and Venetian and Puglian regional cuisines, not as a bowdlerized, debased, or ersatz version of a single classical, authoritative Italian cuisine. This position challenges the authenticity fetish of latter-day foodies prone to dismiss a delicious bowl of spaghetti and meatballs on the grounds that the dish does not appear on restaurant menus in Italy. Much of this brand of anti–red sauce ideology equates, consciously or not, to a class-inflected bias against southern Italian food, a capitulation to the northern Italian tilt in recent elite American food culture.

Mario Batali, the most visible Italian American celebrity chef of the past two decades, has fashioned himself an antielitist, even a populist. Even as he evangelizes an old school Italian code of authenticity centered on fresh products that are locally grown and husbanded, fidelity to local traditions, and the advantages of being able to apprentice (as he did) in Italy with masters of fresh pasta, Bolognese sauce, and foraging for mushrooms, he treats all the regional cuisines with equal reverence, even embracing certain Italian American dishes. On his television show *Molto Mario*, which aired on the Food Network from 1996 to 2006, Batali preached the gospel of Italian cooking's rustic simplicity while railing against the rococo prissiness of the French. Among the anti-Gallic lessons Batali dispensed while showing off his formidable kitchen skills: never (*ever!*) truss a bird. "The French would disagree," Batali mused while loading the cavity of a duck with a stuffing of the bird's own liver mixed with bread crumbs soaked in milk, thyme, and rosemary, "but *they're* French." Batali's show was full of such lessons. Others included how to listen to risotto ("there's an auditory component to the dish: when you hear the rice kernels crackle and pop, that's when it needs a stir"); how to roll gnocchi into perfect specimens of plump softness with a silken "mouthfeel" (because "chewy is not where you want to be in gnocchi town"); and how to handle a bunch of basil properly—to tear it, not chop it, because "we're not afraid of the basil," and anyway, cutting things up small and precise is "just not part of my culture." Batali, a gifted entertainer and effortless conversationalist, in clear contrast to the imperial authoritarianism of classic European master chefs, nevertheless delivered culinary lessons whose painstaking, sometimes persnickety exactitude made them seem very, well, French.[42]

The tensions, if not full-blown contradictions, are obvious: Batali pushes very hard on themes of simplicity and "you can do this too," even while there is no mistaking his cooking school–trained (Cordon Bleu in London), restaurant-honed kitchen awareness—the supple knife skills, visual and tactile senses, and practical chemistry expertise that can take years to develop. *Molto Mario* was a series of filmed live performances, with Batali in a studio kitchen cooking for three friends (often fellow Italian Americans who work in the media arts) seated at a counter in front of him. The idea was to project a casual home cooking vibe—the home, not the restaurant, being the temple of Italian food, as Batali says repeatedly throughout the series—and an image of the food as an integral strand in the general social weave rather than an end in itself. It was a scene that recalled Frank Sinatra, in his glory years, inviting his buddies into the Capitol studios to create just the right social ambience for his recording sessions. But just as we wouldn't expect Jilly Rizzo or some other Sinatra crony to step up to the mike and knock out a killer take of "I've Got You under My Skin," we shouldn't expect one of the *Molto Mario* guests—or ourselves—to step into the kitchen and easily produce a servable quail spiedini with sage polenta and Asiago, no matter how "simple" Mario Batali says it is.

The bigger tension in Batali's persona and practice is between his deep immersion in elite restaurant culture and a warm, soulful, frankly appetitive spirit that aligns him with Mamma Leone and the food/music/sex constellation of early jazz and blues culture. The first tendency is marked by his apprenticeship under Jeremiah Tower, former executive chef at Chez Panisse, and by the hefty prices at his own New York restaurants Po and Babbo; the second is somewhat better represented by B&B Burger and Beer, the Las Vegas faux-dive bar Batali owns with Joseph Bastianich. Ponytailed, habitually shod in red or orange clogs, married and a doting father but still proud of his reputation as an inveterate skirt chaser, Batali is well known for wild, drug-abetted disco dancing and Olympian drinking bouts capped off with a few rousing Italian harvest songs or Broadway show tunes. He's a carnivalesque character, a creature of excess. His personal credo—as he tells journalist Bill Buford in Buford's book about his apprenticeships with Batali and some of Batali's Italian mentors—goes like this: "Wretched excess is just barely enough."[43] Buford describes the off-camera scene at the Food Network studios during the taping of *Molto Mario* as an "anarchic spilling out of naughtiness," a randy debauch of "dancing, butt-slapping, kissing and extra meaning found in ponytails." Female prep cooks run for cover as Batali announces that an ample artichoke or a choice cut of meat has given him "so much wood . . . *big* wood, strong-like a tree wood."[44] It's all for fun, this madcap scene reminiscent of backstage and hotel room high jinks in the rock world, thick with unchecked male prerogative. What Batali parallels in rock culture is not just the phallocentric posturing; it's also the gender bending license. Think of Elvis's hair styling and his obsession with pink; Mick Jagger's mascara and swishy stage gestures; the spandex, long hair, and girlish torsos of the cock rockers. Batali's massive girth puts rock's anorectic, androgynous beauty ideal out of reach, but he shares in the pansexual abandon and polysensual excess known to many a rock star.

Fred Pfeil, writing about 1970s rock culture, suggests that for white male rock musicians authenticity means "being a free agent with ready access to the resources of femininity and Blackness yet with no obligations to either women or Blacks."[45] Black culture does not appear to be one of Batali's readiest resources, even as his outsized appetites recall white minstrelsy's caricatures of black men. Though he codes physically as a plump disco queen or theater doyenne, he expresses no self-conscious affinity with gay culture.

Femininity, on the other hand, is an important dimension of the Batali style, one he is keen to own up to. "I know it doesn't make sense, and I don't understand it," Batali tells Buford, "but it is consistently the case that women are better cooks. They approach food differently." He's convinced that what gives his flagship restaurant Babbo its reputation as one of the best Italian eateries in the country is a style that is "more feminine than masculine." What makes an Italian restaurant great? For Batali the answer is simple: "People think there are grandmothers in the back preparing their dinner."[46]

The Italian grandmother Batali invokes is a stock character straight out of central casting: a *balabusta* figure, thick in the upper body from years of muscling pots around the stove, gruff, plainspoken, asexual—in short, the Italian version of the black mammy. That today's Italian (and Italian American) grandmothers are women who came of age in the 1960s and absorbed many of the same countercultural influences as Batali did a decade later has yet to overturn the image. A notable exception is Lidia Matticchio Bastianich, mother of Batali's business partner and herself a successful television chef/cookbook author. She's a stylishly elegant woman of robust figure, not unaware of food's erotic associations ("What else do you put in another person's body?" she asks), and a businesswoman of considerable savvy (proprietress of Felidia and Becco in New York, Lidia's Kansas City, and Lidia's Pittsburgh).[47] As cooking shows go, her PBS series, *Lidia's Italy*, is a big-budget affair. Multiple film crews capture Bastianich in a home kitchen, resplendent in jewelry and silk blouse, and on site in Italy, returning to places that capture the childhood taste memories that continue to inform the flavor profile of her dishes. (Bastianich immigrated to the United States from Istria in the 1960s.) She plays the *nonna* card to good effect, closing episodes with a food tasting by her grandchildren. It's packaged sentiment, to be sure, but on *Lidia's Italy* (and her other PBS shows) there's no mistaking Lidia Bastianich's cooking chops. I watched Mario Batali religiously, but never once did I jump up and try to make one of his dishes; his art does not translate easily to the home cook.

It's Lidia Bastianich's show, with dishes that are truly simple but well prepared—a zucchini lasagna made with leftover bread, say, or a simple tomato sauce for shrimp, made by carmelizing a little tomato paste and deglazing it with white wine—that prompts me to start peeling the garlic and cutting up the onions.[48]

A big part of what's at work here, of course, is a surrogate exchange in which Bastianich stands in for my mother and my grandmothers, whose recipes have worked their way down to me and now mingle in my kitchen practice with what I pick up from food shows and blogs, cookbooks, and friends. For those of a Freudian or biologically essentialist bent, the transference runs even deeper: the connection we forge with our mothers starts not from the fact that women are more likely to produce the food we eat as children, but from the fact that women *are* food; they are the nourishment we get in utero and for as long as we might suckle at a breast. Therein resides our unrivaled primal joy, our pleasure, our plenitude.

Mario Batali's "women are better cooks" bromide rings especially hollow when we consider that these days most of the people working in New York City restaurant kitchens, including Batali's—most of the people laboring for our pleasure and plenitude—are immigrant men from Latin America. The disingenuousness here is clear. Batali's music, in this respect, is sharply dissonant. This does not mean (except, perhaps, to his employees) that it is unpleasant or unjoyous. Batali's songbook is never so dissonant, and never so uncomfortably pleasurable, as when, in his roles as restaurant baron and celebrity chef patriarch, he trades on his masculine privilege while simultaneously draping himself in the mantle of womanhood, cross-dressing as mammy and mamma.

Bad Mamma

A tavola si sta sempre in allegria. No one wants more to believe the adage—and no one is more aware of its falsity—than Louise DeSalvo. In *Crazy in the Kitchen*, the family table of her 1950s

New Jersey childhood is a space of punishment, cruelty, and torture; a space where insults are hurled like spears ("you no good motherfucker"; "you son of a bitch"; "you atrocious bastard"); a space where parents and children menace each other with forks and knives; a space where blood is shed. "We stood chest-to-chest, so close to one another, that we swallowed each other's saliva," DeSalvo says of the operatic shouting matches in her natal family's kitchen. In this home there was "no happy Italian family gathered around the table stuffing themselves with meatballs and spaghetti, sausage and peppers, everyone talking at the same time." Instead there was "a can of Campbell's soup diluted with an extra can of water to 'stretch' it'" or "two burnt toast cheeses for the four of us." "Our supper table," DeSalvo vividly writes, "was like that of a badly run prison where someone is putting the food money in their pockets instead of on the table. My sister and I waited through meals like two inmates watching the guards through half-closed lids, to see whether or not they were dangerous."[49]

DeSalvo's description of her mother's inability to feed and nurture is premised on a concept of motherhood that puts food and feeding at the center of family interdependence and obligation. This concept of motherhood cuts deep in DeSalvo's memoir, taking shape not just at the micro level of her own family but at the macro level of the entire southern Italian diaspora. *Crazy in the Kitchen* is a memoir of self and family that connects the family table to history—in this case, to the history of southern Italian poverty and hunger. In DeSalvo's imagination, Italy *itself* is figured as a bad mother, indeed the worst kind—a mother who starves some of her children.

Crazy in the Kitchen opens with a stunning prologue, a lyrical rebuke to the beautiful but counterfeit romantic ideal of Italian land and spirit as maternally based nurturance found in the standard cookbook photographs and cooking show travelogues. "Wild Things," DeSalvo titles this section, which she has stitched together out of recovered memories of her grandparents' stories triggered by her reading about the *mezzogiorno*. The wildness this prologue evokes in its poetic cataloging of southern Italian nature and culture—flora, fauna, weather, history, social relations—is brutally elemental, primordial, scary. We hear of raging seas, earthquakes, sandy winds from Africa, scorching sun, swarming mosquitoes, vipers, tarantulas, feral cats, wild dogs, baby-stealing wolves. We read of ferocious armies, brigands, bandits, and anarchists; raging men who beat their wives and sisters; peasants so poor and dispossessed they "did not even own their own shit," which the landlords used to fertilize the fields. "They spit on that place," DeSalvo says of her grandparents' feeling toward their homeland, "because there, no matter how hard you worked, you stayed poor." "The place they came from," DeSalvo writes in words she heard from her grandfather, "was like a parent who wouldn't feed its hungry children, a parent who cast out its daughters and sons to scavenge for food in other places."[50]

Could there be a more definitive antidote to the romanticized Italy of the aristocratic Grand Tour, of countless artists' and writers' bohemian adventures, of the heritage vacation tour packages we see advertised on television during our favorite Italian cooking shows? In contemporary US culture, "Italy"—when it is not mafiosi or Silvio Berlusconi's sex life—is super Tuscan wines and agritourism, *Eat, Pray, Love*–style self-help escapades, helicopter parents on eating-tour rambles behind their children on junior year abroad in Florence or Bologna. In the early pages of DeSalvo's book, "Italy," by contrast, is the long arm of *la miseria* reaching from the killing fields of Calabria and Puglia to the crazy kitchens of Hoboken, Ridgefield, and Teaneck. Not fantasies of bourgeois pleasure in the wealthy urban north, but painful memories of the oppressed agricultural south leading to much unpleasantness in New Jersey. Not *la dolce vita* but "you no good motherfucker."

As readers of *Crazy in the Kitchen*, we are asked to drink and eat young Louise's pain and suffering in the kitchen and at the table of her parents' home. We are asked to acknowledge, in the hunger and misery of her grandparents' generation, an Italy and an Italian history that belie pleasurable images of Mediterranean and Tuscan beauty and abundance that prevail in contemporary bourgeois food culture. DeSalvo has struggled mightily to become the sort of person who delights in her Williams-Sonoma cookware and knows how to put the crucial citrus grace note on a veal piccata. She's a foodie not out of consumer envy or class status anxiety but out of retaliation, a lifelong vendetta against her mother's bad food and the brutal mistreatment of her grandparents in Italy. "I want the food I make to be perfect," she writes, because "with each perfect meal I make, I can undo the past . . . undo my ancestors' history."[51]

When DeSalvo fantasizes about undoing her ancestors' history, she really means that she wants to memorialize her ancestors' experience; to redeem, honor, and dignify that experience by reconfiguring *her own* relation to history. In this effort, DeSalvo extends the work she and Edvige Giunta began in their 2002 anthology *The Milk of Almonds: Italian American Women Writers on Food and Culture*, a volume whose purpose, in part, was "to begin to trace and establish a sense of cultural legitimacy and dignity for ourselves, equivalent to that accorded to women of other displaced and oppressed peoples."[52] The poems, essays, and stories in *The Milk of Almonds* ("Kitchen Communion," "Dealing with Broccoli Rabe," "Coffee an'," "She's Doing the Dishes," "Italian Grocer," "We Begin with Food," to sample just some of the wonderfully evocative titles) poignantly testify to the myriad ways Italian American women living in the twentieth century have engendered and commandeered food customs, rituals, and material culture at the very foundation of Italian American social life: the routine labors of gardening, shopping, and daily cooking; the handcrafting of tablecloths and other linens central to the aesthetic and ceremonial significance of the family table; the shrewd diplomatic finessing of that table's arcane, often treacherous personal politics. At its best, such literature eschews the hackneyed image of the "apron-clad mamma" spoon-feeding us her gustatory love in favor of brutally honest, fearless reflections on the terrible and the wonderful and everything in between. At its most acute and penetrating, such literature is about the fundamental politics of gender and power. This is because control and mastery of food and food spaces historically has often been, as food writing editor Antonia Till has said, "the only kind of power women are permitted to employ."[53]

In the absence of other forms of power, alas, power over food can be its own form of powerlessness: witness the apron-clad mamma trapped in a life of thankless subservience. But it can also be the most awesome power of all: the power over life itself, power over the body and what sustains it. Behind DeSalvo's desire to intervene in her ancestors' history lies the premise that food—what we eat, and how we organize our lives around the production and consumption of what we eat—is nothing less than our embodied essence, the self-identity created first through our ancestral family body, our lineal flesh and bones, the shared blood and mother's milk coursing through our veins and arteries.

In *Crazy in the Kitchen*, DeSalvo is careful to distinguish between her intellectual understanding of her immigrant family's poverty and oppression—garnered from reading recent scholarship on the southern Italian diaspora—and her deeper corporeal knowledge of her ancestors' hunger, with its attendant traumas: "Perhaps we knew these things in our bodies. Perhaps my mother relived the life of her ancestors in the way she treated food. Perhaps my father's rage began there." And it is here, in her keen visceral awareness of the hungry, suffering family body, that DeSalvo locates her fervid desire for the emotional comforts of food abundance: "Perhaps this is why I hoard food, treat it as if it's sacred, revere it, let it nourish me. Let it excite me, calm me, placate me, spend as much time with it as I can; perhaps I do this because my people could not."[54]

Crazy in the Kitchen links the dramatized intensity of DeSalvo's persona to the acute existential struggle of poor southern Italian American immigrants. Her psychic connection to food is outsized—in the parlance of American food culture, her passion about food is supersized. The supersized abundance of her food emotions is directly correlated with the outsized food deprivation her ancestors suffered. In this way DeSalvo's narrative recapitulates the whole history of Italian and Italian American food. In their introduction to *The Milk of Almonds*, DeSalvo and Giunta observe that "the history of food in Italy is often marked by the intertwining narratives of abundance and deprivation."[55] In fact, the economic dialectics of hunger and plenty created *both* Italian America and modern Italy. Several recent books—among them Carol Helstosky's *Garlic and Oil: Food and Politics in Italy* (2004), John F. Mariani's *How Italian Food Conquered the World* (2011), and Simone Cinotto's *The Italian American Table: Food, Family, and Community in New York City* (2013)—explain how the emigration of millions of hungry southern Italians was the precondition for creating abundance for all Italians, both on the peninsula and in the Americas. The mass exodus of fully a quarter of Italy's population left more food for the three-quarters who remained. These emigrants, using the wages they earned in the New World to import foods they never could afford at home, furnished the capital that spawned an Italian mass-produced food industry. Tomatoes, dried pastas, cheeses, and other products were exported and became the foundation for a nationally unified (if greatly simplified) globally popular Italian cuisine.[56]

This is the core story of how twentieth-century Italian economic modernization was inextricably intertwined with Italian American consumer culture and entrepreneurialism. It's a core story of how the most fundamental form of consumption, eating food, produces the nation. As such, it's also a core story of US ethnicity. America is a country that receives abused and deprived immigrants and then abuses and deprives them some more. It's also a country where many of those immigrants achieve comfort and prosperity and along the way both reinvigorate and redefine the national culture. Nowhere is this truer than in the history of American eating. In her book *We Are What We Eat: Ethnic Food and the Making of Americans* (1998), Donna Gabaccia shows how generation after generation of immigrant groceries, restaurants, and family cooking traditions begin as cultural and economic pillars of their ethnic communities, quickly draw in culinarily curious neighbors, and eventually attract the interest of corporate managers and advertisers who market the food to the rest of the country. Today one would be hard-pressed to find an American middle-class household whose refrigerator is not stocked with frozen pizza, bagels, or burritos. In gastro-hip American cities, certainly, but even in the small-town hinterlands, a good number of those refrigerators on any given day will contain leftover Thai noodles, Korean kimchi, Moroccan couscous, or some other au courant ethnic food. When it comes to what Americans eat, we are, as Gabaccia cleverly puts it, "not a multi-ethnic nation, but a nation of multi-ethnics."[57]

In focusing her memoir on the female-centered domain of the kitchen, DeSalvo taps directly into the visceral emotional core of Italian and Italian-American culture, into ancient mythologies of maternal succor that connect the icon of the *pietà* Madonna to the cult of the Sunday gravy mamma. As a feminist, DeSalvo is well aware of the danger inherent in linking motherhood primarily with nature and the body, the danger of reducing women to a natural essence that defines them by their biological role in birthing and nurturing their children. Not only does such thinking limit women's opportunity for self-realization and achievement, even in their roles as mothers, it also obscures the capacities and obligations that men should exercise and embrace in the work of nurturing their children. As an Italian American, on the other hand, DeSalvo is heir to an Italian culture whose most sacred image is that of the Madonna and child—a culture in which, as Maria Laurino has written, to be a mother "inherently means to sacrifice a piece of oneself for another."[58]

Laurino's feminism has been informed by her experience growing up with a mother who had "inherited the Mediterranean instinct to keep young and old close to home," as well as by her own experience as the kind of mother who seeks "intimate communication with my son through food."[59] Her book *Old World Daughter, New World Mother* criticizes mainstream American feminism for having uncritically accepted assumptions about freedom and independence derived from rationalist and capitalist notions of individual autonomy born in post-Enlightenment, Protestant northern Europe. "A feminism that is chiefly about autonomy is bound to liberate one person at the expense of another," Laurino declares, believing that "if equality is truly to be within reach for women—we must rid ourselves of our fictive notion of independence; we are nested in a complex, ancient, and biological system of attachments and dependencies."[60] She cultivates for herself a "connection-based feminism" that honors the virtues of compassion and sacrifice inherent in the noblest ideal of the Italian family, an ideal that centers on the needs of mothers and children. Hers—and DeSalvo's—is a savory Mediterranean-flavored, Catholic-inflected feminism that starts with food and feeding.

In *Crazy in the Kitchen*, DeSalvo tells of driving from Rome to Florence with her husband and their two sons when the boys are young adults. They're all hungry, and when they are stuck for hours in a traffic jam, they start screaming at each other—a distinct echo of the kitchen fights of DeSalvo's childhood. DeSalvo looks into the other cars, wondering why the Italian families are not fighting. "Mothers," she sees, "are pulling out little treats and snacks for their families and handing them around. Biscotti and bottles for the babies. Panini and Orangeade for the grown-ups. These mothers, Italian mothers, understand what happens to Italians when they are hungry."[61]

To dramatize her childhood pain and suffering, DeSalvo trenchantly deromanticizes both Italian American immigrant life and Italy itself. But then, to capture her hard-won late middle age happiness as a mother and grandmother, DeSalvo, in an abrupt and perhaps contrived narrative turnaround, romanticizes Italy again by renegotiating her own and her family's relation to it. She trades *la miseria* for *allegria a tavola*, as it were, redeeming Italy in a way that makes her sound like a righteously ethnocentric Slow Food propagandist. The Italians, she writes in breathless rapture, "caress eggplants the way a mother caresses a baby's bottom. . . . They care about food in a way my mother never cared about food."[62]

We might think of DeSalvo's late-blooming romance with Italy as rooted in the Homeric concept of *nostos*, the longing to return to the ancestral home. This concept, as Joanna Clapps Herman reminds us, lies at the heart not just of *The Odyssey* but also of the immigrant experience.[63] What is most at stake in DeSalvo's *nos-*

tos is motherhood. *Crazy in the Kitchen* was written in the wake of DeSalvo's mother's death; the memoir embodies (among other things) DeSalvo's effort to learn to love her mother, to love the memory of her. It also captures DeSalvo's effort to learn to love the mythical Italian motherland, which has been dead to her much longer.

On their travels to Italy, and in their cooking back home in New Jersey, the now middle-aged Louise and her stalwart husband Ernie dispense with small-time symbolic gestures of heritage nostalgia (photographs, souvenirs, and the like) and concentrate on a campaign of full-scale culinary vengeance. The mission is this: in retaliation for Italy's starving their ancestors, they undertake to *eat Italy*. To even the score for poor southern Italians who were denied a place at the Italian national table, the married couple master Italy's regional cuisines, gourmet home cooking their way from a Puglian period to a Tuscan period to a Ligurian period, and so on across the peninsula. Whereas their Italian forebears left the homeland penniless and bereft of food, they check in at Milan's Malpensa Airport for a flight home weighed down with fifteen pounds of expensive specialty food items. "With every excellent meal I make using my special ingredients," DeSalvo reasons, "I drive away the phantom of my mother's kitchen, try to obliterate the want of my ancestors." Overcoming her dislike for restaurants ("If my own mother fucked up my food, why should I trust a stranger?"), DeSalvo and her husband eat at some of Italy's finest, indulging in "pastas my family never tasted."[64]

There is glibness, of course, in Louise DeSalvo's retaliatory gourmandism, as if her buying luxury medallion-embossed pasta *really* makes up for Italy's brutalizing of her ancestors. And yet even the illusion of vengeance is sweet and just: "It is here, in a land that starved my grandparents until they were forced to leave for America," DeSalvo declares, "that I truly learn the pleasure of the Italian table."[65] To forgive and redeem her family, DeSalvo has had to forgive and redeem Italy. And for that to happen, Italy has had to feed her, to mother her, to recognize her as part of its family.

Who's Your Mamma?

In *A Feast Made for Laughter: A Memoir with Recipes* (1982), long-time *New York Times* food and restaurant critic Craig Claiborne writes of his mother, "She was born into a southern world in which the family was not composed of individuals but the body entire, one bond, one blood."[66]

In her fascinating chapter about Claiborne in *Black Hunger*, Doris Witt dismantles what she calls Claiborne's "plantation school ideology" by a deft analysis of the psychosexual forces that shaped his identity as a gay man. The upshot is that when Claiborne felt a strong need to separate from his mother, a "devouring white woman obsessed with the bonds of blood," he bonded with the family's black servants through food. Growing up amid the southern cult of martial virility, "a powerful black woman in the kitchen was necessary to enable the young, queer misfit 'Craig' to establish a coherent identity as 'Mr. Claiborne.'"[67]

In his best-selling cookbook *Craig Claiborne's Southern Cooking* (1987), Claiborne speaks of "Joe and Blanche and Sally and Hugh" as "my friends and playmates" in "that kitchen . . . where I spent my childhood." Even so, as Witt points out, none of the recipes in the book are credited to these family employees.[68] Witt assigns special significance to the biscuits made in that kitchen that Claiborne's mother enjoyed serving to friends with afternoon coffee or tea. These were known in the South as "beaten biscuits," old-fashioned biscuits whose flakiness and rich texture derived from the labor-intensive process of building the gluten through extended, arduous whacking of the dough rather than through modern leavening agents like baking powder. The sound of "Mammy and her rolling pin" strikes Witt as a primal plantation scene straight out of the Freudian playbook, where beating fantasies are said to help children resolve their fluid position in the triangulated family romance. These fantasies ostensibly serve as "flagellatory penance" for the child's incestuous desire toward the parent (in Claiborne's case, his desire for—in a fetching complication of Dr. Freud's theory—his father rather than his mother).[69]

Admittedly this business of needing to escape a suffocating white mother while developing a psychic investment in a black mammy is uncannily ready-made for race-inflected psychoanalytic theory. I'll modestly settle instead, however, for the more straightforward way Claiborne's "southern cooking"—for instance, the creamed chicken livers he claims as "my first *original* dish" two clauses before saying that Joe (whose last name Claiborne never uses and perhaps never knew) prepared it for young Craig "to my great delight"—exemplifies an appropriation of black labor and culture perfectly in tune with Greg Tate's "everything but the burden."[70] And though the figures of mammy and mamma I invoke throughout this chapter are mostly female-embodied, the roles of nurturance, material and spiritual feeding, and affirmation of body and soul—the roles we tend to code as maternal—have been carried out on behalf of the larger culture by black men and Italian men (as in my take on Mario Batali's cross-gender channeling), not just by women. Reflecting on the connotations of intimacy and availability inherent in such terms as "Earth Mother" and "Brown Sugar," Hortense Spiller muses: "My country needs me, and if I were not here I would have to be invented."[71] Spiller is speaking specifically as a black *woman*, and surely she is right to do so. But the same is true of black culture writ large and (to a less fundamental and as yet less storied extent) of Italian culture too.

The title of the song, remember, is "Everybody Eats When They Come to My House." Listen to the song and hear Cab Calloway's yoking of swing and humor to food consumption and the comfort of home as part of a larger narrative in which the people who labor the hardest and suffer the most in the making of America become the people whose talents and generosity of spirit underwrite American pleasure, gratification, and joy. The people most pained and deprived—Africans treated as chattel, Italians caught up in *la miseria*, migrants from many lands escaping their own unspeakable horrors for a place in labor-hungry sectors of the American economy, only to be marked as aliens and abused accordingly—are the people who produce the abundances of rhythm and tune, flavor and soulfulness, that mark the best of the nation's culture.

The hidden debts we incur in our eating, our listening, our dancing go unrecognized in a narrative of US ethnicity that comes to be all about the pleasures of consumption, abundance of choice, and heartwarming spectacles of multicultural diversity. Louise DeSalvo can't cut into a loaf of crusty Italian bread without thinking about *la miseria*, but most of us can. Who wants to think about Agent Orange while tucking into a plate of savory Vietnamese spring rolls flecked with lemongrass and baby basil leaves? Certainly not the American gourmand unburdened by any sense of national guilt, but also not the Vietnamese American immigrant trying to make a new life for his family. Once spaghetti ceased to be an "ethnic" food in the United States, Italian Americans were happy if that meant they too could be real Americans rather than despised "ethnics." We would all be better off if Calvin Trillin got his way and spaghetti carbonara replaced turkey on the Thanksgiving table.[72] But there would still be little appetite in the United States for any official national reckoning with the memory of the scores of Italian Americans who were classified as enemy aliens during World War II.

When we have the likes of Cab Calloway feeding us, it's not very sporting to bring up histories of deprivation, loss, theft, and injustice. The frittata in the pocketbook, an occasion for madcap theater and raucous laughter, is a story that originates in hunger and insecurity. The enslaved woman in the canefield, a scene of barbarous cruelty, becomes the occasion for iPhone sexual titillation. Greg Tate knows that the bill for the "long-standing, ongoing, and unarrested theft of African American cultural properties by thieving, flavorless white folk" is so far beyond calculation as to be absurd: that is why his sardonic, funky wit is precisely the right register for discussing it.

"Our music, Our fashion, Our hairstyles, Our dances, Our anatomical traits, Our bodies, Our soul"—the ourness itself is what makes *everybody* want it so badly.

Everybody wants that breast. Everybody eats.

THREE

Spike and His Goombahs

"Because We Are So Much Alike"

It was with some measure of his characteristic iconoclasm that Chicago newspaper columnist Mike Royko declared Spike Lee's 1989 movie *Do the Right Thing* a classic cinematic study of Italian American life.[1] Royko's line drew a laugh because everyone knew that Spike Lee was Hollywood's Jesse Jackson: a media-savvy race man, a mediator between the black community and the white establishment, a black artist who had arrogated to himself the responsibility of representing black people and black issues to mainstream America. It was well known that Lee had written the script for *Do the Right Thing* remembering a brutal tragedy in 1986 in the Howard Beach section of Queens. According to the sketchy story publicized by the victim's activist attorneys, a posse that included several Italian Americans wielded baseball bats and tree limbs to clear out a local pizza joint and chase a black teenager to his death.[2] In Lee's movie a black teenager (Radio Raheem) dies on the sidewalk outside an Italian pizzeria, victim of a vicious nightstick choke hold administered by a brutal policeman. This comes after Sal, the pizzeria owner, in a fury of physical rage and racial invective that belies his live-and-let-live image, has grabbed a baseball bat and smashed Raheem's radio to bits. Throughout the movie, the pizzeria—with an Italians-only photographic Wall of Fame (Sinatra, Pacino, DiMaggio, and others) hovering over a black-only Bedford-Stuyvesant clientele—serves as a symbol of economic and cultural colonialism. Sal and his sons drive in daily from Bensonhurst and park their Cadillac out front, where it looms as the emblem of an economic sovereignty seemingly far out of reach of the blacks who patronize the restaurant, none of whom appear to hold jobs. If this was a movie about Italian Americans, then at least on the surface it was mostly about Italians as economic and cultural oppressors and crude racists.

In *Jungle Fever* (1991) and *Summer of Sam* (1999), Lee continued to traffic in images of Italian Americans at their loathsome worst. *Jungle Fever*, Lee's movie about a doomed affair between a black architect from Harlem and an Italian office temp from Bensonhurst, took as its backdrop the 1989 murder of Yusuf Hawkins, a black teenager set upon by a mob of Italian youths in Bensonhurst. But in this movie the Italians visit violence only on each other. The racist father of the woman with "jungle fever" for the black man is a paragon of Italian male hotheadedness: discovering his daughter's race treachery, he beats her bloody. When the woman's spurned Italian boyfriend turns his desire toward a black woman, he gets a garbage pail upside the head, compliments of the guidos who hang out at his Bensonhurst candy store all day seething with racial paranoia. Given Lee's evident penchant for the coarser breed of Italian, he must have drooled over the Bronx primitives served up by Victor Colicchio and Michael Imperioli, authors of the original script for *Summer of Sam*. These Italians are so intellectually challenged that John Turturro, in his off-camera cameo as the voice of the dog who addles the mind of Son of Sam killer David Berkowitz, is about the most cerebral of the lot. Film critic David Denby, in words that might have been delivered by the Italian Anti-Defamation League, said that for Spike Lee "Italianness is mostly a disgrace."[3]

But is it really? How then can we explain Lee's deep reverence for the film artists Martin Scorsese and Robert De Niro? Or his key professional collaborations, especially in the first decade of his career, with the Italian American actors John Turturro, Annabella Sciorra, Danny Aiello, Giancarlo Esposito, Michael Badalucco, Nicholas Turturro, and Michael Imperioli? Actors and directors often find themselves at loggerheads personally, but a basic respect for each other's ethnic identity and heritage seems to be a prerequisite for a functional working relationship. With Spike Lee, and with the black-Italian relationship, there was much more than that. "I think it's a very interesting, complicated, sometimes volatile, violent interaction over the years," Lee said. "That's the reason we have explored it in some of my films. I was always amazed by the similarities between African-Americans and Italian-Americans, and that's why we've come to blows so much—because we are so much alike."[4]

I've purposely misrepresented my own readings of *Do the Right Thing* and *Jungle Fever* in the opening paragraphs of this chapter to underscore Mike Royko's ironic characterization of those films, as well as to emphasize that Lee *does* traffic in certain obnoxious, demeaning images of Italian Americans. I distrust readings of Lee's films such as David Denby's critique of *Jungle Fever* not just because its implied good image / bad image approach to assessing ethnic/racial themed art is unbecoming to a great critic, but also because I find Lee's Italian American characters, even at their most loathsome, far more absorbing and compelling than most of his black characters. Why do I get the feeling that Lee knows these Italian characters (at least the men) as well as many of his black ones, if not better? More important, why do I get the feeling that Lee has a keen intuitive sense for the larger historical forces shaping the relationship between New York Italians and blacks? Surely this has to do with Lee's having grown up in a multiethnic Brooklyn neighborhood among many Italian American friends and enemies, his having experienced the "undercurrents of attraction, disappointment, and mutual implication" that Robert Orsi attributes archetypically to the black-Italian relationship.[5] But it also has to do with a set of cultural vectors that, while much bigger than Spike Lee himself, converged almost perfectly in Lee's creative work, personal experience, and public persona: the New Hollywood, a New York–focused national narrative of urban decline and an equally potent narrative of black middle-class mobility, the white ethnic heritage revival, the death of New Deal/

Great Society liberalism and the rise of Nixon and Reagan-era neoconservatism, and the new black aesthetics and politics of the post–Civil Rights era.

Spike Lee's first commercial feature film, *She's Gotta Have It* (1986), was released during a period of achievement and high visibility for Italian Americans: New York governor Mario Cuomo's extraordinary speech at the 1984 Democratic National Convention; New York congresswoman Geraldine Ferraro's rise to become the first woman on a presidential ticket; the national championships won by college basketball coaches Jim Valvano and Rollie Massimino and football coach Joe Paterno; Antonin Scalia's ascension to the position of Supreme Court justice; Bartlett Giamatti's presidency of Yale University; Lee Iacocca's much-ballyhooed success as a business CEO; Robert Venturi's leadership in the postmodern architecture movement; the high-quality literary and cinematic art of Don DeLillo, Gay Talese, Francis Ford Coppola, Martin Scorsese, Brian De Palma, Robert De Niro, and Al Pacino. And yet in retrospect we can see this period as one of decline for Italian Americans, especially New York working-class and lower-middle-class Italian Americans—a period in which, as crystallized in the Wall of Fame in Sal's Famous pizzeria in *Do the Right Thing*, and as symbolized by the pizzeria's being located in Bedford-Stuyvesant while its family owners live in Bensonhurst, Italian American culture had moved into a period of stale heritage nostalgia and vexing neighborhood dislocation. We can also see this as a period when black urban decline and crisis coexisted with black social mobility and a powerful "new black aesthetic." Spike Lee's *Do the Right Thing* and *Jungle Fever*, whatever their shortcomings as representations of blackness and Italianness, poignantly capture something important about the historical trajectories of these two groups and their relation to each other on the changing landscapes of American politics, urban life, and popular culture in the late 1980s / early 1990s.[6]

Filming the White Ethnic Urban Village

The New Hollywood is the term assigned retrospectively to the generation of directors who transformed American film culture in the 1970s by challenging the producer-driven system of the old-line studios and imbuing movies with the values and sensibilities of the 1960s counterculture. Many of these directors were educated in film schools where they studied the American canon but also absorbed the influence of the Italian neorealists, the French auteurs, and Asian cinema traditions whose narrative styles, modes of characterization, and ideological frameworks often dissented from the classic Hollywood formulas. The new aesthetic favored realist scenarios crafted from location shoots, nonheroic and antiheroic characters, and messy politics. Dream factory fantasy eventually would survive and set new (and very expensive) standards of technical sophistication in blockbuster hits like George Lucas's *Star Wars* (1977) and Steven Spielberg's *E.T. the Extra-Terrestrial* (1982), but not before a new ethic of on-the-ground authenticity found expression in gritty, unromantic depictions of urban life. New York City emerged as the cinematic paradigm of urban decline, with films such as William Friedkin's *The French Connection* (1971) and *Cruising* (1980), Martin Scorsese's *Mean* Streets (1973) and *Taxi Driver* (1976), and Sidney Lumet's *Serpico* (1973), *Dog Day Afternoon* (1975), and *Prince of the City* (1981) strikingly dramatizing the corruption of politicians and police, the physical blight of streets and neighborhoods, and the wholesale fraying of the social fabric.[7]

The urban decline narrative of the 1970s and '80s reflected a deep anxiety about crime and public disorder that was coincident with, and often a camouflage for, a deep anxiety about racial proximity. Heroin and crack cocaine epidemics fueled a sharp increase in violent crime, decimating black and Latino communities and sharpening middle-class perceptions of the "ghetto" as an alien, treacherous, and unredeemable badlands. Long before drug abuse and crime reached alarming rates, however, many urban whites already had mounted stalwart resistance to people of color moving into or even close to their neighborhoods. Government efforts to integrate schools and neighborhoods fostered deep resentment and intensified resistance campaigns, often to a hysterical pitch. Urban renewal projects and antipoverty measures, once a signal feature of the Johnson administration's Great Society, now were widely dismissed as a by-product of liberal fantasy and profligacy. Self-appointed custodians of respectability saw the city streets as a cesspool of graffiti, clamorous music, and menacing bodies. The very gait and mien of black men were read as off-putting if not actually threatening, an offense against propriety and civility.

Richard Nixon's law-and-order conservatism had garnered huge popular support by fashioning itself as a bulwark against all the threats to public order ostensibly unleashed by 1960s liberalism, from the Black Panthers to the antiwar movement to the drug culture on college campuses. In 1973 New York governor Nelson Rockefeller, calculating that his brand of genteel liberal Republicanism was a detriment to his swelling presidential ambitions, proved himself "tough on crime" by signing a law that mandated draconian minimum sentences for the sale and possession of illegal drugs. Over the next several decades the "Rockefeller Drug Laws" exercised a grossly disproportionate impact on blacks and Latinos, who came to constitute the vast majority of inmates in a prison system that grew at an astronomical rate. The wider "War on Drugs" initiated by Nixon and amplified by Ronald Reagan targeted urban minority communities with high-tech, military-style law enforcement. At the same time, a parallel arms race ensued within the drug trade, and random gun violence became a staple of the print and broadcast tabloids. Neoconservative intellectuals chalked it all up to innate moral and cognitive defects among the urban minority poor, while Republican strategists deployed a series of racial bogeymen (welfare cheats, rapists on the loose) to secure vast white voting majorities.[8]

Obscured in this narrative—and far too rarely spelled out by liberals thrown on the defensive by a superior conservative propaganda machine—were the deeper economic forces dooming inner-city neighborhoods. Chief among these was the collapse of the domestic manufacturing sector as capital moved overseas for cheap labor and favorable tax arrangements, consigning the domestic US working class to a tightly constricted job market and expanding an unemployed underclass.[9] The new American capitalism of the Reagan era brought a substantial realignment of the nation's class structure in general, and that of New York City in particular. Huge fortunes amassed by Wall Street financiers created growth in certain allied industries but failed to trickle down to the city's workers, who were doubly victimized by the shrinkage of the organized labor movement. Growing income inequality fueled a parallel distortion in the real estate market as well-educated, mostly white, young urban professionals sought housing in gentrifying neighborhoods, financed by money borrowed from banks that (in the practice called redlining) programmatically denied loans to black inner-city applicants. In *Do the Right Thing*, Radio Raheem and the other black teenagers who loiter in Sal's Famous pizzeria are at risk of ending up in the Bed-Sty underclass; meanwhile, a white yuppie on a neighborhood brownstone stoop (his whiteness symbolically doubled by his Larry Bird basketball jersey) stands poised for upwardly mobile gentrification.

These socioeconomic class dynamics were powerfully inflected by race and ethnicity, notably in a long history of New York City housing, neighborhood formation, and labor market competition that decisively shaped the relationship between Italians, blacks, and other groups.[10] Owning their own homes had always been an exalted goal for Italian Americans; even before World War II, they did so at higher rates than other European immigrant groups. As early as 1930, fully a third of New York City households with an Italian-born head owned their homes; the vast majority of these families already had left the original "Little Italys" of Manhattan to settle in the outer boroughs of Brooklyn, Queens, and the Bronx. Italians went to the end of the subway lines they themselves had built, bought cheap land, built houses, planted gardens, and sometimes even grazed livestock. After World War II, buoyed by GI Bill benefits and highly favorable, racially discriminatory federal mortgage policies, New York Italian Americans moved out to parts of Long Island, Westchester County, Connecticut, and New Jersey where Italian communities had already been established by early twentieth-century Ellis Island immigrants.

This diaspora was only part of the story, however. For Italian New York, participation in what became known as "white flight" took a different course than it did for other white ethnic groups like the Jews and the Irish: Italians colonized the more "suburban" sections of the city's outer boroughs (Staten Island, the "better" parts of Bay Ridge in southwest Brooklyn, Howard Beach in Queens), and they created a new Little Italy in the Brooklyn neighborhood of Bensonhurst, where thousands of post–World War II immigrants from Italy helped shift the ethnic character of what had previously been a largely Jewish neighborhood. All this was happening while blacks and Puerto Ricans were pouring into these same outer boroughs (some from Manhattan, most from the South and the Caribbean), settling in less desirable neighborhoods that often abutted the Italian ones. As Jonathan Rieder, Jerome Krase, Simone Cinotto, and others have argued, Italians became known as the toughest "defenders of place" among urban white ethnics, yoking their communal identity to an aggressive, at times violent territoriality, zealously guarding against a perceived threat of property devaluation and moral decay posed by blacks and Puerto Ricans. An Italian sense of moral superiority over these racial others expressed itself in sanctimony about home, family, neighborhood, and work. Italians took great pride in their family tables, their gardens, and their success in the construction and restaurant trades—even as their high school dropout rates were comparable to those for the blacks and Puerto Ricans they measured themselves against.[11] When Rieder lived in Canarsie in the 1970s while conducting his study of white ethnic antiliberal backlash, he heard a woman voice a sentiment he understood to be widely shared: "I'm Jewish and you know as well as I know that the only place to buy a house in this city is in an Italian neighborhood, because the Italians have more guts than the Jews." In Rieder's analysis, Jews maintained a streak of idealistic humanism, a cosmopolitan spirit, and a faith in liberalism; Italians, known more for "unpretentious warmth" than for high-minded idealism, saw the world as being "neatly divided between loyal kin and perfidious strangers, with an implicit threat of swift reprisal for betrayal."[12]

New York Italian tribal territoriality entailed toughness (the threat and sometimes the actuality of violence) as well as sentimentality (the allure of strong family bonds and cultural pride). This potent combination, steeped in authenticity but also ready-made for tragedy, kindled the imaginations of the two leading Italian American directors in the New Hollywood, Francis Ford Coppola and Martin Scorsese. With his book *Starring New York: Filming the Crime and Glamour of the Long 1970s* (2012), film historian Stanley Corkin helps us think about Coppola's *The Godfather* (1972) and *The Godfather II* (1974) and Scorsese's *Mean Streets* in the context of urban decline, the postindustrial economy, and racial space. For Corkin, these films speak to a longing for an ethnic urban village of yore, an idealized Little Italy of neighborhood intimacy, small-scale family businesses, and social homogeneity. Nostalgia for this romanticized "ethnic white city" takes cinematic form in close-ups of details defining time and place (an antiquated meat slicer in a deli in *Mean Streets*; the juicy orange Vito Corleone buys from a fruit vendor just before getting gunned down), coupled with ground-level camera placements that frame intimate establishing shots across neighborhood streets rather than impersonal wide-angle ones down the city's broad avenues. *The Godfather*'s pre–World War II scenes in lower Manhattan's Little Italy radiate the sociable, face-to-face, personal warmth of the immigrant community theater, the delicatessen, the café, the street *festa*. This is the context in which Vito's violent overthrow of the Mulberry Street gangster Fanuccio plays out as a victory for community-minded benevolence over selfish avarice. *Mean Streets* depicts this same neighborhood in the early 1970s as a place rotting with spiritual decay and social paranoia. While shots of the city at large show New York as a pulsing, modern, multicultural metropolis, Scorsese portrays Little Italy as a "medieval fortress" whose inhabitants devote themselves to keeping outsiders (racial others) from breaching neighborhood borders.[13]

The temporal and thematic scope of the first two *Godfather* films is measured in the succession of business models employed by the two dons, Vito and his son Michael, particularly in how these models change the relationship between the dons and their families, neighborhoods, and ethnic cultures. The Vito Corleone we meet at the start of the saga is a formidable potentate, a man who controls judges, politicians, and even movie studio executives on the other side of the country. But the business interests and lifestyle that engendered this power bespeak modesty and prudence; he's an olive oil importer and commander of old-fashioned vice trades; he sleeps at home every night and finds time to tend his tomato plants. Don Vito is no hidebound Mustache Pete: he moves his family out of lower Manhattan's Little Italy to a compound on Long Island; he collaborates with Jewish gangsters in the invention of Las Vegas. But it is in these moves, according to the sociogeographic logic of these films, that the trouble begins. The Corleone compound in suburban Nassau County is a proto-gated community, a citadel that ensures the safety of the family within but also removes it from the vital sociality of the old urban neighborhood. Because the Corleone rackets are still centered in lower Manhattan, however, family business involves commuting into and out of the city. Not incidentally, it is in acts of commuting that the movie's first instances of violence take place: traitor Paulie Gatto's execution on the highway shoulder; the machine-gunning of Sonny Corleone at a tollbooth. Vito resists involvement with the heroin trade that would entangle the family in a far-flung international trading network, but the Corleones' imperial expansion into the Las Vegas and Havana pleasure industries figures as the backdrop for fraternal treason and family dissolution. Michael Corleone becomes "the model of the traveling businessman in the age of globalization, the father who is never home." When he throws a lavish first communion party for his son at the new family compound on Lake Tahoe in Nevada, it falls to Frank Pentangeli, an old family associate who reeks of New York ethnic authenticity, to try to teach the band to play a tarantella.[14]

Coppola and Scorsese's ascension in the New Hollywood (along with fellow Italian Americans Brian De Palma, Michael Cimino, Robert De Niro, Al Pacino, Sylvester Stallone, and John Travolta and Jews like Harvey Keitel and James Caan who burnished their acting reputations playing Italian American characters) coincided with the Italian American ethnic heritage and antidefamation movements of the 1970s. No single message or agenda emerged from these movements, and their often absurd incoherence can be glimpsed in the fact that the organization that fashioned itself the Italian-American Anti-Defamation League (later renamed the Italian-American Civil Rights League), founded in 1970 with the stated goal of combating pejorative Italian American stereotypes, was led by Joseph Columbo, a crime family boss who ended up being shot and left paralyzed at a rally billed as "Italian-American Unity Day." Then again, there was a certain cognitive dissonance at work when a story like the one represented in the first two *God-father* films, a story that culminates in fratricide and conjugal rupture, could emerge as a popular symbol of the exceptional fortitude of the Italian American *famiglia*. Matthew Frye Jacobson, in *Roots Too: White Ethnic Revival in Post–Civil Rights America* (2006), argues that we can understand the popular reception of *The Godfather*, going back to the publication of Mario Puzo's novel in 1969, only against the backdrop of the 1965 Moynihan Report and the national discussion it provoked about the alleged deficiencies of the black family. With every major organ of the American print media running stories on what Moynihan called the black family's "tangled web of pathology," the Corleones' "strict code of honor, patriarchal authority, family loyalty, sense of duty, and—perhaps above all—self-help" recommended itself to the nation as an ideal for other groups to emulate—notwithstanding the high body count.[15]

Indeed, in a national culture reeling from the spectacular failure of its political and military leadership in prosecuting the Vietnam War, the unprecedented constitutional crisis unleashed by

Watergate, and what intellectuals ruefully diagnosed as the atomization and rootlessness of American social life, it was a propitious time for traditional patriarchy, even in the form of organized crime, to assert itself as a bastion of wise and steadfast moral authority. Hence the devastating implications of the moral (not just economic) calculus by which *The Godfather* represents the don of Detroit's decision to vote in favor of the Sicilians moving into the heroin trade: "In my city I would try to keep the traffic in the dark people, the colored. They are the best customers, the least troublesome and they are animals anyway. They have no respect for their wives or their families or for themselves. Let them lose their soul with drugs." Flesh-and-blood black characters are virtually absent from *The Godfather* saga and are only a token presence in Scorsese's New York films. But blackness looms large in all these films as an absent presence: not just as proximate outsiders threatening Italian tribal purity, but as a group-affirming antitype, as the essential other that defines and bolsters tribal integrity and power through negative example. "Negroes were considered of absolutely no account, of no force whatsoever," Puzo had written in his novel. "That they had allowed society to grind them into the dust proved them of no account."[16] Puzo wrote these lines just after the civil rights movement, through a campaign of heroic physical courage and bracing moral witness against violent massive resistance, had forced on America the most important legal and social changes in its history. Nevertheless, in the wake of the Moynihan Report (not to mention a history of high-placed calumny against black moral character dating back at least to Thomas Jefferson), and with inner cities exploding after the assassination of Martin Luther King Jr., the stage was set for Italians and other white ethnics to fashion themselves not just as defenders of their own turf but as redeemers of the nation.

This was the crucial point missed by the Italian antidefamation lobby: to hold *The Godfather* to account for its pejorative stereotypes was to play small when the big action was at the level of epic myth, the dream space where a nation reimagines itself. The gangster noir of Coppola's two films was but a stylish vehicle for

his majestic historical narrative, a paradigm of the kind of bootstrapping immigrant family saga that vitalized the ethnic revival
movement and, as Jacobson shows, helped shift valorized notions
of American national identity from Plymouth Rock to Ellis Island.
In contrast, there were no such sentimentally glorifying family
and group backstories in any of the "blaxploitation" films that
constituted Hollywood's effort to capitalize on the 1970s vogue
for funky urban fashion, deep-grooved soul music, and "stick it
to the Man" politics. Corkin observes in the original New York
City–based blaxploitation cycle—*Cotton Comes to Harlem* (1970),
Shaft (1971), *Across 110th Street* (1972), *Superfly* (1972), and *Black
Caesar* (1973)—a pattern in which black gangsters' vanquishing
Italians for control of the Harlem vice trades does little to contra
vene Italians' power as exemplars of family cohesion and neighborhood uplift. Tommy Gibbs, the protagonist of *Black Caesar*
(titled *The Black Godfather* in its UK release), outguns his Italian
rivals, wreaks vengeance on the Irish cop who'd exploited him as
a teenager, and even rewards his mother with temporary owner-
ship of the swanky Upper East Side apartment where she'd served
as a maid. But his triumphs are all about the individual glory of
violent retribution and flashy enrichment: he has no significant
connection to (or even safety within) his own neighborhood, no
connection to a deeper historical narrative, no humanizing pretense of working for broader community betterment. His alluring
masculinity—this is a common trope across the blaxploitation
genre—comes in large part from his ability to occupy normatively
white space (downtown lawyers' offices, luxury apartments) with
swashbuckling swagger rather than to ameliorate the substandard
condition of black urban space. These films feature frequent wide-
angle shots of Harlem streets blighted with abandoned buildings,
strewn garbage, and groups of idle, loitering men. Where the Italian gangster films routinely show neighborhood folks working in
restaurants, delis, corner stores, funeral parlors, and construction
sites, blaxploitation films are virtually free of employment outside
crime and policing. The Harlem pictured in these films, as Corkin
puts it, is clearly a ghetto, not a neighborhood.[17]

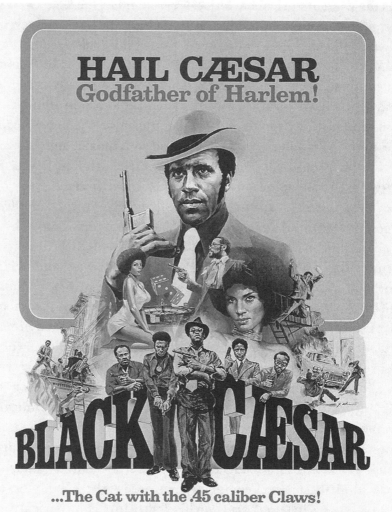

FIGURE 9. *Black Caesar*, a 1973 blaxploitation crime drama starring Fred Williamson and featuring a James Brown/Fred Wesley soundtrack, was a remake of *Little Caesar*, the 1931 gangster classic in which Edward G. Robinson plays a bootstrapping Italian hoodlum who ascends to the upper reaches of organized crime.

Black Brooklyn Renaissance

The distinction between ghetto and neighborhood was an implicit, abiding theme in Spike Lee's first decade as a filmmaker, shaping the visual and sonic design of his films and heightening their relevance to contemporary debates about black urban life. Lee's emergence into national consciousness came as the urban decline narrative attached itself to the crack cocaine scourge, the AIDS epidemic, rising rates of teenage pregnancy, and deteriorating public schools. A series of grim tragedies luridly framed by the tabloid press—Tawana Brawley, Yusuf Hawkins, and the Central Park jogger served as headline fodder—pointed to the most fractious racial landscape since the late 1960s. Hip-hop culture began to segment in ways that reflected strategic positioning in relation to what cultural critic and filmmaker Nelson George called "ghettocentricity." While mainstream media selected out the safest, most innocent forms of racial crossover in suburban teenager–friendly concoctions like the NBC sitcom *The Fresh Prince of Bel-Air*, politically informed message rap, building on Grandmaster Flash and the Furious Five's seminal "The Message" and percolating with Public Enemy's "Don't Believe the Hype," framed black urban America in terms that unmasked the falsifications of Reagan's "Morning in America" propaganda. By the end of the 1980s, as the conservative establishment either wrote off the inner city or encouraged police departments to regard it as enemy territory, West Coast gangsta rap eclipsed East Coast Afrocentric rap as hip-hop's ascendant style. This heralded a new code of authentic black masculinity—one much mimicked by white teenagers—steeped in images of violent criminality, police brutality, and predatory prison life.

Lee would not fully engage this part of the urban landscape until his 1995 film *Clockers*, a crime drama that renders a hellishly dark portrait of the drug trade in a Brooklyn housing project. That film, based on a Richard Price novel, had been in development at Universal as a collaboration between Martin Scorsese and Robert

De Niro before Lee inherited the project. The first of Lee's films not to originate from his own screenplay, *Clockers* is an anomaly in his oeuvre both thematically and tonally. High-quality ghetto-centered drama was the calling card of other emergent film-makers, notably John Singletary in his debut film *Boyz in the Hood* (1991) and, later, long-form premium cable TV series like David Simon's *The Corner* (2000) and *The Wire* (2002–8). A common criticism of Lee before *Clockers* was that he was presenting a selective, even didactic vision of black New York, sanitizing the contemporary city—excepting only the harrowing junkie and crack house sequences in *Jungle Fever*—of its highly publicized pathologies. In *She's Gotta Have It* (1986), *Mo' Better Blues* (1990), and *Crooklyn* (1994) in particular, the warm, sumptuous cinematography by Ernest Dickerson and Arthur Jafa makes black Brooklyn, with its tree-lined blocks of majestic brownstones, look like the American Paris. In the several Brooklyn-based Lee films scored by bassist Bill Lee, the director's father, a romantic jazz orchestral sound full of the enchanting melodies characteristic of early '60s Blue Note and Riverside records bathes neighborhood scenes in an aura of history and nostalgia.[18]

Another way of saying this is that Lee was invested in the romance of the neighborhood as an antidote to the tragedy of the ghetto, a counter to the urban decline narrative that treated city-based stories of black dignity and bourgeois achievement as rare, heartwarming exceptions. Lee's portrayals of black Brooklyn and Harlem gave the lie to the widespread misconception that black America had cleanly fractured into an underclass living in hopeless urban poverty and a suburban middle class of successful college graduates. Lee himself grew up in a family of educators and artists in the largely Italian neighborhood of Cobble Hill, adjacent to bustling downtown Brooklyn and upscale Brooklyn Heights; he later graduated from Morehouse College in Atlanta, historically one of the main training grounds of black leadership. With his first commercially released feature film, the groundbreaking *She's Gotta Have It*, Lee became Brooklyn's most visible booster and creative entrepreneur, eventually producing and marketing several lines of "BK"-themed merchandise and turning his own character in that film, the nerdy bicycle messenger Mars Blackmon, into a television advertising icon. Lee now made his home and built his business in Fort Greene, the neighborhood that is as much the focus of *She's Gotta Have It* as any of its characters. The presence of Lee and his production company, 40 Acres and a Mule Film-works, which occupied a converted firehouse on De Kalb Avenue in Fort Greene, helped ignite Brooklyn's post-1990 renaissance, generating an aura of vitality and hipness that attracted talented, educated, upwardly mobile young people.[19]

What made Fort Greene such a compelling story was its juxta-position of the most alarming signs of urban decline with an en-chanting vision of cultural rebirth. The neighborhood has a rich cultural history whose dignitaries have included Walt Whitman, who lobbied for the creation of Fort Greene Park in the pages of the *Brooklyn Daily Eagle* in the 1840s; Richard Wright, who penned his classic novel *Native Son* while living there in the 1930s; and a number of prominent jazz musicians of the post-bebop gen-eration such as Betty Carter, Cecil Taylor, and Lester Bowie. Since the 1960s the neighborhood had been a beacon of black pride for its relatively high rate of homeownership, as African American families circumvented redlining practices to take advantage of undervalued properties, many of them distinguished examples of nineteenth-century Italianate and Eastlake architecture. Still, by the 1970s Fort Greene and adjacent Clinton Hill had fallen vic-tim to soaring street crime connected to the exploding drug trade. Vernon Reid, founder of the rock band Living Colour, remembers the area, where he has lived since his high school years, as "full-on ghetto" with a "feral environment after dark."[20] This description resonates with the yuppies, buppies, and bohos (black bohemians) who started flocking to Fort Greene in the 1980s, when the devas-tating effects of the crack epidemic and a flood of cheap handguns often made the nightly walk home from the local subway stop an exercise in terror.

Nevertheless, Fort Greene in the 1980s and 1990s attracted a steady stream of black writers (Nelson George, Kevin Powell, Carl

Hancock Rux, Touré), musicians (Wynton and Branford Marsalis, Terence Blanchard, Donald Harrison, Steve Coleman, Greg Osby, Erykah Badu, Meshell Ndegeocello, Mos Def), visual artists (Lorna Simpson), actors, comedians, and other performing artists (Wesley Snipes, Roger Guenveur Smith, Chris Rock, Saul Williams), and arts collectives (the black women's group Rodeo Caledonia, the Black Rock Coalition).[21] Fort Greene's wide range of interdisciplinary, cross-arts creative work exemplified what Trey Ellis dubbed, in a widely discussed essay, "The New Black Aesthetic."[22] This new art making was inspired by the 1960s black arts movement but rejected its narrow strictures of racial purity; it absorbed the fresh energy of hip-hop while drawing on a much bigger archive of cultural influences and resources; it collapsed boundaries between high and popular art, connected with parallel movements in the East Village downtown music club and art gallery scenes, and openly embraced commercial success. Here, arguably, was the most concentrated cohort of cutting-edge black artistic talent, and the most place-specific moment of black cultural production, since the Harlem Renaissance of the 1920s.

Outer Borough Agita

For all their emotional investment in the ethos of neighborhood, all their justifiable pride in the food culture, sociality, clean and well-ordered stoops, yards, and streetscapes of their communities, Italians could claim no part of the borough or the city at large that came close to matching this level of hip mystique and cultural panache. Indeed, the Brooklyn Italian neighborhoods that generated the most interest in these years did so not because of their surging real estate markets or beguiling artistic production, but because of their benighted image in popular media culture. Brooklyn had a long Hollywood history, starting with the 1950s sitcom *The Honeymooners*, television's pioneering depiction of East Coast urban working-class life focused on two couples living in a Bensonhurst apartment building where the governing mode of communication is screaming out the kitchen window. In the 1970s, in the sitcom *Welcome Back, Kotter*, set in Bensonhurst, and the feature film *Saturday Night Fever*, set in Bay Ridge, the southern region of Brooklyn became Hollywood's locus classicus of New York ethnicity. John Travolta launched his acting career playing two working-class Brooklyn characters, colorful ethnics who garnered enormous popular recognition. Vinnie Barbarino, in *Welcome Back, Kotter*, is a goofy but sexy teenage delinquent, a blend of post-hippie antiestablishment attitude and Brooklyn ethnic street style. The ultimate academic underachiever, Barbarino represents Italian American lower-class anti-intellectualism incubated in a New York City public high school (modeled on Bensonhurst's Utrecht High School) whose farcical dysfunction lends itself to the show's latter-day Borscht Belt humor. Tony Manero in *Saturday Night Fever*, for his part, is nothing less than an American icon, the slick-haired, white leisure-suited discotheque habitué whose gyrating hips and diagonal arm thrusts became the global image of the white disco hero.[23] For most of the film he is also the prototype for the figure later called a guido, a primping and preening peacock who treats his body as a site of "narcissistic perfection" and lives for the see and be seen buzz of the nightclub.[24] Crucially, however, by the end of the film Travolta's Manero has used his dancing skills to quit his parochial neighborhood for cosmopolitan Manhattan. The Italian Brooklyn he escapes is a nightmare of screaming fathers, dead-end jobs, ethnic turf battles, rape, and suicide.

Italian Brooklyn's image was yet more severely—indeed permanently—tarnished by the Yusuf Hawkins murder in 1989. Hawkins, a black teenager from Bedford-Stuyvesant, had come to Bensonhurst with three friends to inquire about a used car. Lying in wait was a posse of young Italian American men supposedly protecting the honor of a local girl thought to be dating African American and Latino men. One shot Hawkins twice in the chest with a handgun, leaving him to die. As had happened in 1982 when Willie Turks, a black transit worker, was beaten to death by a group of young Italian American men in the nearby neighborhood of Gravesend, African American civic leaders organized protest marches on the main thoroughfares of an Italian American neighborhood. The Bensonhurst marches, led by the controversial activist Al Sharpton, attracted massive media attention, showing the world the spectacle of Italian American men and women of all ages jeering and spitting epithets while young men in their sleeveless guido-style "guinea T-shirts" hoisted watermelons over their heads in racist derision toward the marchers.

This spectacle of uncouth behavior was acutely embarrassing to liberal and progressive Italian American elites who now questioned the ethical moorings of a neighborhood that represented their own ethnic immigrant saga, whether or not they or their families had ever lived there. Several writers and scholars have written movingly of the painful personal reckonings occasioned by the events in Bensonhurst following the Hawkins murder. Literary critic Marianna De Marco Torgovnick, who grew up in Bensonhurst in the 1950s and '60s, heard her father asking about Hawkins and his Bed-Stuy friends, "What were they *doing* here? They didn't belong." This reminded her of the whispers she heard as a child about the Mafia protecting the neighborhood from "the coloreds." In *Crossing Ocean Parkway* (1997), Torgovnick reflects on her journey from Bensonhurst to her career as an English professor at several of the most prestigious colleges and universities on the East Coast—a journey made possible, she asserts, only by shedding the parochialism of her home and neighborhood and clothing herself in the cultural values introduced by her Jewish husband, whose family lived across the parkway in Sheepshead Bay. Torgovnick struggles to reconcile the simultaneously "choking and nutritive powers" of her old neighborhood, a place where people who rationalize murderous racist rage also lovingly tend the tomato plants and fig trees in their modest, well-manicured yards and congregate nightly on their front stoops for saucy gossip ("Did Anna wear black long enough after her mother's death? Was the food good at Tony's wedding?").[25]

Journalist Maria Laurino covered the Turks and Hawkins murders for the *Village Voice* in the 1980s and found herself deeply alienated by the Bensonhurst racism she calls "a detestable part of my culture." Years later, after serving as chief speech writer for David Dinkins (in 1989 Dinkins defeated his Italian American opponent Rudolph Giuliani to become New York City's first African American mayor; Giuliani won a rematch against Dinkins in 1993), Laurino returned to Bensonhurst to study the neighborhood for a chapter in her book *Were You Always an Italian?* (2000). She's appalled by the "truculent maleness" of the teenagers she meets who model their speech and behavior after the gangsters in *Goodfellas* (1990), *A Bronx Tale* (1993), and *Donnie Brasco* (1997). She rues finding parents telling their children that the point of school is to "show respect" rather than to secure the education that will lead to college and upward mobility. She observes the neighborhood's changing economy (a loss of traditional union jobs) and demography (an influx of immigrants from Asia, the Middle East, Eastern Europe, and South America) and concludes that Italian Bensonhurst has become mired in a cultural identity crisis. While residents proudly call themselves "Italian" to distinguish themselves from Wonder Bread–eating "Americans," only the most recent immigrants speak Italian (Sicilian dialect in most cases) or have other connections to a foreign homeland comparable in depth to those of the newly arrived Albanians, Russians, Chinese, and Ecuadorans. In their fear for the future, the Bensonhurst Italians conjure a belief "that once upon a time there was bread and wine and boccie and laughter that, without their fortitude and determination, will be lost forever." Anxious and unmoored in the neighborhood they worked so hard to make secure, they cling "to a distant culture they will never know."

Laurino grew up in a multiethnic, middle-class neighborhood in suburban New Jersey where, in high school, she imitated the Jewish girls, trying to come as close to the WASP ideal as her olive skin would allow. Like John Travolta, who came from a bootstrapping Italian-Irish family in a predominantly Irish American neighborhood in Englewood, New Jersey, she sees nothing of herself or her family in Vinnie Barbarino, Tony Manero, or any of the characters in *Goodfellas* or *Donnie Brasco*. She both acknowledges and disavows her affiliation with Bensonhurst, aligning herself with its identity as a traditional urban ethnic village of crunchy sfogliatelle and leisurely bocce, but sternly condemning its racism, an offense to the foursquare liberalism she inherited from her socially conscious mother. "Brooklyn," she poignantly muses, "was the place where my family never lived but had to leave."[26]

The urban anthropologist and folklorist Joseph Sciorra has lived in Brooklyn most of his life. His parents were born in New York in the 1920s, were raised in Italy, and returned to America in the early 1950s. Living in the nearby Flatlands district, Sciorra and his younger siblings had "intimate ties" to Bensonhurst— shopping for Italian specialty foods and produce on Avenue U and Eighty-Sixth Street, visiting *compari*—during their childhood years in the late 1950s and '60s. A temporary family relocation to Connecticut confirmed Sciorra's mother's conviction that the suburbs were an "antiseptic wasteland" while Brooklyn was "where civilization thrived right outside one's doorstep." When the family moved back to Brooklyn, Sciorra enrolled at South Shore High just in time to witness the race riots that spilled into the school from neighboring Canarsie. With friendships and loyalties confusingly divided between his black and Puerto Rican classmates and his Italian and Irish neighbors, Sciorra found himself gravitating toward Jewish kids. Rather than following the trope of the scion of an Italian "book-hating family" seeking cultural capital and intellectual stimulation from the "people of the book," Sciorra's connection to the "JAPs" (Jewish American princesses) and Jewish "freaks" hinged on their shared interest in sex, drugs, and rock and roll. At Brooklyn College he fell in love with Puerto Rican culture and people. After a year playing hooky in Bologna and Milan at the height of the late 1970s Italian radical student movements, he returned to college determined to use his training in visual culture and anthropology. His plan was not, as would have been customary, to clinically examine far-away non-Western cultures, but rather to study the people and culture of Brooklyn itself ("the most tribal place in the world," he told his adviser). He went on to become a leading scholar of New York City Italian material culture, religious artifacts, and urban vernacular expressive arts.

What others may find vulgar about the plastic Madonnas and other baroque statuary adorning Bensonhurst stoops, the hyperwattage Christmas light displays in Dyker Heights, the oily sausage and peppers at the *festa*, and the lowbrow "Brooklynese" dialect of the streets, Sciorra enthusiastically embraces as a local people's art and culture, fully authentic expressions of regional *italianità*.[27]

Though culturally simpatico with Bensonhurst and similar Italian American neighborhoods, Sciorra nevertheless found his populist ethic vexed by the ethnic chauvinism he heard voiced by many of his neighbors and research informants. "I had both a personal and professional desire," he writes, "to understand why Italians in New York had come to base their identity in direct opposition to people of color." The stakes were significantly heightened in the wake of the Hawkins murder. Sciorra found the Italian response to the black protest marchers "a blatant exhibition of xenophobia in defense of parochial village values." Fed up with "cautious politicians, out-of-touch academics, and aloof *prominenti*" mired in "deep denial and paralysis," he resolved to step personally into what he diagnosed as a gaping void of Italian American moral leadership. Four days into the protests, Sciorra joined the marchers, carrying a homemade sign that read "Italians against Racism." Italians lining the Bensonhurst sidewalks cursed and spat at him; one enraged man hurled the ultimate Italian curse, "*sfaccim*" (sperm of the devil). Sciorra resented the media's broad-brush depiction of Bensonhurst as a sanctuary for "monosyllabic bigots," and he was pleased to later hear about residents (virtually all women) who spoke out against the killing. But on this occasion, eventually joined in the march by a lone Italian woman and a multiethnic smattering of allies, Sciorra was a pariah among his own people, a race traitor.[28]

Giancarlo and "the Opera of the Streets"

The media buzz around *Do the Right Thing* at the time of its 1989 release (this is true as well of the small cottage industry of ethnic studies and cultural studies scholarship on the movie in subsequent years) focused almost entirely on issues of black politics and black cultural representation: Was Spike Lee aligned with Martin or Malcolm, and what did such a choice mean for contemporary race politics? When Lee's own character Mookie threw the garbage can through the window of Sal's pizzeria, did this symbolize the heroic anticolonialism of oppressed people of color, the tragic black inner-city nihilism lamented by philosopher Cornel West, or the black fascism alleged by cultural critic Stanley Crouch? Did Lee romanticize the street life of Bedford-Stuyvesant? Was he too concerned with black cultural style at the expense of nitty-gritty issue politics? Were his female characters too passive and powerless? Were such literalist questions missing the significance of the film as the vehicle of a new black cinematic aesthetic?[29]

Compelling as such questions were and might remain, they were of no interest whatever to two Chicago Italian pizzeria owners interviewed by movie critic Gene Siskel after a preview screening. For veteran dough tossers Al and Nick, this was a movie about an Italian pizza parlor—its proprietor and his family, its behind- and over-the-counter social dynamics. On this score, Lee got a big thumbs-up. "It's got a lot of characters I've worked with, a lot," said Al. "We used to have somebody who worked with us who was just like Da Mayor [Ossie Davis's character], sweeping up out front, spending the money on liquor. I can't believe how much of our world [Spike Lee] got on film." Nick concurred: "This Spike Lee has real talent. They ought to give this thing the Oscar. It really shows the way it is. . . . Even the Italian was good. I mean it. I put this picture in the same class with *The Godfather*. But I don't think it's going to do as much business. I think the white people who see it are going to tell other white people it's a 'black picture.' That would be too bad."

Siskel's dispatch traded on a tacit cultural understanding: he knew he could count on his readers to smell the goombah authenticity wafting from the words of pizza men who worshiped at the altar of Don Corleone. Such is the iconographic power of pizza and the Mafia in America's imagination of the Italian. Siskel knew also that Italians are as deeply invested in these images as anyone else, perhaps at some cost. In this case the cost was a self-serving vision that translated into a kind of moral blindness. So thoroughly did Al and Nick identify with Danny Aiello's portrayal of Sal as a benevolent small-business patriarch that Siskel had to remind them that in the movie they just saw a young black man gets choked to death by a policeman. "I'll be honest with you," said Nick, "I completely forgot about that kid dying. This Spike Lee is brilliant. He put so much violence in the destruction of the restaurant that I didn't think about the kid. He died for no reason." A chastened Al replied, "I'm really embarrassed I didn't think of him," but he quickly blamed the death on the blacks themselves for stirring up trouble: "He got it because his friend Buggin' Out wanted to be like Martin Luther King or Malcolm X." When Siskel gently suggested that the real issue was police brutality, Nick was happy to shift blame onto the cop—anything to absolve Sal of all guilt. "I'm still upset at the way they [the black kids] treated Sal," said Al. "I was brought up to respect my elders no matter what color they were."[60]

Many Italian Americans were far less enchanted with Lee's film than these Chicago pizza men. Peter Bondanella, in *Hollywood Italians: Dagos, Palookas, Romeos, Wise Guys, and Sopranos* (2006), praises the film for its powerful depiction of racial conflict yet argues that "its premises seem to be based on the same racial attitudes it condemns." George De Stefano, in *An Offer We Can't Refuse: The Mafia in the Mind of America* (2006), laments that while just about every character is a bigot, "Lee has singled out Italians for particular animus." Bondanella and De Stefano share Al and Nick's solicitude for Danny Aiello's character, Sal. Bondanella invokes the trope of the preternaturally overpowering black man to explain why Radio Raheem dies not because of Sal's racism but because of his own physical resistance to the police: "Raheem resists arrest and dies from a choke hold instigated by his stubborn refusal to stop fighting and his superhuman strength that requires an entire squad of police to subdue." De Stefano, assessing the larger political dynamic of the film, sees Sal as a straw man: "Lee holds that the overworked owner of a small, downscale pizza parlor, a man who could have joined the white flight from a once-Italian now black neighborhood but who continues to work there, is emblematic of the oppressive white power structure that kills innocent black men."[31]

Whether endorsing the film or not, all these responses speak to a strong investment in Sal's fundamental decency, a desire to celebrate what he symbolizes at his best and to absolve him of guilt for what he may have helped to wreak at his worst. For Italian Americans (and not just Italian Americans), Sal and his pizzeria represent the abiding virtues of hard work and family-centered business, the moral and spiritual value of the communal table. Sal is tough and profane, a man's man. But when he passionately claims responsibility for feeding the neighborhood kids—"These kids have grown up on my food. *My food*"—he sounds more like a proud Italian mother. When he sits down for a friendly chat with Mookie's sister, the affection they share is not the illicit sexuality Mookie suspects, but the mutual caring of a doting elder and a self-possessed young woman. Sal's Famous is more than an entrepreneurial venture, more than a business Sal can leave to his sons, more even than an emporium of epicurean delight. Sal's restaurant is a community center, a public square, a scaled-down piazza. It's a pillar of neighborhood in a community that lacks sturdy social institutions but radiates a spirit of sociality. Kids hang out and act up. Attachments form and break up. Feelings ebb and flow. Bodies and voices jostle. Time and sound and smell are shared.

Spike Lee seems to have found himself at cross-purposes. He wants to evoke the racism of Howard Beach and Bensonhurst, but he can't help also showcasing the more humane and salutary qualities of those neighborhoods and of untarnished Brooklyn Italian areas like Cobble Hill and Carroll Gardens. "Spike grew up around all these Italians and it was in his blood more than he even knew," suggests Giancarlo Esposito. "I felt that Spike really understood the consciousness of Italian people, probably even more so than he understood black people, which to me was surprising. Bottom line, the reason I think that Spike understands Italians is because they are good people, people who really care about the community.

They're very different from what Spike would probably coin 'white people,' and I think that's why he relates to them."[32]

This may help explain Lee's strong rapport with his Italian American actors and characters. Even as Lee set out to craft an unflinching portrait of Italian racism, he couldn't mask his liking and respect for Danny Aiello—in spite of Aiello's warning him, "My politics are on the right of the most right-wing person you know."[33] In the journal Lee published after the film's release, we learn how Lee's character, Mookie, was influenced by some advice he received from Aiello. "Spike, you're a good actor," Aiello told Lee, "very natural, you just have to get an *activity*. Your body, you have to work on it." Lee Strasberg might have put it differently, but it was advice Lee took to heart. "Danny was 100% right," Lee writes. "Mookie has to have an activity. Maybe he's always shuffling his feet. He has to do something. Another idea just came to me. Mookie might sound a little bit Italian—his intonations and the expressions he uses. He's worked at Sal's for so long, it's rubbed off." Press reports from the *Do the Right Thing* shoot dwelled on rumors of friction between Lee and Aiello over the issue of Sal's feeling toward his black customers. "He shows by his deeds that he is not prejudiced," Aiello told the *New York Times*. "[Sal's racial insults] are not the work of a bigot, but the words of a man who has a limited vocabulary and grew up on the street." Lee's journal evinces mostly good feeling between himself and Aiello. After meeting initially with Aiello when Robert De Niro turned down the part of Sal, Lee wrote: "We hit it off right away. Danny had me dying. Next to blacks, Italians curse the best."[34]

The journal also documents Lee's high esteem for Robert De Niro and Martin Scorsese, whose films he studied closely in NYU film school and who later appeared as guest lecturers at Lee's film institute at the Fort Greene campus of Long Island University. Again and again Lee cites scenes from *Raging Bull* as his inspiration for a particular screenwriting or directorial decision in *Do the Right Thing*. He notes with exacting precision small tics of language and physical nuance that De Niro brought to his portrayal of boxer Jake LaMotta: this seems to have been Lee's cinematic model for the poetics and kinesthetics of ethnic machismo. Lee fancied himself such an honorary goombah—the journal tells us— that he toyed with temporarily changing his film company's name from 40 Acres and a Mule to Da Moulan Yan Picture Company, a barbed inside reference to the Italian term for eggplant, which in slang becomes "moulies," a racist epithet for blacks.[35]

John Turturro credits his affinity with Lee to complementary life experiences: "We're both the same age, we grew up in similar kinds of family situations—my friends were black growing up, his friends were white growing up—we definitely have things in common. I think we were even born a few weeks apart." When Turturro was six years old, his family moved from Brooklyn to an Italian neighborhood in Queens. There he was "like the darkest kid and they thought that I was Arabic or maybe a mulatto. I had a lot of fights. Then I got bussed out to high school, which was all black. When I was growing up, my friends were black. I'm actually not that comfortable if I'm in a completely white situation—I feel a bit ill at ease." In *Do the Right Thing*, this ease with blackness is characteristic of Sal's son Vito, played by Richard Edson. Turturro turned down that role, preferring to play Vito's racist brother Pino. Pino, for Turturro, is "the more interesting of the two brothers."[36] What makes him interesting is the frisson between his antiblack racism and his own darkness. Mookie knows how to get under Pino's skin: he intimates that his kinky hair gives away the tar brush in his family history. Pino frames his racism in geographic terms: "We should stay in our neighborhood and the niggers should stay in theirs." But he himself is the literal embodiment of a geography—the physical proximity and the human intercourse between southern Italy and Africa—that belies strict racial segregation and purity.

Such racial mixing registered on an even deeper personal level for Giancarlo Esposito. Esposito's parents met in Italy in the 1950s when his mother, Elizabeth Foster, an African American opera singer from Alabama, performed at La Scala, the Milan opera house where his Neapolitan father, Giovanni Esposito, worked as a stage technician. Giancarlo was born in 1958 in Copenhagen, where his mother was splitting a nightclub bill with Josephine Baker. He spent his first five years in Naples, Rome, and Hamburg, following his mother's career. The family later moved to Elmsford, New York, just north of New York City, on the border between the town's black and Italian neighborhoods. "The black guys didn't understand me," Esposito remembers. "They didn't understand how I spoke. I didn't walk with a little dip. I didn't wear my hair in an Afro and I had a name like Giancarlo Alessandro Esposito. They couldn't relate. Same with those little guinea guys who I so wanted to relate to because of my boyhood with my dad in Italy. I had to wind up telling them, listen, I'm *more* Italian than you are."[37]

You need only hear Esposito speak his name—which he pronounces, as they do in his father's Naples, with the *r* languorously rolled and the emphasis on the *spo*—to understand how strongly he embraces the musicality at the heart of his Italian heritage. He proudly tells the story of his paternal Italian grandfather, a man of the opera who worked backstage at Naples's San Carlo Theater. With Mussolini's ascendance in the 1920s, fearful of the Black-shirts' running riot over the theater, he hid the sets for the company's operas all over the south of Italy. It was this kind of commitment to art that Esposito's mother found so bracing when she went to Italy to pursue her singing career. Giancarlo describes her as a "beautiful, dark, stately" woman who "adopted European consciousness," turning to high culture as a refuge against American racism.

Esposito's maternal grandmother played organ in a rollicking Pentecostal church in Alabama where his mother sang in the choir. His love of performance owes as much to this vernacular tradition as to the formal vocal training he received from his mother while appearing as a song-and-dance Broadway baby during his adolescent years. In the late 1970s, after shifting to drama, Esposito won an Obie for his performance in the Negro Ensemble Company's *Zoo Man and the Sign*. It was during that show's run that Spike Lee, then a recent film school graduate making ends meet by cleaning films for Maxie Cohen at First Run Features, came backstage to introduce himself and compliment Esposito on his work. Lee talked with fervor about his vision for making films that plumbed black life and culture from the inside. He talked about a script he was working on called "Homecoming," a musical that explored fraternity and sorority life at historically black colleges modeled on Morehouse and Spelman.

"Homecoming" became *School Daze* (1988), the first of four films in which Esposito worked under Lee's direction.[38] The most absorbingly personal of these roles was his character in *Do the Right Thing*, Buggin' Out, a hip-hop generation black nationalist who looks and sounds like a hybrid of boxing promoter Don King and rapper Flavor Flav. As the movie unfolds, Buggin' Out patrols the Bed-Stuy sidewalks with an exuberance more comic than menacing. His signature valediction, "stay black," comes with a soul brother handshake so elaborately choreographed that it suggests parody as much as solidarity. When the white yuppie wearing a Celtic-green Larry Bird basketball shirt rudely bicycles over his just out of the box Air Jordan sneakers, then compounds the insult by repairing to the stoop of his brownstone and intoning about *his* property rights, Buggin' Out stands tall for the neighborhood against this boorish representative of white privilege. He stops short of unleashing vengeance, however, cooling out his posse of b-boys and b-girls with an appeal to the moral superiority of the "righteous black man" with "a loving heart."

For Lee, as we've seen, Sal's pizzeria symbolizes not just the persistence of economic colonialism since integration, the flow of capital out of the black community into the hands of nonblack ethnic entrepreneurs—the Korean grocery across the street from Sal's carries that theme just as well. At Sal's the stakes are higher than what the cash register tape reveals: here the coin of the realm is *respect*. Buggin' Out is plenty miffed by the two-dollar surcharge for extra cheese on Sal's slices, but what really incenses him is Sal's Wall of Fame, his photographic shrine to Italian American achievement made up of publicity shots of Frank Sinatra, Dean Martin, Perry Como, Liza Minnelli, Al Pacino, Joe DiMaggio, and Luciano Pavarotti. "Yo, Mookie," Buggin' Out calls to Lee's character, "how come there ain't no brothers up on the wall?"

Sal's response to Buggin' Out shows none of the loving heart we see elsewhere in the film, none of the simpatico Mediterranean benevolence he shows when he speaks sentimentally about feeding the neighborhood kids. With Buggin' Out he musters only spiteful defensiveness: "Get your own place, you do what you wanna do. You can put up your brothers and uncles, nephews and nieces, stepfathers and stepmothers, what you want. But this is *my* pizzeria. American Italians on the wall only." To which Buggin' Out responds: "Rarely do I see American EYEtalians eating here. All I see is black folks. We spend much money here, we should have some say."

Lee's depiction of Bed-Stuy's Stuyvesant Avenue leans heavily on representations of black consumer culture: a billboard of heavyweight boxer Mike Tyson looming over the pizzeria, Magic Johnson T-shirts, Air Jordan sneakers, Afrocentric body ornaments, and the ubiquitous black music sound stream flowing out of DJ Señor Love Daddy's (Samuel Jackson's) storefront radio station two doors down from Sal's. Every bit as much as the blessings, dispensations, and seasoned wisdom offered by local elders Da Mayor (Ossie Davis) and Mother Sister (Ruby Dee), what is presumed to hold the black community together is their shared (albeit mass mediated) popular culture. The formidable transracial power of that culture becomes evident when even Pino, Turturro's combustible bigot, identifies Magic Johnson, Eddie Murphy, and Prince as his personal heroes.

Against this backdrop, one might hear Buggin' Out's call for a change in the iconography at Sal's as a gesture of "hip black separatism," as political columnist Joe Klein, the film's sternest critic, suggested. But Thomas Ferraro has brilliantly argued in an opposite vein that the nuances of the film instead reveal a Brooklyn urbanism founded on the interethnic common ground shared by the Franzione family and its customers:

> On the strip along Stuyvesant Avenue between Quincy and Lexington lies a habitus of stoops and windows, street mingle, store flow, and music: less a mean street than a boulevard of what Herbert

Gans once called an "urban village," its open hydrant the fountain of an elongated *piazza*—and what we see there is the syncopated congress, the *opera* of the streets: where the individual is constituted not so much outside of group interaction as through it—as one or another archetype or ethnic persona, realized in competitive display, in oral inventiveness or eloquent silence, in the airing of family linen, intrablock melodrama, or neighborhood defense; and where the ethical imperative that emerges is a formidable combination of love and irony, respect and suspicion, absorption and wariness.[39]

Lee's pizzeria opera evokes a larger New York social drama in which Italians and blacks are the most passionate of intimate strangers: others who are almost the same. Biological mixing is prelude to the cultural weave. Bensonhurst guidos and Bed-Stuy homeboys inhabit overlapping urban style worlds of syncopated streetwise lingo, body posturing, and a visual vernacular of hair, clothing, and ubiquitous gold jewelry. They treat their Air Jordans and their Cadillacs as organic extensions of their bodies, using them for purely expressive purposes. They groom and they strut and they emote.

And they scream. None louder or uglier than Buggin' Out and Sal in the pivotal showdown that grows into one of the most incendiary racial conflagrations in recent American cinema. Buggin' Out storms the pizzeria in league with his homey Radio Raheem, whose signature boombox blasts Public Enemy's "Fight the Power" at ear-splitting volume. Sal yells that he wants the music off. Buggin' Out holds his ground. The two start spewing a stream of racial epithets in each other's faces. Sal grabs a baseball bat (a grim reference to Howard Beach) and smashes Raheem's radio to bits. The ensuing melee takes a grisly, tragic turn when a policeman's brutal nightstick choke hold squeezes the life out of Radio Raheem. After a moment of eerie calm, the hitherto placid Mookie strikes his blow for the revolution, flinging a trash can through the pizzeria's front window, sparking a riot that ends with Sal's Famous pizzeria and the Franziones' Cadillac in ruins.

FIGURE 10. In *Do the Right Thing*, director Spike Lee's 1989 film, Lee (as Mookie) mediates between the Bedford-Stuyvesant black community and the Bensonhurst Italian American family played by Danny Aiello (Sal), Richard Edson (Vito), and John Turturro (Pino). Here Mookie, Sal, and his sons brace for the neighborhood rioting that will burn down Sal's Famous pizzeria.

Lee's movie was a big cinematic public mural: loud, messy, provocative. Joe Klein, among the most provoked, worried that the film would incite the city's black youth to riot; he denounced Lee as a reckless threat to public order. Others perceived something highly original and piercingly insightful. Joseph Sciorra recalls that "the film had a profound effect on me because it looked at the Italian American version of racism I had experienced firsthand in New York. [Turturro's character] Pino was an incredibly accurate portrayal of the confused and angry youth I had grown up with and interviewed."[40] For Esposito, there was a devastatingly intimate reality beneath the film's colorful surface and controversial reception. At the time of the Howard Beach incident, Esposito's father was teaching Italian at a public school in that very same neighborhood in Queens. Giancarlo had grown estranged from his father after his parents divorced years earlier, and he craved a stronger bond with him. "I didn't know if I was doing him proud as a son, because I could never be as Italian as he is—I can't speak the language as clearly as he does." Curious to check out Howard Beach, but as fearful as any other brown-skinned person of setting foot there, Giancarlo joked with his father about coming to visit one of his classes—the joking a mask to cover an undercurrent of pain. In his Italian neighborhood in Howard Beach, Esposito senior had assimilated into white America, but the son remained persona non grata—which is to say, neighborhoodless.

The script of *Do the Right Thing* heightened Esposito's inner conflict. "The movie was part of the catharsis I went through to release a lot of anger that I built up. Playing an angry black man allowed me to say: 'I refuse to live in that space that says I am not good enough, a world that will not accept me because of the color of my skin.'" Complicating matters was the easy rapport Esposito enjoyed with Aiello, Turturro, and Edson, the Italian family that represents the racist regime against which his character mounts a neighborhood insurgency. The bonding ran deepest with Aiello, a man "who was the same color as my dad," and who seemed able to relate to Giancarlo in ways his father had lacked.

The camaraderie worried Lee, who tried to keep the two from mixing. "Spike's style," Esposito explains,

> is to make the actors enemies [off-camera] because he wants the real thing to appear on-screen. In *School Daze* he separated the "jigaboos" from the "wannabes" and even put them in different hotels. It was freaking everyone out because people had friends on the other side, but Spike wanted war. I understood it. He's a new filmmaker, and that's his way of creating the tension he needs. But it was frightening to me because he was manipulating people in a way that's different than just directing. It was about manipulating who people *are*. If you can do that as a director, you probably get a better scene or a better movie. But I didn't agree with it. I felt that what I do is *act*. I don't have to carry that hate inside me.

Whatever the virtues or defects of Lee's approach—call it method directing—the upshot was a powerful blowup between Buggin' Out and Sal. Beyond Lee's directorial reach, the scene also served as a poignantly shared personal epiphany for Esposito and

Aiello. "We got to that scene and an amazing thing happened," Esposito discloses.

> Everyone is going nuts and screaming. All of a sudden I felt all these years and years of rage. And Danny, who I never heard curse, started cursing. Not a typical epithet, not just "nigger." It reminded me of what my mother had taught me. She said, "When someone calls you something, you have to say something back." Danny had learned that lesson, too. We started screaming at each other, and some of the things that came out of his mouth I had never heard before. I could not believe it. Some of the things that came out of *my* mouth, I also couldn't believe.
>
> It was a really harrowing moment for both of us. We were staring into each other's eyes, and all the anger from all those years came right out. Needless to say, we got an amazing scene. Spike was going nuts. He loves it. Danny starts to cry. I start to cry, and we start to hug. We hugged each other for at least twenty minutes. We didn't want to take that anger out of the scene, didn't want to take it with us.

Brecht in Brooklyn and Harlem

Spike Lee explained his thinking behind *Jungle Fever* as a straightforward matter of race and sexuality pitting two New York neighborhoods against each other. "Harlem and Bensonhurst for me are more than two geographic locations," he told *Newsweek*. "Yusuf was killed because they thought he was the black boyfriend of one of the girls in the neighborhood. What it comes down to is that white males have problems with black men's sexuality. It's as plain and simple as that. They think we've got a hold on their women."[41] In the film Flipper Purify (Wesley Snipes), a married black architect from Harlem's Strivers Row, has an affair with the Italian office temp Angie Tucci (Annabella Sciorra), who has been forced on him by his white business partners after his regu-

lar African American secretary leaves. In Harlem, the affair up-
ends Flipper's picture-perfect black upper-middle-class nuclear
family life; meanwhile his crack-addicted brother, Gator (Samuel
Jackson), drives their father, the Good Reverend Doctor Purify
(Ossie Davis), to filicide. In Bensonhurst, the affair throws Angie's
lower-middle-class family into chaos as she suffers contempt and
physical violence at the hands of her father (Frank Vincent) and
brothers (Michael Imperioli and David Dundara). The relationship between Flipper and Angie commences in steamy sexual congress on a midtown Manhattan office drafting table, but thereafter
it falters on the shoals of Flipper's guilt and arrogance. Lee tries to
frame the relationship as fraught and doomed owing to family dis-
approval (at dinner at Flipper's parents' home, Angie suffers the
Good Reverend's arch sermonizing about the sinfulness of interracial coupling); the racial politics of public space (after Flipper
and Angie take an apartment in Greenwich Village, they are set
upon by two white police officers, weapons drawn, while engaged
in innocent sidewalk horseplay); and Angie's naïveté (she impetu-
ously argues with the policemen, stoking Flipper's fear and dis-
may).

For Lee the relationship could function only as a projection of
racial mythology: a white woman's fantasies about sexual equipment, a black man's curiosity about forbidden fruit. Some who
were close to Lee believed his attitude toward interracial relationships had been poisoned by his own father's marriage to a white
woman not long after his mother's death. Esposito, whose entire
family life had been built around interracial marriages—he married the Irish American producer Joy McManigal in 1995 and
had four children with her before they divorced—later said he
found Lee's thinking narrow-minded. "I was just crushed about it,
crushed. I thought, get smart, get some serious issues out there.
When I confronted him, he said to me, 'Look, Giancarlo, it's called
Jungle Fever. That's all it is."[42] Annabella Sciorra (Joseph Sciorra's
younger sister) held a very different view of Angie's motivations
than Lee did.

At some point we discussed the characters' attraction to each other, and Spike said, "This movie is about fear of the big black dick." That just made me laugh—maybe there are some people out there who are afraid of Spike's dick, but I didn't understand that from the character. If I had, I would have addressed the character differently. But I was under the impression she was falling in love with the *man*. He was different from what she was used to. She had these brothers who were kind of bullies and racists, and so was her dad, and she was the girl who came home from work and cooked and cleaned for her family. I think that in Flipper she saw something that she hadn't come close to before. He was educated and opening up another world for her.[43]

Lee has been a famous person with a public platform ever since *She's Gotta Have It*, and his pronouncements on social issues often have demonstrated a blustery radical chic rather than deep and careful analytical thought. Part of Lee's entrepreneurial energy manifests itself in quasi-political agitprop that often serves as effective publicity for his films. His adoption of the "jungle fever" theme as an idée fixe invoked an undeniably important phenomenon in the history of US race relations; in connection with his film of that title, however, it came to take on something of the atmosphere of the shrewd carny barker. The fact is that the interracial sex motif ostensibly at the center of *Jungle Fever* is simply not as interesting, nuanced, or resonant as other themes that unfold in the film outside Lee's public framing of it.

Sciorra's Angie not only is a more multidimensional character than the director envisioned, she embodies a narrative of class, culture, and geography that makes *Jungle Fever*'s Manhattan/Brooklyn racial schema ethnographically richer and more insightful. She is joined in this by John Turturro's character, Paulie Carbone, Angie's Bensonhurst boyfriend, who also develops an interracial romantic interest that reveals a deep hunger for education and social experience far beyond what the traditional ethnic neighborhood offers. Angie and Paulie are trapped in situations than consign them to perpetual family obligation: each is playing the role of surrogate wife/mother in a wifeless/motherless family. Angie dutifully cooks and cleans for her father and brothers; it is their prerogative to reverently bless the spirit of their dead wife/mother and to entomb their daughter/sister in that reverence. Paulie's father (Anthony Quinn) wails hysterically over the loss of his wife and smothers his son with his emotional neediness. Paulie, no less than Angie, takes on the traditionally feminine tasks of nurturance and domesticity.

Angie and Paulie are not given much screen time together: we implicitly understand that their relationship is over; were it to continue, they would remain trapped in unfulfilling, family-suffocated Bensonhurst lives. As it is, Paulie grudgingly runs his father's candy store, where he earnestly reads while a group of neighborhood layabouts (Nicholas Turturro, Michael Badalucco, Michael Imperioli) pour out their hatred of blacks and their insecurity vis-à-vis WASP men. "What's with this reading?" Nicholas Turturro's character Vinny asks Paulie, in American cinema's purest distillation of Italian American anti-intellectualism, "Some guy writes a book, fuck him." Paulie explains that he's reading about how, in 1899, the Sicilian owners of a Louisiana factory "gave blacks equal status until the regular white people found out about it and lynched the Italians." "Good," Vinny seethes. "They got what they deserved. They shouldn't have gotten involved with no niggers in the first place." The candy store chorus harasses Paulie and brands him a race traitor when he has friendly interactions with Orin, a neighborhood black woman played by Tyra Ferrell. The candy store sells only the daily tabloids and the racing sheet; Orin pushes Paulie to order the *New York Times*, signaling her education and sophistication. She also implores Paulie to apply to Brooklyn College, and his eagerness is catching. He's also eager for Orin.

"Before there was a script," Turturro recalled, "Spike interviewed me about my relationship with girls. Originally I thought that I was going to be the main character—that's the way Spike appraised it. To this day I think that this would have made a better movie. I had a lot of black girls that used to like me when I was a kid. I'd fool around with them and stuff, but I never went out with a black girl because, with my parents, that would have been a difficult thing. [But] I lost my virginity to a black girl."[44] Paulie and Orin's budding relationship is given context and pacing that gild it with romance. In spite of the odious candy store race talk that clouds the atmosphere around them, Paulie and Orin push for a space of purity and innocence. He asks her out on a proper date, and as the two stroll through the neighborhood, it is possible to temporarily forget Bensonhurst's reputation as a northern urban version of Mississippi, a last bastion of the American race line. Whether Orin's interest in Paulie reaches beyond her cheerleading for his education is unclear: Farrell plays the role with guarded emotion. But this did not prevent certain viewers from *wanting* to believe in a romance that blossoms above the racial maelstrom and other obstacles. "That relationship, that was what made the movie for me," said Giancarlo Esposito. "John and Tyra, they were in love. It was beyond anything you can label. It doesn't matter how different people are. Did you ever meet people who don't speak the same language, yet they are in love? It's magnificent. That kind of love is the language of the world."[45]

If there was a place in Spike Lee's imagination for that kind of love (and for a black woman living in Bensonhurst in the first place), he was steadfast in his conviction that black men and their sexuality threatened the fundamental order of things in places like Bensonhurst. This, for him, was the unassailable truth revealed by the Hawkins murder. "I don't care what people say," Lee said in 2005, "the year *Jungle Fever* was made—some Italian girl brings a black guy home? Maybe you can do that *now* in Bensonhurst. But back then? Hell . . . no. Now these white kids are into rap, hip-hop, black culture. They weren't into it that much back then."[46] Lee seems here to have forgotten about the black culture-loving, albeit racist, Italian characters he created in his own films—John Turturro's Pino in *Do the Right Thing* and Nicholas Turturro's Vinny in *Jungle Fever*, who drives up to the Carbones' candy store in a 1970s powder blue Cadillac with his girlfriend Denise (Debbie Mazar) screaming at him to turn down the rap music (Public Enemy) thundering from the car stereo. But few Italian Americans would deny the underlying validity of what Lee was saying about the community's deep-seated attitudes. The issue is whether those attitudes were monolithic and permanent or whether the progressive voices of people like Marianna De Marco Torgovnick, Maria Laurino, and Joseph Sciorra heralded the possibility of transformation and redemption.

It is in this context that Annabella Sciorra's Angie Tucci figures as a more complex and intriguing character than the "jungle fever" trope foretells. The film was a big score for Sciorra—casting director Robi Reed reported that she and Lee considered "practically every white actress in New York," including Marisa Tomei, Linda Fiorentino, Kelly Lynch, and Gina Gershon—but it proved difficult as a working experience. "[Spike] really bad-mouthed me in the press," Sciorra said. "He and Wesley [Snipes] went around saying I wouldn't reveal my sexuality in the relationship because I'd never been with a black man before. Then they'd say, 'It's just for publicity.'" The shooting of the office scene where the relationship with Snipes's character is consummated was "just awful" for Sciorra. "I kept saying, 'This isn't sexy'" when the performance played out as a rape scene before an acceptable take finally emerged. Overall, there was a basic disagreement over what sort of person Angie should be. "Spike wanted Angie in lipstick and high heels," Sciorra recalled. "He expected me to play Angie as a sexy but ignorant woman and I wouldn't do it. I'd improvise lines, talk about current events, Farrakhan etc., and he would cut them. He'd say, 'Angie wouldn't say that; she's from Bensonhurst.'"[47]

The candy store scenes were shot not in Bensonhurst proper, but on Avenue N not far from the neighborhood in Brooklyn where Sciorra had grown up. The neighborhood is not Italian—it is predominately Irish, German, and Jewish—but when an unidentified truant apparently threw a rock through the store window during the shoot, Lee hyped it to the press as proof that "it was the Italians in the neighborhood who didn't want the black people there." It also appears that Lee resisted cast efforts to humanize Angie's father (Frank Vincent) and show that he could still love his daughter in spite of her interracial affair. Sciorra told writer George De Stefano that when she met actor Joe Pesci ten years after the making of *Jungle Fever*, Pesci told her he had been slated to play her father in the film but dropped out when Lee would not guarantee a scene in which he reconciles with his daughter. "Joe felt," Sciorra said, "that even if he would beat me up and throw me out of the house, and disown me, he felt there should be some sort of reconciliation, that after all, it was his daughter and that he would have to accept her back because culturally that's what he would do as an Italian."[48]

Despite all the friction and contretemps, in the end "Spike gave me all of my moments," Sciorra told De Stefano. "Everything I wanted to do with that character is in the movie, so in the end, Spike saw what I was doing and put it in the movie—and he didn't have to."[49] Angie is far from physically unattractive, but she is not the sexpot Lee initially fantasized. What makes her seductive in the office scenes is her sheer sparkle, her spirited insouciance. At home in Bensonhurst, she leans over the kitchen sink with an air of ennui and circles the dinner table stoically going through the motions; she doesn't seem resentful or passive aggressive toward her father and brothers, just disengaged, uninspired. In the architect's office, by contrast, her countenance glows, her eyes twinkle, her voice enchants. Cinematographer Ernest Dickerson photographs the office in chilly, sterile tones, perhaps to underscore an aura of cultural whiteness that confounds Flipper's professional ambitions—in contrast, for instance, to the warm tones he brings to the Bensonhurst candy store scenes, perhaps to signal the suffused, affective warmth of Italian social space (even when ugly sentiments are voiced). Against the wintry whiteness of the Manhattan office, Angie is a spring flower pushing up from the soil, drinking in the air and light. Her smart professional appearance, her organized desk, her efficient typing, even her alert posture as she sits at her desk—this is a young secretary from the outer boroughs for whom the Manhattan corporate office represents opportunity, significance, excitement, social mobility.

This young woman is feeling her power to live in a bigger world, to dream of a life beyond the limitations of her parochial village, even as she retains her ethnic pride (bragging to Flipper about the great Italian American boxers Marciano, Graziano, LaMotta) and the spunky pugnacity characteristic of women from her neighborhood (mouthing off to the policemen who racially profile Flipper and rough him up).

Ed Guerrero, a scholar of black cinema, laments that Lee did not give Angie more space to express her liberated self beyond the affair with Flipper. He is not convinced, as the denouement of *Jungle Fever* frames it, that with the end of the affair she would simply go back to her old life in Bensonhurst. "It is highly implausible," Guerrero writes, "that a woman of Angie's adventurous character, whose miscegenous affair can, at least in part, be read as an act of rebellion against all that Bensonhurst has come to stand for (including the violent beating she takes at the hands of her father), would not foresee the possibilities of her freedom beyond the dead hearth and home of racist patriarchy."[50] The point is well taken and underscores how Lee's fixation on the "jungle fever" trope restricted his capacity for a nuanced understanding of the full humanity of his characters. But it has always been Lee's strength and value as a filmmaker to shape blunt-edged microcosmic framings of American racial (or at least black-white) logic so as to distill and clarify what is most fundamentally at stake in a very complicated cultural and political landscape. His racial logic, like his conception of "blackness," is often limited to either/or choices (Martin or Malcolm?) that aggressively streamline and simplify messy social and personal realities. Douglas Kellner likens Lee's method to that of the German modernist playwright and director Bertolt Brecht, both artists producing "didactic learning plays" that dramatize the need to make clear-cut and decisive choices, no matter the intricacies and ambiguities involved.[51]

The main choice that *Jungle Fever* implicitly poses is between two New York City neighborhoods and their respective cultural and historical trajectories. Lee views Harlem and Bensonhurst through a Fort Greene black middle-class lens that functions as a kind of Brechtian didactic filter: Harlem as a space of both out-sized black dignity (Strivers Row) and degradation (the crack den), Bensonhurst as a space of tribalism, social stasis, and injustice. Lee's moralism reveals itself in his pointed depiction of Harlem street chaos, wanton graffiti, the two-dollar crack whore played with brio by Halle Berry. At the same time, he fetishizes the upwardly mobile, bourgeois lifestyle enjoyed by Flipper's family and their Harlem neighbors. The atmosphere and decor in the film's Bensonhurst homes seem all the more grim and dated when contrasted with what we see in the home of Flipper and his wife Drew (Lonette McKee). There an attractive, ambitious young couple make love in the morning before heading off to their jobs in an architecture firm and an upscale department store, while their lovely school-age daughter giggles in furtive delight. The daughter wears a Spelman T-shirt, telling us her parents expect her to end up at an elite black women's college if she doesn't get sidetracked into the Ivy League. The designer kitchen in their brownstone apartment looks like something in a late 1980s lifestyle magazine. After Drew discovers the affair and throws Flipper out, she convenes her girlfriends for a crisis intervention summit. These black women, all stylishly dressed, speak with passion and sophistication as they bemoan patriarchy, sexism, skin-tone colorism, and other factors complicating their love lives. Drew's sisterhood circle looks and sounds like a cross between a hip uptown soirée and an elite college gender studies seminar—fittingly, insofar as the scene feels like a direct response to bell hooks and other black feminist scholars who had lambasted Lee for his gender politics.[52] By contrast, when Angie seeks emotional support from *her* neighborhood girlfriends, the informal gathering takes place on a Bensonhurst sidewalk next to a schoolyard.

These class distinctions do not speak just to the matter of uneven cultural capital. *Jungle Fever*'s Harlem and Bensonhurst signify divergent historical vectors for blacks and Italians writ large. One gains a sense from the film that the Italian American story has already been written, while the African American one is still evolving. Bensonhurst stands for the ethnic primitivism that darkens and deromanticizes the American immigrant narrative. Harlem represents the black cultural glory of a romantic past *and* black adaptation for a bright future. Bensonhurst is perpetual epilogue; Harlem is perpetual renaissance. Even Harlem's crack and crime epidemics contribute to a sense of purpose and motion: more black lives to save, more social problems to solve, more stereotypes to combat, more need to rewrite the American story from black perspectives, more black perspectives in play.

We *hear* this black-Italian divergence in *Jungle Fever* as much as we see it. The Italian American music in the film is nostalgic, canonical, classically beautiful—which is to say, Sinatra, but a very specific Sinatra. It's the Sinatra of the 1965 concept album *September of My Years*: not Sinatra the swinger, but Sinatra, in the year of his fiftieth birthday, in a sentimental, ruminative, looking-back frame of mind. Lee shrewdly uses three ballads from the album—"Once upon a Time," "Hello Young Lovers," and "It Was a Very Good Year"—to give several of the scenes with the Italian characters a burnished aura of wistful melancholy. The music is extraordinary, but the power it holds and expresses is the power of memory, the memorializing of romantic feeling for the past. The pastness hits our ears all the more acutely because we've already heard in this film a very different music, the always and eternally present sound of Motown perennial Stevie Wonder. Wonder's original soundtrack for the film is far from his best work, and as an album it is not remotely the same achievement of musical art as Sinatra's *September of My Years*. But its method and sound—its grooves, instrumentation, stylization, lyrical content—are utterly contemporary, fully in sync with early 1990s black popular music, and by extension American popular culture. Not since the late 1950s/early 1960s, the era of Sinatra, Dean Martin, Tony Bennett, Vic Damone, Bobby Darin, Connie Francis, and Dion and the Belmonts, would it be possible to identify and talk about an Italian American popular music that was anything like a thriving pulse at the heart of American popular culture. And only in the decades after Lee's films, with the launching of *The Sopranos*, the resurrection of the Rat Pack, the sanctification of the Italian "slow food" ethos, and the advent of Italian American studies programs in American colleges and universities, has Italian American culture achieved renewed currency and status.

Crossover Dreams and Delusions

In *One Nation under a Groove: Motown and American Culture* (1995), Gerald Early argues that Motown, which became the paradigm of racial and cultural "crossover" in the 1960s, initiated its cross-racialism by modeling the figure of the Italian pop ballad singer. Between 1961 and 1965, at the same time that Felix Cavaliere—soon of the Rascals—was fantasizing about being a black soul singer, Marvin Gaye cut four "ballads and standards" Motown albums for which the obvious touchstones were Nat King Cole, Sinatra, and above all Perry Como, whose casual dress Gaye imitated in this period.[53] These were also breakout years for Dion DiMucci, a former Bronx street gang member, a dark haired tough with a love for the vocal group harmonizing of black R&B groups like the Orioles, the Ravens, the Flamingos, the Wrens, the Cadillacs, and the Teenagers. Dion and the Belmonts (Carlo Mastrangelo, Fred Milano, Angelo D'Alea) were one of a slew of Italian-led New York groups (Nino and the Ebbtides, Vito and the Salutations, Johnny Maestro and the Crests, the Capris, the Elegants) performing in the style that was later dubbed "Italo-doo-wop," or simply "doo-wop." Drawing on the traditions of barbershop a cappella, gospel falsetto, jazz scatting, and jump blues, doo-wop groups sang simple love ballads and upbeat numbers energized by nonsense syllable vocal riffing in the tenor, baritone, and bass registers. The Belmonts and their confreres combined the romance and elegance of standards-centered pop with a grit and moxie born of hardscrabble urban working-class youth experience. Doo-wop resonated organically out of the New York City soundscape; the songs literally were created on street corners and subways, in apartment vestibules and public school hallways and bathrooms— any space with warm acoustics and social intimacy.[54]

Simone Cinotto proffers the beguiling suggestion that Sal, the Italian pizza patriarch in *Do the Right Thing*, "must have been a teenager in Brooklyn in the golden age of Italian doo wop, a fan of the music and/or a singer himself."[55] Cinotto argues that doo-wop was quintessentially a *neighborhood* culture, a music whose sites of production and lyrical evocations together made it redolent of place and community. Yet because of personal connections between the musicians, and because this music, in recorded form via radio and phonograph, crossed racial and cultural lines of consumption, these black and Italian evocations of place and community crossed from each neighborhood over into the other, generating a sense of shared culture. "Sal loves Bed-Stuy and his black regulars," Cinotto says, and part of the reason may be that he came from a generation of New York Italians who, in the early years of rock and roll, made and shared a popular culture together with New York African Americans, even if they were also squaring off against each other in youth gangs.

When Jonathan Rieder lived in Canarsie in the 1970s, he could still behold a "houseproud neighborhood" where "the residents see themselves as the plain, doughty backbone of America—cabbies and teachers, merchants and craftsmen, salesmen and police—who stoically bear their burdens, raise their families, and serve the country."[56] But he also saw widening—even gaping—political and cultural rifts in which large numbers of Italians and Jews had given up on New Deal/Kennedy/Great Society liberalism and, largely because of racial fear and resentment, had become ripe for plucking by Nixon and Reagan. The 1970s disco movement, in some ways unprecedented as an inclusive cultural space in its interracial as well as gay-friendly ethos, was hugely popular among the kind of Italian Americans (not all of them gay-friendly) we see caricatured in *Saturday Night Fever*, and among its most important behind-the-scenes mediators were a number of prominent Italian American DJs. Similarly, the first stirrings of hip-hop culture among pioneering graffiti and turntable artists included a number of Italian Americans.[57] Joseph Sciorra, in his work as the director of academic and cultural programming at City University of New York's Calandra Institute of Italian American Studies, has been the leading chronicler and curator of this Italian presence in hip-hop, including the Staten Island– and Brooklyn-centered subgenre called "hip-wop."[58] As much as these black-Italian intersections in post-1970s youth culture recall earlier affinities and alliances, they carry little of the innocent optimism of the Kennedy and Johnson era: too much has happened to complicate the relationship, too much that has driven many blacks to see Italians as just another part (if not the worst part) of the white power structure and many Italians to see blacks as a scourge and a threat to public safety and order.

This brings us back to the Yusuf Hawkins murder, which in retrospect we would be wise to think about not just as a brutal tragedy but as an important watershed in New York ethnoracial history. At the time of the murder and its ugly aftermath, Nelson George filed a striking piece in the *Village Voice* providing a larger perspective for the racial friction playing out in the Bensonhurst streets. George's *Voice* readers for the most part were racial justice progressives strongly inclined to a knee-jerk condemnation of the Italians who resisted the protest marchers. While devastated by the Hawkins murder and offended by "the everyday anti–Third World bias" in Bensonhurst, George asked his readers to consider the neighborhood's antiblack hostility as the product of "a nagging, evil insecurity." Before ritually denouncing Bensonhurst's Italian youth, they should ask, "Who is addressing their high dropout rate and rising criminality?" George further asked his readers to "imagine the anxiety of a working-class Italian teen in Bensonhurst, getting bum-rushed culturally and physically every day of his life." These youths had "no dynamic role models." The "most written-about Italian in this city" was not "a politician, athlete, or pop star" but the mobster John Gotti. With Italians and other white ethnics losing ground to "tribes of black, brown, and yellow peoples" and "running away or watching ruefully as their European enclaves turn into Third World villages," it is no wonder that for young working-class Italian men "Gotti's turf control" and "nefarious empire" are "welcome proof of potency."[59]

George's story was remarkable for its cross-racial empathy and big-picture acuity in the heat of the Bensonhurst battle. The connections he drew between politics, economics, and gender were confirmed by the observations Maria Laurino made when she returned to the neighborhood later in the 1990s. She found many Italians in Bensonhurst blaming "the Mexicans" for stealing their local jobs—"Mexican" being neighborhood shorthand for all Spanish-speaking immigrants who were not Puerto Rican or Dominican, many more actually being from Ecuador than from Mexico—rather than holding responsible the Italian construction companies that were hiring the cheapest labor they could find. Many of these same Bensonhurst Italians denounced affirmative action and other government programs designed to help historically disadvantaged minority groups, perhaps unaware that, owing to a successful ethnic discrimination lawsuit an Italian American professor brought against CUNY in 1992, Italian American students, faculty, and staff were now a protected "nonwhite" class in the CUNY system.[60] Alas, this business of being classified as "nonwhite" in the New York City official bureaucracy did little to raise "people of color" consciousness among Bensonhurst Italian American teens—such as the group of them, including an honors student and altar boy at Xaverian parochial school, who clubbed a homeless Ecuadoran man to death in 1994.[61]

Roiling currents in social status destabilized Italian American identity, posing a particularly dire threat to Italian American masculinity. Pino in *Do the Right Thing* and the candy store bigots in *Jungle Fever* are men whose ironic coupling of antiblack racism and black cultural fluency is part of a larger complex of inferiority and resentment that constitutes nothing less than a crisis of masculine pride. Even as Frank Sinatra proudly beamed from Sal's Wall of Fame as a symbol of Italian American excellence, the exalted position Sinatra once held in American popular culture was now occupied by the likes of Quincy Jones, Michael Jackson, Prince, and Stevie Wonder. Indeed, Sinatra's own iconic status, if it was to continue to flourish beyond the domain of ethnic heritage nostalgia, now hinged on the reverence accorded him by these established black cultural icons and soon-to-arrive Chairman of the Board hip-hop idolaters like Puff Daddy and Jay Z. Even as John Gotti's local turf control was a sign of continued Italian "potency" in New York City neighborhoods, Gotti's image in the national popular imagination, like that of Italian American gangster legends like Al Capone and Lucky Luciano, now derived mainly from allusions to his gaudy lifestyle found in gangsta rap lyrics.

"Italian Americans Coming into Their Own" was the title of a 1983 cover story in the *New York Times Sunday Magazine*.[62] And while the ensuing decade witnessed a number of personal achievements confirming Italian America's full assimilation into the American mainstream—Mario Cuomo, Geraldine Ferraro, and Antonin Scalia in politics and government; Bartlett Giamatti in education, Tommy Lasorda, Jim Valvano, Rollie Massimino, and Joe Paterno in sports—none of these individuals projected the deep, epochal cultural excitement of a Frank Sinatra, a Joe DiMaggio, or even a Rudolph Valentino or Al Capone. With the exception of Valvano, Massimino, and other Italian American college basketball coaches, the prominence of these individuals testified more to the Americanization of Italians than to the Italianization of America. None, certainly, was anything close to a bracing figure of racial/ethnic difference on the order of Jesse Jackson, the African American political organizer and presidential candidate.

Or, more to the point, the African American filmmaker Spike Lee. In a post-1985 media culture that had yet to launch *The Sopranos* and that had created an ad hoc genre of "mass-market Italian American lite" with such films as *Prizzi's Honor* (1985), *Moonstruck* (1987), *Married to the Mob* (1988), *My Cousin Vinny* (1992), and *Analyze This* (1999), the atmosphere of deep ethnicity cultivated in the first two *Godfather* films, *Mean Streets*, and *Raging Bull* was now hard to find, even in Francis Ford Coppola's and Martin Scorsese's own subsequent work. When it came, in particular, to the matter of the New York City neighborhood as a cauldron of racial and ethnic friction and a theater of social drama, there simply was no Italian American heir to the Coppola/Scorsese tradition. Which is to say: in the absence of an Italian Spike Lee, it fell to the black Spike Lee, in league with his goombahs, to produce new classic cinematic studies of Italian American life.

FOUR

Sideline Shtick

"I Got the Two Kisses on the Cheeks"

Much to the chagrin of the ethnic pride entrepreneurs at the Italian American Sports Hall of Fame, the term "Italian American basketball star" is one we have almost no occasion to use. Not, at least, since the great Paul Arizin, on offensive force for Villanova and the Philadelphia Warriors, hung up his Converse kicks in 1962. This would change if Manu Ginóbili, crafty shooting guard for the San Antonio Spurs, an immigrant Argentinean of Italian descent, or Kobe Bryant of the Los Angeles Lakers, who spent much of his childhood in Italy, were to choose to self-identify as Italian American. Or if Marco Belinelli, Andrea Bargnani, Danilo Gallianari, and other Italians who have recently made it into the NBA were to do the same. Or, best of all, if we look to the women's game, where we can behold the superlative Diana Taurasi, perennial WNBA all-star.

Alas, the place for the heritage industry proselytizers to focus is the sidelines of the college game. That is where we find Taurasi's coach at the University of Connecticut, Geno Auriemma, the azure-eyed, raven-haired dandy with a cocky strut who regularly wins national championships.[1] And that is where in the men's game, for the past several decades, we have seen a parade of vowel-heavy names (Carnesecca, Vitale, Valvano, Massimino, Carlesimo, Pitino, Calipari, Martelli, and more) command attention for charismatic modes of dress, gesture, talk, and interpersonal intimacy that have helped engender new models of masculine sports leadership and celebrity.

As the popularity and profitability of basketball have skyrocketed since the late 1970s, the big-time college men's game has become in many respects equivalent to the professional game. College stars receive as much media coverage as their counterparts in the NBA—college coaches get *more* attention than pros—while the NCAA championship tournament has become a national ritual ("March Madness") that the NBA playoffs rarely match for audience share or intensity. In so many ways this economic and cultural phenomenon owes overwhelmingly to the labor and artistry of African American athletes. Yet as big-time college basketball has become blacker, it also has become more Italian, even while Italian Americans have been among the white ethnic groups whose on-court athletic presence has radically diminished.

Italian American ascendancy into basketball's managerial and media elite has happened at the same time as we have seen a dual, or even bifurcated, African American basketball narrative take shape. In one storyline, megatalents like Magic Johnson, Michael Jordan, and LeBron James have become American sports plutocrats, transforming the game with their transcendent court skills while also becoming media icons and tycoons. At the same time, at the vernacular level—as perhaps best captured in the remarkable documentary film *Hoop Dreams* (1994)—scenes of inner-city schoolyard basketball commingle with images of drug dealing and of struggling black families.[2] Italian Americans have inserted themselves into both these narratives, mediated between them, and in some cases brought them together.

What is being marketed and consumed in the media presentation of big-time college basketball is nothing less than the core national mythology, the "American dream." There's a breathtaking passage in *Hoop Dreams* in which Dick Vitale gives a pep talk to a group of blue-chip prospects attending a summer camp sponsored by Nike, the sports gear merchandiser. Vitale, who grew up in a working-class Italian immigrant family in Passaic, New Jersey, is a former college and NBA basketball coach who has garnered considerable wealth and fame as an analyst for the cable sports network ESPN (Entertainment Sports Programming Network). For better or worse, Vitale's manically exuberant broadcast voice, one of most consumed sports media voices in history, has been the dominant sound of men's college basketball for the past three decades. Vitale oozes a quality of ethnic presence Pellegrino D'Acierno has dubbed dagotude, a style of self-presentation redolent of an extroverted charisma characteristic of many Italian Americans, perhaps especially those from the New York metropolitan area.[3] In the *Hoop Dreams* clip, Vitale's voice quivers and he gesticulates wildly as he delivers his heartfelt homily: "While you're sitting here today, you should feel like a million dollars. You should feel so special. You are one of the hundred best high school players in this country, the United States. My mother, God bless her, she's up in heaven today. She used to always say to me, [the vocal quiver intensifies] 'This is America. You can make something of yourself.'"[4]

Here we are witnessing the machinery of corporate consumer capitalism shifting into high gear, powered by an alignment between black labor and Italian social capital. As a Nike shill, Vitale is selling the American dream through the symbolic power of his ethnicity, an ethnicity positioned both inside and outside the US establishment, inside and outside American whiteness. From his time recruiting inner-city players as a coach at Rutgers and the University of Detroit, through his broadcasting career at ESPN, Vitale (like the other Italian American men I am writing about here) has shown himself to be comfortable among black bodies. This is why his assimilationist pieties of family, hard work, and material acquisition should not be heard as patronizing his audience in the familiar manner of those who hold up a mythical Italian American bootstrapping narrative as a model for African Americans. Vitale has made something of himself, to be sure, but he hasn't done it alone; he has made himself through the American consuming public's huge appetite for the skill and beauty of the players whose performance he once managed and now narrates, interprets, and evaluates. In this sense "Dickie V" is a trick-

UNIVERSITY OF DETROIT

DICK VITALE   HEAD COACH

FIGURE 11. Before "Dicky V's" ESPN broadcasting voice became the sound of men's college basketball, Dick Vitale was the head coach at the University of Detroit from 1973 to 1977. His 1977 team won twenty-one straight games, including an upset of Al McGuire's Marquette team that went on to win that year's national championship. (Courtesy of University of Detroit Mercy athletic department.)

ster, a liminal, transactional figure poised at the intersection of race, economics, and culture.

The man who has best understood the commercial possibilities of this transactional space is a goombah of Vitale's who goes by the name Sonny. John "Sonny" Vaccaro, a self-described "fat little dago," is proud of his mutually enriching relationships with basketball royalty from Michael Jordan to Kobe Bryant and is not in the least shy about his Las Vegas affiliations, including a brother slyly referred to as a "consultant to the gaming industry." Vaccaro's home office is decorated with photographs of his favorite basketball players, Rat Pack publicity shots, and Sands Hotel memorabilia. He made his fortune masterminding a scheme for marketing Nike basketball sneakers: he'd pay college basketball coaches to outfit their teams in the sneakers and other clothing and gear bearing the company's trademark swish, so that television coverage of their games would become, in effect, long-running Nike advertisements.

In 1965 Vaccaro cofounded the Dapper Dan Roundball Classic, an annual all-star game featuring the country's most touted high school players. The game took place in Pittsburgh, not far from the small western Pennsylvania town where Vaccaro grew up. During his college years at Youngstown State University in Ohio, Vaccaro had discovered his skill at the transactional side of basketball by helping the men's basketball coaching staff recruit players out of Pittsburgh. In its forty-three-year run, the Dapper Dan, a forerunner of today's McDonald's All-Star Game, served as a coming-out showcase for such future stars as Patrick Ewing, Shaquille O'Neal, Alonzo Mourning, Chris Webber, Kevin Garnett, Kobe Bryant, Tracy McGrady, and Vince Carter. While forging his reputation as a powerful broker between coaches and blue-chip prospects—at the same time working as a public school teacher in his hometown—Vaccaro built a special rapport with many black players. ("I got the two kisses on the cheeks," said Tracy McGrady.) In the late 1970s Vaccaro grew his hair and teased it out into an Afro: "It was part of me," he explained, "it was part of my person, it was natural." It was also during this period that he worked with a local Italian cobbler to design prototypes for a line of casual sports shoes, including one he described as a "summer basketball sandal." This led to his epiphany about the huge marketing potential in outfitting whole teams in high-quality basketball shoes, a concept he brought to Phil Knight, cofounder and chairman of Nike.[5]

The first coach Vaccaro recruited was his friend Jerry Tarkanian, the colorful Armenian American head coach at UNLV (Nevada–Las Vegas). He proceeded to target coaches at small Catholic colleges in the Northeast, reasoning that the extra money from Nike would keep these coaches from pursuing the bigger salaries they could garner at large state universities. The first of these marks was Jim Valvano, then still coaching at Iona, a small commuter school in Westchester County, just north of New York City. "Picture this," Valvano told the story of their initial meeting:

> Two guys named Vaccaro and Valvano meeting at La Guardia Airport. Vaccaro reaches into his briefcase. Puts a check on the table. I look at it and say, "What's this for?" He pulls a sneaker out and puts it on the table. Like we were putting a contract out on somebody. He says, "I would like your team to wear this shoe." I said, "How much?" He says, "No. I'll *give* you the shoes."[6]

The big breakthrough came in the early 1980s when Vaccaro signed up Georgetown's coach John Thompson just as his team was emerging as a symbol of black authenticity in the burgeoning hip-hop culture. Vaccaro went on to broker endorsement deals with Michael Jordan and other black superstars, leading to Spike Lee–directed Nike advertisements that helped make the new black aesthetic of the 1980s central to US corporate consumer culture. Later, after defecting to Adidas, he brokered the multimillion-dollar deal that established teenager Kobe Bryant as the basketball face of that company (playing on Kobe's "Italian roots" during the negotiation) and maneuvered behind the scenes to help engineer Bryant's much-coveted signing with the Los Angeles Lakers rather than a team in a smaller media market. Meanwhile, Vaccaro tight-

ened down his position as the single most influential force in the
college recruiting process as the architect of the shoe company–
sponsored summer camp—the ABCD camp—where his friend
Vitale colorfully channeled his mother's uplift ethos.[7]

Scorned by his critics as an oily "sneaker pimp," Vaccaro fash-
ions himself as an avuncular "counselor" to young players, especially black boys from disadvantaged backgrounds. Why do inner-
city kids trust the old white guy? According to sportswriter Ric
Bucher, "it's for the same reason *Scarface* and *The Godfather* are
on every NBA player's favorite-movie list. Any minority who has
busted his or her butt to succeed and has suffered that you-must-
be-crooked look can relate. Any old Italian guy with lots of friends
and money must be shady. A young black kid with fresh hip-hop
gear and a nice car must be a drug dealer."[8] The black-Italian affinity here is premised on a shared experience of social stigma—of
being outside traditional American bourgeois normality—that
underwrites a shared code of style, a glamour that carries a whiff
of transgression. Hollywood gangster films and sports media are
among those many culture industry spectacles that have propa-
gated powerfully influential models of masculinity that run
counter to traditional WASP ideals. Basketball's inventor, Presby-
terian minister James Naismith, envisioned the game as an outlet
for young white men's moral education in hygiene and Christian
virtue, a forge for building character. It has instead become, in the
larger cultural framework enabled by its massive media presence,
an arena for the display of personality, style, and image.

It is in this respect that sport is a generative and defining space
of American consumer capitalism. The story of US sports culture
is the narrative of an epochal economic/cultural transition in
which bodies originally built for production (bodies disciplined by
and for work on the plantation, on the railroad, in the factory, and
at other sites of agricultural and industrial labor) became bodies
groomed for consumption (bodies whose labors on the fields and
courts of "play" serve as objects of spectacle, entertainment,
desire, and fantasy). Sport is a space where labor and leisure,

power and pleasure, muscle and grace, sweat and style infiltrate each other in ways that profoundly—perhaps singularly—shape cultural perceptions of race and gender.

Basketball has emerged as an especially fascinating consumer culture since the 1980s as cable television, the Internet, talk radio, and other electronic mass media have enhanced the consuming public's visual, verbal, and imaginative access to the bodies that animate this sporting spectacle. Of all the major team sports, it is basketball—with the relative compactness of its stage and, as a result, its intensively proximate interaction between fleshly athletic (mostly black) laboring bodies and the (mostly white) bodies of coaches who clothe themselves in the uniform of the professional managerial class—which most powerfully dramatizes the intermeshing of capitalism and race.

To spotlight the black-Italian nexus in men's college basketball is to illuminate a spectacle in which producers assert their identities through lavish bodily display of consumption, expressive exhibitions of signature style that mass audiences then consume for themselves. Players and coaches alike construct public personae through their own performances as consumers of music, movies, clothing, and food; in turn, through the shoes and clothes they wear, the language they vocalize, and the personality they express kinetically through their movement, the bodies of the players and coaches literally become sites of public imagination, consumable images that stoke audience desire and fantasy. Understandably, most of the attention paid to basketball as a cultural spectacle has centered on its blunt racial staging, in which exceptional, mostly black bodies meet the gaze of an ordinary, mostly white audience hungry for fantastic displays of athletically erotic beauty. But we make this conventional view much more nuanced and interesting by putting Italian American male basketball coaches center stage, where we see these important actors as brokers and as originators of alluringly consumable, seductively racialized and ethnicized images. For at the center of the mass-mediated spectacle of big-time men's college basketball is a story of the cross-racial fashioning of consumable African American and Italian American masculinities, a story that challenges and complicates simple black-white binaries.

Hardcourt Dagotude

From the 1950s to the early 1970s, the most famous US college basketball coaches were men like UCLA's John Wooden, who never lost his Indiana wholesomeness and reserve while mentoring stars like Lew Alcindor (Kareem Abdul-Jabbar), a devotee of John Coltrane and Malcolm X, and Bill Walton, a Grateful Deadhead and Vietnam War protestcr. Or they were men like Kentucky's Adolph Rupp, who grcw up in rural Kansas, the son of Mennonite German immigrants, and became best remembered as a segregationist whose 1965 all-white team lost to an underdog Texas Western team that featured an all-black starting five. Wooden made his peace with the countercultural and black freedom movements, and perhaps not coincidentally won an astounding tcn national championships in these years; Rupp symbolized what those movements were fighting. But both men performed their role as an act of mid-twentieth-century professional middle-class, middle American whiteness, embodying the same general masculine vocabulary and cultural idioms as small-town teachers, businessmen, and clergy.

This model of white Protestant leadership is deeply rooted in US sports culture. One sees its extremes of nobility and decadence in a figure like Bobby Knight, the Ohio-bred longtime coach of Indiana University. Knight trademarked a style strong on the fundamentals, one that yielded three national championships in the 1970s and 1980s, only to see his career at Indiana end in infamy in 2000 following the public release of a videotape showing him choking one of his own players. Knight's first head coaching position was at West Point; at his best his coaching exemplified an effective military approach, imbuing his players with strong fundamentals and selfless team commitment. At his worst Knight was a bully and a boor, given to embarrassing public temper tantrums.

As basketball became blacker, Knight became whiter. He practiced a kind of racial passive-aggressive behavior: he recruited black players (though not as successfully as his competitors) but then became more of a closed-minded traditionalist than he'd been early in his career, making more of a show of his friendships with local good ol' boys. His arrogance expressed itself in an unwillingness to communicate with the press except to belittle and strongarm reporters. His white privilege revealed itself in a dress code that became more casual as he attracted more public scrutiny. While the newer breed of Italian American and African American coaches dressed in expensive tailored suits, Knight, the standard bearer of the old-school coaching ideal, took to underdressing in a run-of-the-mill college sweatshirt.[9]

Against the middle American, rural and small-town, Protestant basketball coaching tradition stands another one—urban, immigrant working-class Jewish and Catholic. Not surprisingly, given these demographics, the capital of this coaching nation is New York City, with strong orbiting satellites in the ethnic diasporas of Long Island, Westchester County, New Jersey, southern New England, and greater Philadelphia and Pittsburgh. Here the coaches are men who toughened up in the sidewalk and schoolyard ethnic combat zones that make the melting pot a decidedly treacherous and bloody space. Here the coaches are fast and highly demonstrative talkers with stylish flair and a warm, suffused, tactile approach to interpersonal intimacy.

In 1977, in the waning seconds of Marquette's victory over North Carolina in the NCAA championship game, Marquette coach Al McGuire sat on the bench by himself, his face buried in his hands. Coach McGuire, it soon became clear, was weeping. NBC's cameras lingered on the scene, framing it as a canonical moment of real-time sports drama, McGuire's Irish heart and soul laid bare, his joy, sadness, sorrow, and love all of a piece. Feeling ran deep that night because this was McGuire's last game as a coach after many years patrolling the sidelines with inimitable Brooklyn panache. The following year found him in the television broadcast booth. For the next two decades—McGuire died in 2001 of a blood disorder—first NBC then CBS college hoops telecasts jigged and lilted to his trademark New York Irish accent, redolent of the family saloon where he grew up pulling pints and burnishing his storytelling skills. McGuire invented a new art of basketball broadcasting: an elliptical, free-associative, syntactically fractured existential poetry that every once in a while referred indirectly to something vaguely connected to what was happening on the court. McGuire's broadcast partners Dick Enberg, the play-by-play man, and Billy Packer, the analyst, played straight men to McGuire's folk philosopher–comic, a kind of Mark Twain for our time. In sports television parlance, McGuire was a color man; rarely has sports commentary been so colorful.

Not for the first time in American history, an Irish Catholic breakthrough into the Protestant mainstream set the stage for an Italian one that brought yet more ethnic piquancy. This is the context in which Italian American basketball coaches—and certain other figures occupying key sports media and marketing positions—have forged electronic media–friendly aesthetics of theatrical self-display derived from the cultural sensibility I'm calling—with thanks to D'Acierno—dagotude. The pioneers of hardcourt dagotude are well known even to the casual American sports fan. Lou Carnesecca, who grew up slicing salami and cheese in his immigrant father's Italian deli on Manhattan's Upper East Side, achieved renown as the coach of St. John's University in Queens (1965 to 1970, 1973 to 1992) for an expressive face straight out of the commedia dell'arte and a sideline shtick so acrobatic that *Sports Illustrated* described him as "jumpier than a minstrel end man."[10] Bergen County, New Jersey's, Dick Vitale first established his life's goal of "being the most enthusiastic guy about everything" while coaching at the University of Detroit (1973–77); there the only thing louder than his mouth were his clothes, garish checked slacks and gaudy shirts that stood out even in the outré polyester 1970s.[11] Queens-bred Jim Valvano, whose entertainer chops exceeded the combined talents of Lou Carnesecca, Lou Monte, and Lou Costello, first pioneered his postgame "press conference as Vegas lounge" act while head coach at Iona College

(1975–80); later he became the virtual personification of "March Madness" the night his underdog North Carolina State Wolfpack won the 1983 NCAA championship on a spectacular last-second play as CBS cameras followed him frantically running around the court looking for someone—anyone—to hug. Rollie Massimino, whose smelly De Nobili stogies and Frank Sinatra/Jimmy Roselli soundtrack (standard-issue cultural equipment from his central New Jersey upbringing) brought a vivid, not entirely welcome cultural tone to Villanova University's Mainline Philadelphia suburban idyll, achieved sports immortality the night he took down heavily favored John Thompson and Georgetown for the 1985 national championship, to the great delight of a middle-aged white sportswriter corps mortified by the black power overtones of "Hoya paranoia."[12]

The primary stage for Italian sideline shtick was the Big East, founded in 1979 as a made-for-TV basketball conference of schools from the major urban markets of the Northeast. The league originally included mainly Catholic schools (St. John's, Providence, Boston College, Seton Hall, Georgetown) as well as Syracuse and Connecticut. (Villanova, also Catholic, joined the league in 1980, while non-Catholic Pittsburgh joined in 1982.) The Big East's founders recognized that most of the best players on the eastern seaboard were leaving the region for other major conference schools in the Southeast, Midwest, and beyond. To keep these marquee players closer to home, the conference promised not just major television exposure (through its own regional television network along with featured slots first with CBS and then with ESPN), but also a gritty, blue-collar style of play. This required, above all, a special kind of coaching sensibility. Whereas many coaches in the South, Midwest, and West recruited urban players but then tried to leach the "city" (black) element out of their game, Big East coaches embraced many elements of the urban school-yard game. On Big East network broadcasts, league founder and former Providence College coach Dave Gavitt, working as the color commentator, purposely spotlighted the coaches and their personalities in a way unique in the field of sports television. In

1983 the conference's postseason tournament moved to Madison Square Garden, where over the coming decades it became the most buzz-worthy annual event on the New York City sports calendar.

A generation earlier, on the neighborhood courts of the city, black players like Earl "the Goat" Manigault—the schoolyard legend featured in Pete Axthelm's *The City Game* (1970)—introduced a soulful and spectacular improvisatory aesthetic of self-expression that finally killed off any vestigial sense of the sport as a white man's game of late nineteenth-century Scottish Calvinist inspiration. Basketball had come to be associated with both the expressive styles and the social problems (e.g., Manigault's drug addiction) of the post-1960 black ghetto. And yet, throughout the "urban crisis" of the 1960s and 1970s, basketball, in both organized leagues and playgrounds, became one of the few remaining urban spaces of interracial, interfaith contact. "In the 1960s," writes James Fisher, "sports became the main conduit for interaction between urban [white] Catholics and blacks; by the late 1970s, sports talk was providing grounds for the preliminary stages of reconciliation made possible by the profoundly democratic mysticism of the streets and the school yards."[13] As inner-city public schools deteriorated, and as more and more black families opted to send their children to parochial schools, certain of these parochial schools' basketball teams began to operate like college or even semiprofessional programs. Many of the best Big East players were recruited out of these schools.[14]

For Catholic ethnic immigrants in the early twentieth century, playing team sports was tantamount to being an assimilated American. In the 1920s and '30s, the success of Notre Dame and Fordham football was nothing less than an assault on Protestant masculine hegemony.[15] Basketball followed suit. Seventeen Catholic schools have made it to the NCAA Final Four, starting with Villanova in 1939, the tournament's first year. From the late 1940s to the early 1960s was the first golden age of Catholic college basketball, including the national championships won by Holy Cross in 1947, La Salle in 1954, San Francisco in 1955 and 1956, and Loyola in 1963. A generation passed before the next crowning of a Catholic school champion (McGuire's 1977 Marquette team), a period that coincided with the church's realignment after Vatican II. Then, in the 1980s, came a second golden age. Of the forty Final Four spots that decade, seven were taken by Catholic schools: St. John's, Villanova, Providence, and Seton Hall each made it once, while Georgetown made it three times, winning the championship in 1984, the first by a team from the Northeast since La Salle's in the Eisenhower era. Nineteen eighty-five was a Catholic basketball apotheosis. That year St. John's, Georgetown, and Villanova all made the Final Four, with Villanova upsetting Georgetown for the championship in one of the greatest college games ever played. *Sports Illustrated*'s Frank Deford wrote, "For many Americans college basketball is the outward and visible sign of Catholicism in the United States. And because private schools of any stripe tend to be smaller and more focused than the sprawling public mega-universities that they play games against, basketball has become even more the cynosure on the Catholic campus."[16]

Remarkably, six Big East teams reached the NCAA Final Four in the 1980s; even more remarkably, four of the six (all Catholic schools) were coached by Italian Americans: Massimino at Villanova, Rick Pitino at Providence, Carnesecca at St. John's, and Irish Italian P. J. Carlesimo at Seton Hall. One of the others, Georgetown, the marquee team of 1980s men's college basketball, was coached by the most visible African American coach of the era, John Thompson. This meant that when sports media trained their focus on these major northeastern Catholic schools—schools whose hierarchies, like the other institutions of the US Catholic Church, continued to be predominately, even tribally, Irish—the most visible authority figures were Italian American and African American. These are schools with rich histories, intellectual traditions, and social missions. But for national television audiences tuned in to Big East games in the mid-1980s, Georgetown was a glowering John Thompson with a towel draped over his shoulder; Villanova was a frenetic Rollie Massimino with his suit coat flying; Seton Hall was an intense P. J. Carlesimo in his Nike-emblazoned cardigan. The priests at the end of the team benches perhaps still symbolized something meaningful, but it was the coaches who were modeling what these Catholic institutions of higher education had chosen as their version of mainstream Americanism.

Carlesimo, more than the others, brought his own priest-like sensibility to the coaching profession. His father, Pete, had coached college football and basketball at the University of Scranton; later he served as athletic director at Scranton and at Fordham, both Jesuit institutions, rounding out his career by serving for many years as executive director of college basketball's National Invitation Tournament. Pete's Italian Catholic family and his wife Lucy's Irish Catholic family each had ten children; P. J. himself grew up with nine siblings. P. J., who later lettered in four sports at Fordham, was a well-known type in youth sports culture: the coach's son. "Coaches," Frank Deford wrote of Carlesimo in a *Sports Illustrated* profile in 1999, "were the men who guided him, disciplined him, informed his ethic." That ethic was Jesuit: "the priests even hung around the house," Deford wrote, "a familiar and avuncular presence." P. J.'s sister Cheryl said of her brother, "The Jesuit influence is still very strong in his life. P. J. is a humanist. And he very much believes that acts have their consequences and that work should pay off." Carlesimo's coaching became what Deford calls a "secular Jesuit" mission: he remained unmarried until well after his sideline career ended, becoming well known for a bachelor lifestyle marked by nightly restaurant parties with other coaches, with male camaraderie and the "hearty laughs and the tall tales and the fine red wine" flowing deep into the night. Like his Italian father, Carlesimo was known for such sentimental behavior as habitually crying in the locker room at season's end. "Lucy, the stalwart Irish mother," Deford noted, "is bemused by these lugubrious Italian men of hers."

Tip O'Neill, the late Speaker of the House of Representatives, an Irishman known for his rich blarney, called Carlesimo's father the best after-dinner speaker in the world. Pete would end his speeches with a mock-Jesuit poem titled "Rules for the Game of

Life." The last line of the poem offered what we might take to be the heart of the Catholic basketball creed: "Here is the ball. It is your immortal soul."[17]

The Brothers versus the Joeys

"They called me a 'black Italian,'" muses John Thompson in ESPN's documentary film *Requiem for the Big East* (2014), recalling his intense 1980s rivalries with Carnesecca, Massimino, Carlesimo, and Pitino.

Thompson, an imposing six-foot-ten, three-hundred-pound man who'd been backup center to Bill Russell on the Boston Celtics in the mid-1960s, had turned Georgetown into a national power in the late 1970s and had ensured Georgetown's preeminence in the early 1980s by landing the most prized recruit of the era, center Patrick Ewing. Georgetown made it to the NCAA championship game three of Ewing's four college years, winning the championship in 1984. Thompson introduced a new style of play—defensive-minded, rigorously disciplined, physically and mentally aggressive to the point of intimidation. His team projected an aura of purpose, intensity, and menace never before seen in college basketball. "Georgetown has the panzer divisions and the swift tanks and the Luftwaffe and the long bombs," said Lou Carnesecca in a deft spin on the military analogy that became a commonplace of Georgetown commentary. "They just completely destroy people, and, yeah, they scare the hell out of you."[18]

Thompson's hulking body, mean stare, and profane street language enabled him to commandeer the sidelines; he carried a white towel over his shoulder, making him look more engaged in the sweaty labor of the game, his body and his aura another physical force thwarting the opposing team's will. His players, in a tactic new to the sport, used dead-ball time to huddle on the foul line and other spaces in a way that signified both territorial sovereignty and "all for one, one for all" team unity. Georgetown *owned* the court and the sidelines; opposing players and coaches lined up to take their beating.

Either that, or they proved their manhood by standing up to the Hoyas. When Rick Pitino was trying to win respect for Providence, which had been languishing in the lower reaches of the Big East, a key turning point came when he refused to back down from Thompson in a midcourt shouting match. Thompson called Pitino a "young punk." "Fuck you," Pitino fired back. Pitino later said he wanted to send a message to his team: "No more being intimidated by Georgetown. No more being patsies for the Big East teams."[19]

Georgetown University, otherwise best known for training young diplomats for careers in the State Department, had become perhaps the most visible and assertive public symbol of masculine black power since the Black Panthers. Georgetown jackets and caps became de rigueur among urban b-boys and b-girls. The team was celebrated in rap lyrics and counted Grandmaster Flash and the Furious Twelve among its aliases. To their admirers, John Thompson's Georgetown Hoyas stood for dignified, unapologetic self-determination; to their detractors, they looked like thugs and hustlers.[20]

The media framed Thompson's image as a racial warrior, an image that might have synchronized with the military, business, and religious values of Reagan-era America had it been attached to a white authority figure. But for the fact that its patriarch and his charges were black, Georgetown basketball might even have been a model for the family values rhetoric of the Moral Majority. Race changed everything, however. John Thompson's Georgetown existed in the national imagination as a symbol of black power, and for the white majority, the terms "black power" and "family" did not go together.

How very different the situation is when it comes to Italians. In the American mind, Italian American ethnicity is hardly ever imagined outside sentimentalized, stereotypical notions of "the family." The Italian family, in general, is a cultural figure shaped by myth, desire, and lack—perhaps never more so than in the

United States, where tropes of Italian ethnic soulfulness, warmth, and loyalty serve as antidotes to the individualism, materialism, and capitalist instrumentality of the dominant culture. We see this in audience responses to *The Godfather* and other Italian mob films and television shows, when viciously violent men are romanticized as protectors of their families, and even as sentimental and emotionally vulnerable. We see it in any number of media images of Italian men tying their identities to food and fraternal intimacy.

We see it as well, not surprisingly, in the cultural memory of Villanova's win over Georgetown in the 1985 NCAA championship game. Three documents illustrate the point. In March 2004, *Sports Illustrated* published a long article by Tim Layden, headlined "The Upset," recounting Villanova's seismic upset and tracing the legacy of the game over the next two decades. Also published in 2004 was *Ed Pinckney's Tales from the Villanova Hardwood*, part of a series of chatty books on college basketball programs from a midwestern company called Sports Publishing, this one seemingly written by the Villanova sports information department. In 2005 HBO aired its documentary *Perfect Upset: The 1985 Villanova vs. Georgetown NCAA Championship*. Together these documents frame the 1985 game as a battle between two distinct value systems: Georgetown's culture of monoracial homogeneity and paranoia versus Villanova's food- and family-centered culture of multiracial harmony and playfulness.

Villanova's coach, New Jersey-reared Rollie Massimino, son of an Italian immigrant shoemaker, went by the moniker "Daddy Mass." "Every coach has a shtick," *SI*'s Layden writes, "Massimino's was family. Come to Villanova to play basketball and you'll be part of a family. We'll eat pasta dinners together and talk about life. We'll win because you'll love one another like brothers. If it was a sales pitch, it was nonetheless heartfelt."[21] HBO's *Perfect Upset* features home movie-style footage of Villanova postgame dinners. "We'd cook, eight, nine pounds of macaroni," Massimino says. "You know how many people that feeds?" Tarantella music washes over these images, bathing the scene in the feel-good sentiment of an Italian wedding.[22] Massimino incarnated folk notions of Italian sociality: he needed people around him all the time. "Even on the road Rollie never wanted to be alone," Mitch Buonaguro, his top assistant in 1985, told *SI*. For home games, Massimino brought in celebrities like Tommy Lasorda, Mario Andretti, and Perry Como as "designated Italian" guests for the evening. "Rollie made sure I announced that 'Coach Massimino's *good friend*, Perry Como, is in the house tonight,' remembers Al Elia, Villanova's public address announcer.[23]

Massimino's sideline demeanor was hot and passionate. "By the end of the game he looked like he'd been in a Maytag washing machine," Dave Gavitt says in the HBO documentary. With his bulging waistline and Napoleonic stature, there was something cartoonish about Massimino pacing the sidelines, erupting into a tirade, ripping off his suit coat, stamping his feet. But there was no mistaking his skill at building team chemistry, devising zone defenses, and rallying his players at critical junctures. Stories about Massimino's motivational techniques circulate like folklore. The classic Daddy Mass folktale has become known as the "Pasta Bowl Speech." Earlier in the 1985 NCAA tournament, in the regional final against North Carolina, Villanova had been thoroughly dominated in the first half, scoring only seventeen points. The players were tight, lifeless, maybe scared. In the locker room at halftime, Massimino tried to loosen up his team. In HBO's *Perfect Upset*, Massimino remembers starting his halftime speech: "You know what I want more than going to the Final Four? I want a big bowl of pasta with clams." The players looked at each other, puzzled, as Daddy Mass went on talking passionately about eating. Win or lose, there's always pasta, the coach seemed to be saying, so why not relax and just go out there and have fun? The speech seemed to work. In one of the most dramatic turnarounds in NCAA tournament history, Villanova came out in the second half and ran Carolina off the court.

Stories of Massimino's prowess as a recruiter also saturate the memory of Villanova's championship; there's fascination with the spectacle of a short, pudgy, well-dressed man flapping his lips, flailing his arms, and baring his heart in the living rooms of prospective players, many of them from black, mother-headed households. "His family atmosphere was key," Harold Pressley recalls of Massimino's visit to his Connecticut home. "He came in, lounged around with my mother, seemed real comfortable."[24] This was the soft, sociable Daddy Mass; he could also go hard and play the role of the tough-loving father. According to the account in *Tales from the Villanova Hardwood*, when Massimino visited Ed Pinckney's home in the Monroe Housing Projects in the Bronx, he told Pinckney and his mother that Ed would not play as a freshman; first he'd need to get his academic game in order. "When he left that day," Pinckney recalls, "my mom said, 'You should go to Villanova. That little Italian coach—he'll make sure you graduate.'"[25]

In the early 1980s, Massimino built a strong Villanova team around his undersized but strong and deft-footed center John Pinone, an Italian American from the Hartford area whose mother cooked the team pasta dinners when Villanova came up to play the University of Connecticut. Pinone's toughness and intensity defined a team that often played above its talent level. In his senior year, Villanova beat both Patrick Ewing's Georgetown and Michael Jordan's North Carolina. After Pinone left, Pinckney, Pressley, and point guard Dwayne McLain became Villanova's leaders. These three players ("The Expansion Crew," they called themselves) each had big-time quality, but none had the Big East notoriety of Ewing or Chris Mullin of St. John's. The year they won the championship, Villanova had finished the regular season with a disappointing 19–10 record, barely qualifying for the NCAA tournament. Pinckney had played several strong games against Georgetown, but critics persisted in drawing unfavorable comparisons between his languorous style ("E-Z Ed") and Ewing's fiercely intense one. In popular perception, Georgetown exemplified the gold standard of black masculinity: everyone else's manhood was open to question. The Hoyas' stylistic affinity with urban rap culture, combined with John Thompson's antiaccommodationist posture, meant Georgetown was the authentically "black" team no matter how well black players on their opponent's teams performed.

The brute fact was that the success of Catholic school basketball hinged on the performance of athletes who were, for the most part, black Protestants. But even at Catholic universities, it was race, not religion, that was the most salient identity category shaping campus culture. And in this respect the demographic dissonance between court and campus was striking. Frank Deford noted that most people who watched Villanova's black starting five—the rest of the team was almost completely white—play Georgetown's totally black team "would probably be startled to learn that, notwithstanding what appeared on the court, Villanova is so white (98%) and so suburban upper middle class that it is known in its own bailiwick as Vanilla-nova."[26]

Villanova and Georgetown were more like Notre Dame than like traditional Catholic basketball powers such as Marquette and Big East rivals Seton Hall and St. John's, urban schools with melting pot student bodies reflecting a continued institutional commitment to bootstrapping working-class and immigrant populations. These instead were elite bastions of white privilege, charter members of a kind of Catholic shadow Ivy League, complete with Gothic architecture and preppie cliques. In the mid-1980s, Villanova's student culture was perfectly in tune with the careerist materialism of the Reagan era. Asked to characterize her fellow students, the editor of the school newspaper replied, "They're looking to make it big."[27] Georgetown students, for their part, were accustomed to thinking they'd already made it big merely by enrolling at the university. Theirs was an institution with a confident sense of its importance: the oldest Catholic university in the United States (founded in 1789) and, abetted by its location in the bosom of the federal government, a powerhouse in the fields of political science, law, economics, and foreign affairs.

Georgetown is a city school, but until the early 1970s it made little effort to integrate itself into the life of the city where it resides. Because Washington, DC's, local population is overwhelmingly black and the federal government is overwhelmingly white, Georgetown's affiliation with political elites inside the Beltway, the main source of its prestige, implicated the school in the city's history of racial segregation. It took the racial unrest of the late 1960s to arouse impulses for racial justice in Georgetown's Jesuit leadership. The ensuing reform campaign centered on efforts to recruit and retain black students through a "community scholars" program and, in general, to try to see the local population not as a danger but as a potential asset.

Basketball excellence was an ingrained feature of black Washington, but traditionally the best players took their talent elsewhere—Elgin Baylor to Seattle University, Austin Carr and Adrian Dantley to Notre Dame, Dave Bing to Syracuse, to name a few of the most prominent examples. Meanwhile, the teams Georgetown put on the floor up through the early 1970s were, as one writer put it, "a bit too slow, a bit too small and, to get to the heart of the matter, much too white."[28] John Thompson had grown up in Washington. Like Elgin Baylor and the other black prospects, he'd left the city for college—Providence in his case. Thompson disdained the NBA lifestyle, retired early, returned to Washington, DC, in the late 1960s, and was hired by Georgetown in 1972.[29]

Inevitably, Thompson's performance became a referendum on the changing balance of racial power and presence in a still overwhelmingly white institution. More than a few alumni grumbled when Thompson, in his first year, started five black players, all from the District of Columbia. This established a pattern: throughout his career at Georgetown, Thompson's teams mostly, sometimes exclusively, comprised black players, leading critics to accuse him of harboring a bias against whites. Thompson countered that his only bias was in favor of a particular style of play that required a particular kind of athlete. Like all coaches, Thompson recruited players who appeared to share his own culture and values. As it happens, a handful of those players happened to be white. One, Jeff Bullis, a Georgetown forward from 1978 to 1982, told *Sports Illustrated*, "On this team the black-white thing just doesn't come up until some reporter starts asking questions. It's hard to explain how close we are, but we're closer, I think, than any of the teams we've played. That's how Mr. Thompson wants it, and that's the kind of people Mr. Thompson recruits. We're like a military unit that has gone through the fire together. Mr. Thompson is the fire. He's very tough, but if you can take it, he'll make a man out of you."[30]

Bullis's language is revealing: to his players Coach Thompson was "Mr. Thompson," connoting a style of authority as much professional as paternal, the relevant professional code being that of the military. This led to a paradox of racial coding: Thompson's "black" teams played a brand of basketball usually associated with "white" habits like discipline, order, and control. Thompson was well aware that his emphasis on discipline undermined prevailing stereotypes of the black player: "Undisciplined, that means nigger. They're all big and fast and can leap like kangaroos and eat watermelon in the locker room, but they can't play as a team and they choke under pressure. It's the idea that a black man doesn't have the intelligence or character to practice self-control." The ironic corollary is that the basketball style coded as "black" is more likely to be encouraged by a typical white coach. "A white coach recruits a good black player," Thompson explained. "He knows the kid's got talent, but he also knows—or thinks he knows—that because he's black he's undisciplined. So he doesn't try to give the kid any discipline. He puts him in the freelance, one-on-one, hot dog role, and turns to the little white guard for discipline. Other black kids see this and think this is how they are expected to play, and so the image is perpetuated."[31]

Thompson was also bent on challenging conventional assumptions about the educability of urban black athletes. He insisted that his players approach their studies with the same intense focus and discipline he was cultivating on the court. One of his tactics was to quell postgame locker room celebrations by telling his players that while the big win was great for *him* and might even get him a raise, it probably wouldn't do much to improve *their* lives— meaning the bargain they'd made with Georgetown wasn't a smart one unless they left with a degree. Alas, the high graduation rate among Thompson's players—90 percent or more in most of his recruiting classes—didn't erase a widespread perception that these players did not belong in Georgetown classrooms. Thompson's campus allies couched their support in liberal terms that may or may not have made the players feel more comfortable. "The main way I see Georgetown," said Father James Redington, a theology professor who served as the basketball team's scorekeeper, "is in terms of the increased commitment by Catholic universities, and by Jesuits in particular, in support of social justice. Or specifically, it's what we Jesuits call an option in favor of the poor."[32]

This option in favor of the poor seemed especially compelling when it came to Patrick Ewing, the most highly touted big man since Lew Alcindor. Ewing came from an immigrant Jamaican family in Cambridge, Massachusetts, and had done well academically at the city's highly regarded Rindge and Latin High School. Because he had shown interest in local Boston University (a basketball lightweight), and because Boston College (like all major basketball programs) had shown interest in him, when Ewing opted for Georgetown some powerful Bostonians felt betrayed and turned on him in ways that others could only see as carrying an unfortunate racial subtext. "As long as Patrick Ewing went to one of the Boston colleges, he was fine," said Georgetown president Reverend Timothy Healy. "The Boston newspapers wanted him to stay in Boston. But as soon as he went to Georgetown, he became an illiterate to them. Well, if he was an illiterate, then why did the Boston papers want him to stay in Boston in the first place?"[33] A racist misperception of Ewing's intelligence quickly hardened into conventional wisdom, abetted by several factors. Ewing— who later emerged, especially after his playing career ended, as friendly, sweet-natured, sometimes even garrulous—was shielded from the press with intense vigilance by coach Thompson. Coupled with his fierce, warriorlike mien on the court, Ewing's silence fed into benighted perceptions not just of his intelligence but of his fundamental humanity. Put simply, Ewing's detractors saw him as an animal. Throughout his college career, Villanova fans had been among the worst in taunting Ewing with heinous racist slurs. During the pregame warmup at a January 1983 game at the Palestra in Philadelphia, someone from the Villanova cheering section unfurled a banner that labeled Ewing an "ape." When Ewing walked onto the court during the player introductions, someone from the same section threw a banana peel toward him. The travesty brought to the surface a deep racial substrate, intensifying the feeling that the Georgetown rivalry was a proxy for a deeper battle between blackness and whiteness.

During the Final Four weekend in Lexington, Kentucky, Georgetown maintained an air of secrecy and menace in the style of the rap group Public Enemy. The Villanova camp, meanwhile, struck a tone closer to a doo-wop revival. "Rollie had more fun down at the Final Four than any other coach I could possibly imagine," recalled a Villanova athletic department associate.[34] Photographs of the Villanova team and their "extended family" lounging in front of their Ramada Inn headquarters circulated through the sports media. At an open practice in front of 15,000, Massimino staged a team scrimmage with a cagey twist: he pitted the team's seven black players and seven white players against each other. The team came up with a name for the event: "the Brothers versus the Joeys." "The spectators couldn't believe we were cutting up like that," said backup center Chuck Everson, "but it was a terrific idea and it turned into a really effective practice session. It kept us loose and brought us even closer as a squad."[35]

In the narrative that has been forged retrospectively, Villanova's riveting upset win over Georgetown vindicates Massimino's family holiday atmosphere and sly mockery of Georgetown's black power ideology. The first half of the game was a dead heat, with Villanova holding a narrow 29–28 lead going into the locker room. Pinckney and the Villanova forwards challenged Georgetown inside right away, making it clear that they weren't intimidated by Ewing. Just as important, point guard Gary McLain did an excellent job at controlling the pace of the game and protecting the ball. This was the last year the tournament would be played without a shot clock—the Big East had experimented with a forty-five-second shot clock during its regular season—and Massimino figured his team's best chance at winning was to minimize the number of shots taken in the game and simply outshoot Georgetown from the field. Unable to dictate the pace and tone of the game, Georgetown seemed tentative and frustrated. At the very end of the first half, Hoya forward Reggie Williams gave Everson a rough shove to the face. Massimino went ballistic, defiantly pumping his right fist while screaming at the Georgetown contingent as both teams ran through the arena tunnel to their locker rooms. Massimino used the incident to fire up his team. "Who do they think they are?," *Perfect Upset* recalls his emoting in his locker room oration. "They can't do that shit to us. That's it. We're going to kick their ass!"[36] Here was a distinct echo of Pitino's showdown against John Thompson, only now a national championship and a national racial mythology were at stake. To reach right up to the edge of caricature: Rollie Massimino was now playing the same role as another iconic Philadelphia Italian American underdog— Sly Stallone's Rocky Balboa—in standing up against the fearsome black colossus.[37] Unlike Rocky—in the first movie, anyway—Rollie took home the crown, as his team hit nearly 80 percent of its shots and squeaked by with a 66–64 win over Thompson's more talented and heavily favored Hoyas.

All in the Family

It had been just two years since North Carolina State's Jim Valvano dashed wildly around the court looking for someone to hug after winning his national championship. In another two years a new generation of Italian American coaching would rise to the top when Rick Pitino led Providence to the Final Four. Two years after that, P. J. Carlesimo's Seton Hall would make a run all the way to the title game. Meanwhile John Calipari, an acolyte of Sonny Vaccaro and Rick Pitino, was set to steer the University of Massachusetts into the big time. In the lore of men's college basketball, the 1980s are remembered—properly—as the decade of John Thompson and Georgetown. That was also the decade of the Italian Americans.

But the decade was only half over, and its second half would bring knotty twists to the Rollie Massimino story and the Italian

American college basketball narrative writ large. I lived in Philadelphia during these years and became a connoisseur of what is known as the Big Five. Locals will tell you these were diminished times for the unofficial city rivalry between Villanova, Temple, Penn, St. Joseph's, and La Salle. No longer were all the Big Five games played at the Palestra on the University of Pennsylvania campus, one of college basketball's legendary sites. No longer were these teams composed almost exclusively of players from the Philadelphia area who had competed against each other in youth and high school leagues and in the city parks. Television exposure had given these teams (especially Villanova and Temple) a national recruiting profile, while the sudden ubiquity of televised games on ESPN and the traditional networks kept more and more basketball fans at home.

The many Philly wags who thought Rollie Massimino was never as committed to the city basketball tradition as he should have been scorned his Big East celebrity status as a slighting of the Big Five. Some critics seized on every piece of evidence—and such evidence was not hard to find—that Massimino's already sizable ego had ballooned to unseemly proportions following the 1985 championship. Inevitably, as had happened with Jim Valvano, the glory of the championship crown brought Massimino a much higher media profile, enticements from bigger and better-endowed colleges, and—in what was emerging as a standard perquisite for successful Italian American coaches—flattering interest from the hapless New Jersey Nets of the NBA.

None of this got in the way of my robust pleasure in observing Massimino during these years. Decades on, I still vividly recall loud, boozy nights and weekend afternoons watching Villanova games in Philly bars, thrilling again and again to Massimino's late-game tactics and theatrics as he micromanaged the clock, keeping his team in the game as long as possible, all the while looking like an exploded piñata spilling all over the court. I wasn't a Villanova fan; I was a Rollie fan. To watch him was to feel him, to channel his energy and passion. If I too fell under the "Daddy Mass" spell, for me he was more like an uncle—the crazy uncle, a stock character in Italian families, who looms large in a child's life by heightening the ritualistic power of social gatherings through sheer force of his charismatic personality. In a lifetime of sports spectatorship sometimes bordering on the manic-obsessive, I have never been so enthralled by a *coach*. Watching Massimino in those Philly bars gave me some of the most intense feelings of participatory rapture I have ever experienced outside music and dance.

And so I couldn't help feeling chagrined that the 1985 fairy tale suddenly and surprisingly unraveled when, two years later, a controversy erupted that threatened the "Daddy Mass" image and family narrative. In 1987 Gary McLain published a first-person cover story in *Sports Illustrated* revealing a cocaine addiction that went back to his days playing for Villanova.[38] It was a recovery memoir rich in sordid detail, a play-by-play account of major college basketball experienced through the haze of a drug habit. McLain's description of his own experience was startling, but he also painted a culture of deception and cover-up at Villanova. McLain claimed he wasn't the only Villanova player involved with illegal drugs. Worse, he alleged that Massimino was aware of his problem but never faced up to it squarely. There were denials all around, but the damage was done. The sentimental image of Massimino's Villanova as an old-fashioned, morally superior ethnic family had been tarnished—to be resurrected only in historical memory.

Try as Villanova might to dismiss McLain as an anomaly, in fact he was its team's inspirational leader, its coach on the court. He'd come from a broken family and was living with his high school coach's family outside Boston when Massimino recruited him. As much as anyone, he fit the symbolic role that validated Massimino's reputation as a surrogate father. One of Massimino's own sons was one of McLain's teammates; he like the others had to clear his name in the face of McLain's allegations. But certain difficult questions still linger, including the biggest of all: What was the true nature of the Villanova team culture underneath the "one big happy family" rhetoric? None of the retrospective accounts address this at all. *Ed Pinckney's Tales from the Villanova Hardwood* buries mention of the McLain episode in a wincingly credulous postscript ("The incident has not caused his teammates to replace or rethink the fond memories they have of Gary as a person and teammate").[39] *Sports Illustrated* and HBO treat the McLain incident as an afterthought, sealing it off from their general feel-good pasta bowl narratives. HBO's *Perfect Upset*, in fact, does its best to cast the McLain story as one of forgiveness and redemption. It shows footage of Massimino and McLain embracing at the 2005 Villanova team reunion and ends the segment with the words "We're always going to be family."[40] Such, evidently, is the scandal-proof power of the sentimental Italian family image.

The Killer Vees

Massimino, Valvano, and Vitale emerged as celebrity ethnics at a time when the advent of ESPN permanently increased the size, scale, and cultural influence of US sports media. ESPN changed the landscape in no small part through the resonance of Italian American personality and voice. According to Michael Freeman, author of *ESPN: The Uncensored History* (2000), the veteran New York sportscaster Sal Marchiano commanded one of the network's first six-figure salaries for a Thursday night boxing program and various other events because "ESPN needed a New York voice to appease rich Manhattan advertisers, and few broadcasters in New York were better known than Sal Marchiano."[41] Through the years, sportswriters Al Morganti, Sal Paolantonio, and Mike Lupica have cut their broadcasting teeth at ESPN. When the network moved into talk radio in the 1990s, its first major personality jock was Tony Bruno, one of the "Morning Guys" at Philadelphia local station WIP, along with Morganti and Angelo Cataldi. Such sports talk radio programs—like the several Valvano hosted and like the "Mike and the Mad Dog" show on New York's WFAN hosted by Mike Francesa and Chris Russo until their breakup in 2008—provide a forum for pungent, ethnically accented, almost entirely male sports banter such as one might otherwise hear in the gym, on the street corner, in the saloon, and at the kitchen table.[42]

Even against the elevated standard of Italian American garrulousness, Vitale—ESPN's longest-lasting star—is in a class by himself. "For its volume of work," said *Sports Illustrated*'s Rick Reilly, "Vitale's mouth should be studied and preserved by the Smithsonian."[43] The pitch and energy of his voice would not be unusual coming from a boardwalk barker on the Jersey Shore, but it seems completely out of sync with almost every other human vocal utterance on national television. Vitale does not analyze the action of a basketball game; he emotes and embodies it, absorbs it into his heart and moves it up through his throat and out his mouth in wacky turns of phrase often punctuated with Sinatra-like use of the snappy word "baby." When a coach has reason to be agitated, it's "Maalox Time, baby." When a quick-handed player steals the ball, he's "All-Pickpocket Team, baby." When a team hits the soft part of its schedule, it's "Cupcake City, baby."

While Vitale's manic exuberance has won him a legion of detractors—"Can I get a V-chip that specifically screens out the most unpleasant things on sports television? In other words, is there a Dickie V-chip?" quipped one[44]—his supporters claim he's one of the biggest factors in college basketball's explosive rise in popularity starting in the 1980s. There's a larger point here: when a retired college basketball coach turned television sportscaster *himself* becomes the subject of extensive sports media debate and scrutiny, something significant has happened in the perception of what basketball is really all about. It's not just the players engaged in a performance: the ninety-four-foot wooden floor where the game is played is just one of multiple stages (locker room, arena tunnel, sidelines, courtside seats, press row, television screen, network studio) for the increasingly theatrical, multimedia spectacle of the game. Starting in the 1980s, many of the elite college basketball programs no longer played their games in the sturdy brick campus gymnasiums students used for recreational sports; they now played in flashy professional-style arenas or even domed stadiums featuring elaborate scoreboards and audiovisual systems designed to incite fan response. Pregame player introductions became rituals of staged bombast using music and lighting techniques drawn from rock and rap concert productions. As ever, African Americans took the lead in exploring innovative stylistic possibilities, using the player introductions to perform the latest 'hood-certified handshakes, fist bumps, and mock strip-search riffs.

What has this meant in the past two decades for dagotude sideline shtick? In my reading, it has meant a shift in cultural dynamics in which a traditional ethnic image rooted in "family"-centered sentimentality and folksy humor, while by no means absent from the college basketball landscape, has to some degree been eclipsed by a newer business-centered corporate image. Lou Carnesecca, Rollie Massimino, and Dick Vitale personify the first type, Rick Pitino and John Calipari the second. Jim Valvano represents an intriguing transitional figure between the two.

By the 1990s, the Duke–North Carolina rivalry emerged as the top one in college basketball, owing not just to the consistent excellence of those two teams, but also to ESPN's hyping of the "Tobacco Road" storyline and its obsessive fawning on the two coaches. In the early 1980s, however, neither Dean Smith of North Carolina nor Mike Krzyzewski of Duke was the ACC coach with the biggest star power. "Back then, there was no bigger star in college basketball than James Thomas Valvano," John Feinstein writes in his best seller *A March to Madness*. Feinstein describes Valvano as "a wisecracking New Yorker with thick black hair, a prominent nose and foghorn voice, who was so quick and so funny that he was impossible not to like."[45]

Valvano was also one of the best ever to coach the game. "A lot of basketball people would tell you then and will tell you now that if they had one game to play with their entire life on the line, their first choice to coach that game would be Valvano," Feinstein reports. "Not Bob Knight. Not Dean Smith. Valvano. He was that good."[46] *Sports Illustrated*'s Curry Kirkpatrick concurred, labeling the 1983 national championship season the best coaching performance in college basketball history. "No man ever cajoled, connived, whipped, sawed, laughed, sobbed, held together, led and willed his young wards to the national championship in precisely the manner Valvano did." Citing Valvano's masterful management of game tempo, Kirkpatrick concluded, "No one ever won the thing strictly by coaching as much as this man. In the ultimate coaches' sport, V was the ultimate."[47]

For all of his X's and O's brilliance, Valvano won over the sports media with something else: here was a coach with a Vegas-quality lounge act. "V is not just a funny sports guy," Kirkpatrick observed, "V is *funny* funny. After dinner funny. Talk-show funny. Sit-down, stand-up, prone supine, in-your-face, sober-or-high, all-time hall-of-fame funny. V doesn't engage in conversation, he plays the room." Kirkpatrick continued: "V has a sense of the comedic art—precise timing, a special radar to the jugular vein. V is a connoisseur of the greats. Benny. Burns. Mort Sahl. Mark Twain. Richard Pryor. He didn't just laugh at Jimmy Durante. At age seven he was *doing* Durante." Kirkpatrick's backstory on Valvano—"a full-blooded spaghetti-slinger who married the beautiful blonde Jewish princess . . ."—reads like something out of the show business slicks. Valvano's picaresque "up from the urban streets" tale sounds like the plot of an ethnic novel. He was "a have-not walk-on who needed a bank loan to get into Rutgers," where he was both a tough backcourt player and a serious student, an English major with a genuine love of literature. He went on to become a "coach/romantic who carries a book of poetry in his briefcase right next to the scouting reports."[48]

For all Valvano's joyous zest for life, he is now best remembered for his tragically premature, very public death, and in particular for the emotional speech he gave at an ESPN awards dinner—the ESPYs—in 1993, just months before succumbing to cancer at age forty-seven. One of the key lines in the speech—"Don't give up. Don't ever give up"—became the motto for the Jimmy V Foundation, a cancer research philanthropy. Every year since, at the outset of the college basketball season, ESPN sponsors a week of fundraising for the foundation and rebroadcasts Valvano's speech. This yearly ritual has become college basketball's singular performance of sentimentality. The tape of Valvano's courageous, heartrending 1993 ESPY speech shows an audience of the US sports elite, at least half of whom—including the biggest, toughest-looking football players—appear to be crying. Current ESPN personalities use the occasion to reminisce about Valvano with deep feeling. In a December 2005 broadcast, former Notre Dame coach Digger Phelps recalled his visits to Valvano's parents' house on Long Island. Rocco and Angelina had moved from the Corona neighborhood in Queens where Jim grew up, but Angie's cooking was still legendary. "The Irish eat more Italian food than cabbage and ham," Phelps quips.

This canonizing of Valvano as a college basketball saint came not long after he had been tagged as one of the game's most conspicuous sinners. Throughout the 1980s, Valvano and his staff recruited a number of players of extremely marginal academic talent, and the NC State program came to be associated with the widening public perception that big-time college basketball had all but abandoned the pretense of an educational mission. In 1989 a book about Valvano and NC State portrayed the program as an ethical cesspool rife with grade manipulation, point shaving, and other cheating schemes.[49] An NCAA investigation ensued. In the end Valvano was absolved of the most serious allegations, but media scrutiny and pressure from NC State alumni forced his resignation in 1990. Almost immediately, the same media industry that had faithfully charted his fall from grace happily embraced him as one of their own: following Al McGuire's example, Valvano took his place in the broadcast booth for ESPN and ABC. He was occasionally paired with Dick Vitale, and the two were touted as the "Killer Vees." The broadcasts sounded like a cacophonous Sunday dinner at Rocco and Angie's. Comedian Bill Cosby was among those who dug the act: soon Valvano and Vitale showed up on *The Cosby Show* in a cameo appearance as professional movers, parlaying Italian working-class ethnic shtick on prime time TV's parable of black middle-class uplift.[50]

It seemed quite a comedown from his glory days as a star coach, but the truth is that Valvano seemed always to have approached coaching as a hustle, a way to leverage a bigger slice of the entertainment market. It was in the late 1970s, while coaching Iona, that Valvano "conglomeratized himself" as a business entity and media personality. He took on full-time radio and TV commitments—using "Theme from *The Godfather*" as bumper music for his call-in radio show—and wrote a nationally syndicated newspaper column. He incorporated JTV Enterprises and pursued restaurant partnerships, advertising spots, and after-dinner speaking engagements. He loved what he was doing and loved that he was doing it at a place like Iona. "I knew I was home. The Iona kids were second-generation ethnics, commuters who pumped gas at night so they could afford to pay for their books in the morning. They were me."[51] He enjoyed socializing with his players and Iona students and alumni, some becoming his business partners. Not incidentally, he put Iona on the national basketball map, turning a third-rate program into a slayer of big-time Goliaths. The national champion in 1980 was Louisville. In January of that year, Louisville came to New York to play Iona in Madison Square Garden, probably figuring on an easy win and some flattering New York press. Valvano's Iona Gaels summarily thrashed them, winning by seventeen points.

Valvano's NC State teams were mostly black, but they also included Vinny Del Negro, Tom Gugliotta, and Chris Corchiani, three Italian Americans who made it into the NBA in the 1990s. Valvano's ethnic sensibility had a refined particularity: he incarnated New York City outer borough sauciness. In the 1993 ESPY speech, a moment of poignant humor comes when Valvano pauses to say he's going to ignore the signal from offstage indicating that his allotted speaking time is up. "I've got tumors all over my body," he says with a wry smirk, "and I'm going to worry about some guy in the back saying 'thirty seconds'? Hey, *funable*, brother!" By flinging this southern Italian colloquialism (translation: "go to Naples" or, very roughly, "get the fuck lost") along with a well-known Italian hand gesture signaling biting reproach, Valvano shifted the tone of the room: he went to New York Italian American street vernacular, and everyone followed him, laughing hard at the gallows humor.

The 1983 championship had deified Valvano, bringing a proliferation of media exposure, endorsement deals, and corporate speech-making gigs. He did sports on the CBS Morning News. He cut a pilot for a Hollywood variety show. He hosted a cheesy sports bloopers TV show. He occasionally read the commute-time traffic report on a local Raleigh radio station. Meanwhile he increasingly delegated day-to-day coaching responsibilities to his assistants. There is little doubt NC State basketball suffered as a result. Several of his late 1980s teams had more talent than the 1983 edition; none made it back to the Final Four.[52]

Gym Rats Gone GQ

Rick Pitino, the most celebrated Italian American coach of the contemporary era, enjoys the distinction of being the only college coach to have won the NCAA national championship at two schools, at Kentucky in 1996 and Louisville in 2013. Pitino has coached two of the NBA's most storied franchises, the New York Knicks (briefly but successfully) and the Boston Celtics (unsuccessfully). Raised in a working-class Italian American family in New York City and Long Island, he is now transplanted Kentucky gentry, a multimillionaire who trades in racehorses. He pulls top dollar for his Dale Carnegie–style motivational speeches at business conventions and publishes best-selling books on executive leadership bearing titles like *Success Is a Choice*. He's a fashion plate who favors gorgeously tailored dark suits with matching pocket squares and ties ("Lots of coaches don't got style like Coach P," said Louisville forward Earl Clark), but recently he has taken to appearing at one game a year in a luminous white linen suit ("Pitino was looking very guido in the white leisure suit," ran one YouTube comment; another said he looked like "a pimp at P. Diddy's all-white Hamptons party"). One sportswriter has said of Pitino and Calipari—this was back when Calipari was coaching at Pitino's alma mater, UMass—that as young men they'd "become prototypes of the modern basketball coach. They were slick and good-looking. They were sultans of spin and sound bites every bit as they were Xs and Os experts. They were not father-figure coaches [of past generations], but rather the new generation of coaching genius, the gym rat gone GQ."[53]

A renowned motivator, strategist, and administrator ("Rick is more organized than crime," said a former associate), Pitino takes a mix of inferior and superior athletes, works them all to the bone, bending their individual wills to the team system. He breeds an ethic of mutual support and loyalty throughout the team ranks—even, oddly, when his own conspicuous personal ambitions trump his loyalty to his teams. He has been much more successful at the college level: NBA players proved wary of his evangelical fervor ("I expect them to have a boyish enthusiasm for the game"), his urge to constantly teach, and most of all his torturous work regimen. "The basic premise of my system is to fatigue your opponents defensively and [maintain] constant movement offensively," Pitino explained. "You're trying to get up more shots than your opponents by forcing more turnovers. By using multiple substitutions and ten to eleven players, you go into the final five minutes as the superior-conditioned team." Pitino is here describing a corporate system that provides little space for individual ego, totally out of sync with the star system that has come to dominate the pro game.[54]

The one star in Pitino's system is Pitino himself: his goal is to have his team "become an extension of my personality on the court."[55] This would seem even more self-aggrandizing if Pitino did not have such a remarkable passion for the game. For all his success in the broader world of business and media, Pitino, according to intimates, is still truly comfortable only around other basketball people or a select few men from the horse-breeding world. This is a legacy, they say, of all the time he spent as a teenager and young man at the Five Star basketball camp. At that legendary proving ground for both coaching and playing talent, Pitino apprenticed under coaches' coaches like Hubie Brown and Chuck Daly, nurturing his love for the male homosociality of the basketball fraternity. Throughout his career, Pitino has conducted team practices in a more physically engaged style than most of his colleagues, mixing it up with his players as he demonstrates the strategies and formations he wants them to perfect. Al Bianchi, his former boss with the New York Knicks, said of Pitino, "Beneath the expensive suits and the Phoenix tan beats the heart of an old New York street fighter." The gym is Pitino's home; he finds it hard to leave. "At Providence," he recalled, "my assistants and I would play half-court basketball at midnight, then go sit in the sauna, and talk about the next day's practice." On his wedding night, early in his career, Pitino left his wife Joanne behind in a New York hotel lobby to do an impromptu interview for an assistant's position at Syracuse.[56]

On the Sunday afternoon of Thanksgiving weekend in 2008, while visiting my wife's family in Nashville, I sneaked away to attend the Louisville–Western Kentucky game at the Sommet Center, the city's downtown arena. As I took stock of the pregame scene, I was struck with the thought that here at the crossroads of the Sun Belt and the New South, in this massive arena filled with thousands of Kentuckians, a couple hundred local Nashville service and security personnel, a hundred or so media workers, and possibly a handful of souls of my ilk—holiday weekend carpetbaggers escaping the in-laws—it was entirely possible that Rick Pitino, his son Richard (a Louisville assistant coach at the time), and I might be the only Italians in the house. The closest Pitino's Louisville team came to on-court Italian American representation was through a racial passing fantasy: in the team media guide, the six-foot, six-inch African American forward Terrance Williams said that the actor who should play him in a movie is the five-foot, five-inch Al Pacino—physique evidently being less important than gangster iconicity. I chuckled at this, but a theme had presented itself and soon would begin to resonate.

While the players came to the end of their drills and the cheerleaders started tumbling through the air, the arena sound system pumped high-volume Jay Z, a favorite of today's players. Then, all of a sudden, the bass-heavy hip-hop throb let up and I heard something I could hardly believe. It was the Louisville pep band, just to my left, launching into "Theme from *The Godfather*." Just at this moment, with the band's brass section miming the plaintive mandolin lines of Nino Rota's original, Rick Pitino emerged from a tunnel on the far side of the arena, striding confidently to the loud cheers of the Louisville fans. It was a staged celebrity-style entrance, drenched in the rituals of hero worship. Impeccably dressed and coiffed, coolly poised, regal, Pitino was Michael Corleone arriving at a meeting of the heads of the five families. He was Sinatra mounting the stage at the Fountainebleau. He was Julius Caesar making his entrance at the Colosseum.

It was, in short, a spectacle of such bombastic, over-the-top ethnic kitsch, so tonally dissonant from everything I'd heard and seen that day, that I couldn't keep from doubling over in laughter. But the ritual is a serious one for Pitino and his fans, and we should scrutinize it for clues about the deeper cultural flows at work in basketball. One flow was captured in the arena audio track, in the abrupt shift from contemporary black hip-hop to Italian ethnic nostalgia, a segue not nearly as dissonant as one might suppose. Jay Z, one of those hip-hop artists who's also a fantastically successful business entrepreneur, dresses in a high-fashion corporate style very much like Rick Pitino's. His beats may not sync with "Theme from *The Godfather*," but his aura of sovereign discipline and cool toughness echoes something of the posture of Michael Corleone, a gangster persona white America finds safer and more pleasing than its black gangsta derivatives. So, as I sat next to the Louisville pep band, perhaps I shouldn't have felt so whipsawed by the sound cues: there was a cultural logic here, a cross-racial, black-Italian masculinity that's become so seemingly natural and seamless it plays beautifully even here in Nashville, country music heaven.

I'll continue working the "Godfather" masculinity theme pretty hard in a moment, but I should first acknowledge that there's a more straightforward way to hear the movie soundtrack in a basketball arena—that is, simply as the sound of sentimental ethnicity, of Italian American group memory made audible in our so-called postethnic era. Usually when I hear "Theme from *The Godfather*"—even just the signature riff blaring from my New Jersey uncles' car horns back in the 1970s—my thoughts and feelings don't focus on the scenes of tough men smoking cigars and plotting revenge; they focus on the scenes of the vulnerable young Vito Corleone arriving at Ellis Island among his fellow Italians, steerage passengers leaving Old World troubles, hoping for New World opportunities. I think of my father arriving with one small suitcase and the salami his mother had slipped into his pocket. I think of my maternal grandparents, who met each other on Ellis Island—at their own marriage ceremony. *The Godfather* was the first movie my parents ever saw that depicted the Ellis Island experience, and watching it with them connected me to the family narrative. The movie soundtrack usually goes right to my heart. But in Nashville that day it went somewhere else—to my funny bone, as I've said, and to whatever part of me holds the irony and the snarkiness. Maybe it was simply because the tune was being played by a college pep band, an outfit that trades in satirical burlesque. But I think it also had something to do with the crowd I was part of—southern US white and black, with nary a sign of southern or eastern European stock—and the incongruity of having this audience witness, in Pitino's grandiose entrance, a performance of New York-style bravura: dagotude incarnate. What I *heard* in "Theme from *The Godfather*" was a vestigial sound, a nostalgic audio artifact recalling a different America and perforce a different college basketball world, a world dominated by immigrant working-class Irish, Jews, and Italians, a world in which blacks were at best a token presence. What I *saw* in the Sommet Center was the reverse picture, one in which the white ethnics now are the tokens—except for one proud Italian American who refuses to be anyone's token.

Behind such scenes, there's a form of masculinity that governs the relationships the most successful Italian American coaches develop with their mostly African American players—a rapport centered not so much on a mock gangster code of loyalty, with its fastidious parsing of favors and slights, as on a more general style of ethnic homosociality, a schoolyard and locker room idiom of fast talk, cutup humor, hang-loose bodily interaction, and flowing energy. In this milieu Rick Pitino and John Calipari have garnered reputations as master motivators and recruiters, especially adept at strategically deploying what Jack Woltz, the Hollywood tycoon in *The Godfather*, calls, in a dramatically different context, "guinea charm." Early in his coaching career, Pitino set a new standard for recruiting fervor, turning what had been merely an unseemly vocation into a full-fledged manic disorder, relishing the unrelenting travel, the fleabag motels, the happy hour free food. "I was a regular Fuller Brush man," Pitino recalled of his first job as an assistant coach at the University of Hawaii, "filling their heads with visions of alohas and Don Ho." Just a couple of years earlier, as a player at the University of Massachusetts, Pitino was known for getting in fistfights with the two point guards ahead of him on the team depth chart. Off-court, meanwhile, he served as social director of his fraternity. This combination of traits—slick sociality and pathological competitiveness—served him well in his first job. "I loved it. Loved the competition for players, the thrill of the chase, selling myself, everything. I loved living on airplanes and making thirty calls a day, doing the hundred and one things that go with being a college recruiter."[57]

John Calipari apparently has used more than his guinea charm and type A personality in the recruiting game. When Calipari was up for the head coaching job at UMass, Villanova coach Rollie Massimino did his best to spoil the candidacy, casting aspersions on Calipari's ethics in a poison-pen letter to the school's administration. Massimino, a legendary recruiter in his own right, given to a much folksier, sentimental ("you'll be part of a family") approach than his rivals, had lost some blue-chip prospects to Big East rival Pittsburgh when Calipari was an assistant there, and Massimino alleged foul play. (There was also a story afloat, never confirmed, that Calipari had steered a player away from St. John's with the lie that St. John's coach Lou Carnesecca was suffering from terminal cancer.) The first two times Calipari led his teams to the Final Four, UMass in 1996 and the University of Memphis in 2008, the teams were retroactively disqualified when their star players were discovered to be in violation of NCAA eligibility rules.

Yet Calipari is still considered the best recruiter of this era. One of his former Memphis players, Chris Douglas-Roberts, thinks he knows why. When Douglas-Roberts was being courted on the west side of Detroit, his strategy was to line up neighborhood friends on the porch and watch the coach-suitors interacting with them. "I'm from a tough neighborhood and I always wanted to see how the coaches would deal with it. I had a lot of my people on that porch and some of the coaches weren't very comfortable but Coach Cal—he handled it perfectly. He greeted everyone, slapped five, showed he was very comfortable with where he was." This won over Douglas-Roberts, and just as crucially, his mother. "That wasn't easy," Douglas-Roberts said.[58]

Calipari grew up outside Pittsburgh. His paternal grandfather, an immigrant from Calabria, had labored in the West Virginia coal mines. His father worked first in western Pennsylvania steel mills, later with a cargo company at the Pittsburgh airport. John himself, according to his high school coach, was "the gym rat of all gym rats." Calipari was a solid if unremarkable point guard. But he was class president and prom king and had the gift of gab. After Five Star, he started his *own* basketball camp for elementary school kids, hustling sponsorship from a local McDonald's.[59]

In 1988, when the University of Massachusetts was in the market for a new head coach, Rick Pitino, then with the Knicks, urged his alma mater to hire Calipari, who at that point had worked only as an assistant at Kansas and Pittsburgh. UMass basketball had floundered after a brief moment in the spotlight in the late 1960s, when the spectacular dunk artist Julius Erving wore the Minutemen uniform. "If we don't hire Calipari," Pitino argued, "then we're afraid to win." UMass sided with Pitino over naysayers like Rollie Massimino, and Pitino made a personal contribution to Calipari's first salary package. In what Pitino called "the best rebuilding job in college basketball history," Calipari turned UMass from one of the worst Division I programs in the country into one of the best, culminating in the trip to the Final Four in 1996.[60]

Calipari quickly proved himself a first-class evangelist and motivator in the Pitino mold, pushing a "life skills" philosophy in his recruiting and hyping UMass basketball throughout New England in a way that caught the attention of key New York sports media stars, notably the influential talk radio jock Mike Francesa. Calipari's best coaching probably came in these early years, when he seemed to instill his own ferocious will in his mostly journeyman players. Inevitably, however, he seemed less substantial than his benefactor, a perception deepened by an instinct for self-glorification that made even Pitino look modest. Early in his UMass tenure, Calipari actually trademarked his team's motto, "Refuse to Lose," clear evidence of his approach to coaching as a private business venture. In *Going Bigtime: The Spectacular Rise of UMass Basketball* (1996), Marty Dobrow sums up the divided reaction to Calipari's success. For some Calipari was "a modern-day Horatio Alger, a man who rose from modest roots to the top of his profession through an unrelenting work ethic." For others he was "a greedy whiner, willing to step on anything or anyone to get his way . . . a jockish Michael Milken whose 'refuse to lose' bespeaks nothing but arrogance, and whose emphasis on life skills demonstrates only slick self-promotion."[61]

In the UMass years, Calipari demonstrated an uncanny ability to get under the skin of other coaches—especially, it seemed, other tough ethnic coaches. UConn's Jim Calhoun, a crusty Irish American Bostonian who fancied himself the kingpin of New England basketball, resented his rival's upstart ways—not to mention his success in recruiting star center Marcus Camby out of Hartford, Calhoun's presumed jurisdiction. By many accounts he grew to loathe Calipari. UConn and UMass are less than seventy miles apart; with UConn basketball's national prominence, Calhoun knew he had the power to elevate UMass's profile simply by scheduling an annual game with them. Instead, he pretended the idea had never occurred to him. Mike Jarvis, George Washington's coach at this time, also from Boston, was one of the few young African American coaches in big-time college basketball. He developed an intense Atlantic 10 rivalry with Calipari and took to gloating when his team beat UMass. After a big GW victory in Amherst, Jarvis left the interview room preening: "Thank you very much. It's been a wonderful trip back to Massachusetts. God bless everybody, and the commonwealth."[62] Temple's John Chaney, the dean of African American coaches, several times failed to hold his volcanic temper in check during and after hard-fought games with his younger league rival. Once he tried to strangle Calipari in an on-court tussle; another time he broke into a postgame press conference screaming homicidal threats at him.

UMass's run to the Final Four in 1996 at first seemed to vindicate Calipari and his supporters. But a scandal soon ensued, triggered by the revelation that star center Marcus Camby had accepted illegal payments. Facing the prospect of closer NCAA scrutiny of his program, and presented with an alluring offer to coach the New Jersey Nets, Calipari bolted for the NBA. After a short, unsuccessful stint in the pros, he returned to the college ranks, to another rebuilding job, this time at Memphis. His coaching formula had changed. Now he tried to recruit marquee players, flattering their egos with the promise that he'd groom and showcase them (e.g., guaranteeing them their "touches" in his wide-open dribble-drive offense) for early entry in the NBA draft. Riding the back of an extraordinary (but, as it turned out, academically incligible) point guard, future NBA most valuable player Derrick Rose, Calipari arrived at the very cusp of the national championship in 2008, only to blow the game with a couple of crucial late-game tactical blunders.[63] After the next season he moved from Memphis to the University of Kentucky, taking that year's recruits with him. He has had great success there using the same recruiting strategy he employed at Memphis, winning the national championship in 2012 but continuing to provoke heavy criticism from traditionalists (Bobby Knight in particular), who view him as a craven hustler who has tainted the college game.

The "Godfather" trope is a colorful if imperfect metaphor for the role college coaches like Pitino and Calipari play in the lives of their players, but certainly it works better than the traditional image of the coach as father figure, the image most strongly associated with Rollie Massimino. In second-millennium American popular culture, many of the defining qualities of traditional crime family patriarchy (e.g., protectiveness, discipline, "respect") have lost out to an almost purely materialistic, consumerist concept of gangster culture. The imperial grandeur of Don Corleone is a fictional construct, and even this mythic ideal has undergone a harsh chastening through the torturous self-consciousness of Tony Soprano; alas, however, the real-world mobsters who most decisively infiltrated the broader culture are greaseball lowlifes like John Gotti and Nicky Scarfo. Since the 1990s, gangster rap's code of hardcore masculinity has so saturated the basketball world that the NBA saw fit, before the 2005–6 season, to implement an off-court dress code banning the oversized jeans, "bling" accessories, headwear, and sunglasses synonymous with hip-hop street culture. Some saw this an effort to contain and repress the influence of disorderly "bad nigga" figures like Allen Iverson, and to resurrect the image of Michael Jordan, the ultimate noble black man, an athlete of virtuosic artistry and steel-willed competitiveness whose image nevertheless is safe and pleasing to a mainstream white audience.[64]

Coaches often are cast sympathetically as victims of a degraded, egocentric, "I'm the man" culture that has polluted their youthful charges. But the truth is that coaches are an integral part of that culture, not just as enablers but as collaborators. The prevailing Armani-clad sartorial aesthetic in the coaching fraternity symbolizes not just a welcome concern for elegant personal style but also a bid for both legitimacy and cachet among the business-class boosters who underwrite these coaches' gargantuan salaries. These boosters want a return on their investment. They also crave the titillation of being associated with men who share their capitalist values, mimic but then elevate their own codes of appearance, and yet at the same time retain the animal vigor of the sporting life. These boosters—and here's the point, really—by and large are middle-aged white men who like being associated with other white men who have access to young black men and the kind of renegade young white men who masquerade as outlaw black men. Rick Pitino and John Calipari enjoy cachet among business executives because they operate like CEOs serving as the face of a corporate brand even as they maintain proximity to the vital masculine pulse. They are CEOs uniquely endowed with coolness and freedom. They slap five in the hood. They keep their jobs even after being discovered enjoying carnal relations with younger women in restaurant booths after hours. They are Coaches, in short, who are Players.[65]

This is not the only model available of the contemporary Italian American big-time college basketball coach. As it happens, the game I saw in Nashville was not a good one for Rick Pitino and his Louisville Cardinals. They were upset by Western Kentucky in what turned out to be one of their only losses of the season. Later, after earning the top seed in the 2009 NCAA tournament, the Cardinals missed making the Final Four with a loss to Michigan State in the Elite Eight round. This brought more ethnic intrigue: Michigan State's coach, Tom Izzo, hails from an Italian American, working-class family in Michigan, and ESPN, ever alert to alliterative possibility, billed the game as "The Paesan Playoff." Michigan State beat Louisville the same way Western Kentucky did in the game I saw—by neutralizing Pitino's trademark full-court press and exposing soft spots in his half-court defense.

Izzo's midwestern dagotude has none of the big-time flash and corporate sheen of Pitino's or Calipari's. His is a Rust Belt, meat and potatoes, hunting and fishing masculinity more common to football, Izzo's favored sport in his days as an athlete. Like Pitino and Calipari, he's demonstrative and voluble on the sidelines, an intense competitor. Unlike his *paesani*, his wardrobe never receives fawning notice, and he has never been in the headlines for on-court illegality or off-court marital infidelity. Izzo has spent practically his whole life working in his home state, whereas Pitino and Calipari are notorious for leaving high-paying jobs for even higher-paying jobs, wherever it happens to take them. Yet Izzo, who won the national championship in 2000 and who led his team to the Final Four six times in twelve seasons, may well be the best coach of the three. He may, in fact, be the best coach working in men's college basketball today, and as such, Geno Auriemma's only true peer.

Even so, the Michigan State pep band doesn't have "Theme from *The Godfather*" in *its* repertoire.

You Looking at Me?

With a few exceptions such as Angelo "Hank" Luisetti and Paul Arizin, basketball has never been a sport of Italian American male athletic achievement at anything approaching the same level as boxing (Marciano, LaMotta, etc.), baseball (DiMaggio, Berra, Rizzuto, to name just some of the Yankees), or football (Parilli, Lamonica, Montana, Marino, to name just some of the quarterbacks). Italian Americans also made their mark at the managerial level in these sports: witness Cus D'Amato and Angelo Dundee in boxing; Tommy Lasorda, Tony La Russa, Joe Torre, and Terry Francona in baseball; Vince Lombardi, Joe Paterno, and Bill Parcells in football. It is in boxing, baseball, and football that traditional models of the tough and resilient industrial-era male body best matched the sensibility of blue-collar Italian Americans.

Basketball too was an inviting space for the many working-class Italian American male athletes who populated the rosters of urban Catholic Youth Organization, parochial school, and college teams through the 1960s. Yet not a single one of them came close to achieving the renown of figures like Joe DiMaggio and Joe Montana, considered to be among the very best ever to play center field and quarterback. Since the 1980s, only a handful of Italian American men have played basketball at a high level. But during this same period, Italian American college basketball coaches have excelled, hardly a year passing in which one or more of them is not competing for the national championship. Meanwhile, a "fat little dago" named Sonny Vaccaro hatched the marketing plan that transformed college basketball into a multibillion-dollar business, and a loudmouthed *buffone* named Dick Vitale MC'd the party.

I've suggested that this Italianization of men's college basketball at the level of management and media is correlated with changes in the nature of basketball as a cultural form, in particular its shift into a more personality-driven, style-conscious, image-making, made-for-TV consumer culture. Before they went into coaching, Jim Valvano and Rick Pitino were point guards who approached each game as if it were a street fight. This fierce pugnacity carried over into their coaching and made them winners. But it did not make them stars. *This* they (and their fellow Italian American coaches) achieved through their mastery of the basketball court as a theatrical stage, and through their understanding that players and fans alike were hungry for performances of their distinctive brands of dagotude.

"Image is what much of basketball is about—looking good, bad, safe, edgy, cool, tough . . .": so shrewdly asserts Jeffrey Lane in *Under the Boards: The Cultural Revolution in Basketball* (2007).[66] Lane is talking primarily about men who play basketball, and he is thinking about the game as a text that's about more than on-court performance; he's thinking, that is, about basketball as a consumer culture. To think about basketball this way, we should consider players and coaches not just as images we consume, but as actors who work out their complicated relationships with each other through mutually constitutive protocols in which they define each other by consuming each other.

Except for the dramatic arts, there are few if any spheres of American life in which men in positions of institutional leadership cry, hug, sing, dance, versify, or in general use their bodies and voices to express deep feeling and sentiment, at least not publicly as a normal function of their occupation. Such is the enduring power in our culture of traditional Protestant norms of masculine control, rationality, and cool emotional discipline. Perhaps this is why, for many sports fans, some of the most vivid and memorable scenes in men's college basketball have involved coaches—coaching being a profession that combines the managerial and the performative—displaying spontaneity and passion through expansive physical gesture. And perhaps this is why, for many basketball players, Italian American coaches like Lou Carnesecca, Rollie Massimino, Jim Valvano, Dick Vitale, Rick Pitino, John Calipari, and Tom Izzo have proved seductively adept at the level of style, feeling, and attitude. Italian Americans who patrol the sidelines and man the broadcast booths are among the most heavily consumed bodies and voices in the US sports media. As such, these colorful purveyors of sideline shtick have much to teach us about ethnicity, masculinity, and American culture.

FIVE

Tutti

The House We Live In

The soaring crescendos of Enrico Caruso, the bel canto of Frank Sinatra, the soulfulness of the Rascals, the vitalism of Angelo Pellegrini's garden-to-table eating, the kitchen craziness of Louise DeSalvo, the wretched excess of Mario Batali, the maternal paternalism of *The Godfather*'s Don Corleone and *Do the Right Thing*'s Sal Franzione, the brave adventurousness of *Jungle Fever*'s Angie Tucci, the dagotude of Dick Vitale and Jim Valvano—what do these and other performances of American *italianità* throughout this book mean for our understanding of ethnicity, race, and American culture?

We began our journey in earnest at the historical moment when Frank Sinatra emerged as an important national figure. It is perhaps not coincidental that this was the same time—the World War II years—when the concept of ethnicity first took firm hold in American social science and popular discourse as a tool for understanding American social heterogeneity.[1] Anglocentric nativism of the pre-1924 period had cast immigrant Italians as a distinctive and inferior *race* unworthy of American citizenship. By contrast, the late 1930s Popular Front and the 1940s wartime ideology of pluralist Americanism gave second-generation US–born Italian Americans a strong sense of inclusion in the national community (excepting, of course, the several hundred Italian Americans who were interned and the thousands who were declared illegal aliens).

The ethnic distinctiveness of different Americans of European descent became an emblem of national pride, fodder for an ideology of democratic inclusiveness that became a key ingredient of American exceptionalism. But because this new concept of ethnicity was an inherently racialized, Eurocentric formulation of American pluralism, this model of inclusiveness actually operated as a vehicle of exclusion. The national community Sinatra invoked in the propaganda film *The House I Live In*, for example, includes the Irish, Italians, and Jews, makes no mention at all of African Americans, and pointedly excludes "the Japs."

In other words, no sooner did Italian Americans become ethnics than they became *white ethnics*, even though that term did not become commonplace for another couple of decades. A familiar narrative tells us that over time, with postwar suburbanization and class mobility, they become less and less ethnic and more and more white. A related narrative tells us that when Italian Americans self-consciously endeavored to revive and intensify their ethnic consciousness, they did so as part of an effort to resist the advances of African Americans and to create a zone of safety inside a nation they saw as falling hostage to the surging power of nonwhite racial minorities. This was the period of the ethnic revival movement of the late 1960s and '70s, when the terms white ethnic and white ethnicity came into vogue. This movement had far more to do with politics than culture: ethnicity not of the *My Big Fat Greek Wedding* and *Tony n' Tina's Wedding* variety, but as an alignment among working-class and lower-middle-class whites based on shared affective and socioeconomic interests, in particular an antagonism toward state-sponsored measures on behalf of people of color.[2] This was a grievance-based politics, a politics of resentment that found its popular symbols in flag waving, antiliberal "hard hats" and stridently outspoken mothers waging resistance to school busing programs. Michael Novak, the leading intellectual spokesperson for what he called the "unmeltable ethnics," hatched the sardonic acronym PIGS (Poles, Italians, Greeks, and Slavs) to name the ethnic groups at the center of this affective alliance; he excluded Jews from his southern and eastern European immigrant ethnic formation, reckoning that they had become—not least in their sympathy for blacks—part of the elite liberal establishment.[3]

Even as Sinatra broke his ties with the Democratic Party during this period, he did not embody the ascendant tenor of the moment nearly as well as someone like Anthony Imperiale, the Newark civic leader who wielded a baseball bat to defend his neighborhood during the city's racial unrest in the summer of 1967, and who advocated still more robust forms of armed white self-defense against the likes of Amiri Baraka. When Sinatra reemerged on the national scene in the 1980s, it was not just as the regal don of American popular song, but also as Ronald Reagan's ally in a mission to bury the fractious politics of the 1960s and '70s under a refurbished American patriotic nationalism. Thus did Sinatra's singing of "The House I Live In" at the centennial celebration of the Statue of Liberty in 1986 become a landmark event in the crystallization of a European American–centric "Nation of Immigrants" narrative of US national identity.[4]

In *Mean Streets* and *Goodfellas*, his films from 1973 and 1990, Martin Scorsese presented an Italian American neighborhood tribal culture that looked a lot like Anthony Imperiale's vigilantism in late 1960s Newark. By 2004, when he codirected the documentary film *Lady by the Sea: The Statue of Liberty*, Scorsese had moved beyond an obsession with specifically Italian Catholic forms of tribal violence and now appeared fully enthralled with what Matthew Jacobson describes as the "white ethnic myth," the story that has shifted the primal space of US national self-conception from Plymouth Rock to Ellis Island. While thus moving into a position of significance in the shaping of the national imaginary, Scorsese intensified a marked tendency in his work toward racial exclusion and marginalization: where blacks and other people of color are virtually absent from his canonical films (with the exception of the African American boxers that Jake LaMotta defeats in *Raging Bull*), they figure insufficiently and problematically in the portrayal of the Civil War era in *Gangs of New York* (2002) and are completely absent from his rendition of the American experience in the Statue of Liberty documentary.

That Scorsese in *Gangs of New York* and *The Departed* (2006) transitioned to portrayals of Irish gangsters every bit as vividly psychopathic as his canonical Italian ones is the kind of data point one might chalk up to the ethos signified by the buzzwords "multi-culturalism" and "diversity." Those terms arose in the 1980s, a time of conservative retreat from government-sanctioned group rights, to signify a voluntary, individualist approach to racial/ethnic inclusion focused more on cultural heritage hype than on substantive challenges to racial hierarchy. Conservatives have maligned multiculturalism as a pernicious antiwhite ideology, disingenuously ignoring how it has provided space for a conception of American pluralism very much like Sinatra's "The House I Live In" in its erasure of race and its celebration of European Americans as icons of American diversity. In mind of such erasure, Lisa Lowe calls multiculturalism "the national cultural form that seeks to unify the diversity of the United States through the integration of difference as cultural equivalences abstracted from the history of racial inequality unresolved in the economic and political domains."[5]

Equivalence here means treating race as just another form of ethnicity, downplaying historical structures of racism, and arguing that racial minorities would realize the same successes as white ethnics if only they would evince the same qualities of hard work, discipline, and bootstrapping persistence. This was a view that found deep resonance not just among urban lower-middle-class white ethnics in the throes of the 1960s racial conflicts but also among suburban, educated, upper-middle-class white "post-ethnics" in the 1980s and beyond, not least because it enjoyed the sanction of public intellectuals like Nathan Glazer, Daniel Patrick Moynihan, and Arthur Schlesinger Jr. Two fundamental assumptions inherent in this view have strongly permeated American thinking. The first is that while ethnicity (and race as another from of ethnicity) originates in biological and cultural heritage, ultimately it folds into socioeconomic class and should be studied as such by focusing exclusively on measurable factors like income, education level, and marriage and residence patterns. The second is that the ineluctable direction of American history—indeed, the very purpose and destiny of the nation—is one of linear progression in which ever-increasing economic success and social mobility make ethnicity (and race) decline in significance.

One sees these assumptions at work in Richard Alba's *Italian Americans: Into the Twilight of Ethnicity* (1985). In venerable assimilationist fashion, Alba argued that ethnicity was fast receding in salience for Italians since they were intermarrying at high rates, moving into the suburbs and the professions in ever-increasing numbers, and presenting an overall socioeconomic profile that no longer set them apart from other European Americans.[6] Based on interviews she conducted in the 1980s for her book *Ethnic Options: Choosing Identities in America* (1990), Mary Waters concluded that American descendants of Italians in mixed-heritage marriages were strategically choosing their ethnic affiliation based on circumstance—an "ethnic option," she importantly noted, that American descendants of Africans still did not enjoy.[7] In *Postethnic America: Beyond Multiculturalism* (1995), Richard Hollinger suggested that counting ethnicity as the most salient part of one's identity weakened the fundamental tenets of American liberal individualism[8]—thus sidestepping or undervaluing Waters's argument that in the age of multiculturalism ethnicity had become not just a nonstigmatized identity but a very sensible option for individuals to voluntarily exercise, given what she described as "this particularly American need to be 'from somewhere.'"[9] Each of these formulations came in the wake of Herbert Gans's highly influential notion of "symbolic ethnicity," his argument that in late twentieth-century America, ethnicity had largely become a voluntary and malleable recreational activity for comfortable middle-class whites, a form of bourgeois consumerism (ethnic food and couture, heritage travel, etc.) rather than the "real" identity it had been for first- and second-generation immigrants.[10]

In a powerful critique of Gans, Simone Cinotto questions the sociologist's assumption of a strict dichotomy between *contadini* (peasant) immigrants who "had their ethnicity inscribed on their bodies and had to live with it 24 hours a day in their urban ghettos" and latter-day suburban quasi- or postethnics who use ethnicity "situationally and intermittently" like any other leisure activity. Such a formulation condescends to the *contadini*, denying their agency to shape their own cultural identities in the teeming multi-ethnic environments they helped to build. Even more fundamentally—and with grim consequences for an analysis of late capitalist, postmodern ethnicity—it belittles the concept of cultural identity itself, misunderstanding the importance of symbolic consumption as a "code by which people and groups make sense of themselves and their place in society, tell who they are, where they think they came from, and what they want to become."

Cinotto, an Italian cultural historian of Italian America, is mapping out a way of thinking about ethnicity that moves beyond traditional class-centered sociological frameworks to instead foreground cultural experiences and artifacts, texts and symbols, expressive practices and performances. This new direction, which draws on the work of cultural theorists like Dick Hebdige, Homi Bhabha, Arjun Appadurai, and Werner Sollors, conceives of ethnicity as a dynamic and inventive adaptation to forever changing socioeconomic and political circumstances. Ethnicity is an invention (Sollors) through which people make sense and meaning of their lives; an invented tradition that expresses itself as much through cultural and aesthetic stylization (Hebdige) as through shared biological or historical ancestry; an ensemble of experiences, images, and things chosen from what global markets make available in local contexts (Appadurai); and, crucially, a perception of self-identity and cultural belonging that unfolds through interaction with both internal and external others, the creation of shifting boundaries of sameness and difference through opposition or hybridization (Bhabha).[11]

The Italian American/African American contact zone I've explored in this book is a space where grandiose, territorial mascu-

linity vibrates with robust matriarchal energy; where traditions
of singing, dancing, and eating embrace the funky vitality and unembarrassed pleasures of the body; where ear- and eye-intensive
sensibilities mark extroverted, charismatic presentations of the
public self; where blunt acceptance of life's inherent harshness
breeds a tragicomic cast of mind that transmutes suffering into a
powerful capacity for joy and satisfaction. The black-Italian relationship that Jennifer Guglielmo describes as "a very complicated
history of collaboration, intimacy, hostility, and distancing" is
significant, I argue, not only for the challenge it poses to conventional notions of ethnic purity and black-white racial dynamics,
but also for the very strong imprint it has made on American culture writ large.[12]

At least since the 1920s, a period that witnessed the Harlem
Renaissance and the efflorescence of jazz alongside a spike in Ku
Klux Klan violence and enactments of racial purity legislation, we
have known that the essential argument about American culture
is the argument about race—specifically, whether blackness, as
supporters of jazz asserted, is an essential ingredient of American
cultural indigenousness or whether, as white nativists warned, it
is a dangerous threat to national identity, a force of cultural de-
generacy.[13] Italians figured into this calculus too, their dark sensuality, exoticism, and rituals of festivity imagined by Victorian
traditionalists as a threat to the nation's cultural tone and by bohemians and artists as a boon to modernist cultural invigoration.[14]
After World War II, the southern black energy unleashed in rock
and roll and the urbane swinger ethos set in motion by Sinatra
and the Rat Pack together bucked and bristled against the norms
of Cold War conformism. Cold War strategic policy dictated that
America cultivate amicable relations with African anticolonial
movements, even as the US government could not figure out how
to position itself in relation to the civil rights and black freedom
movements at home.[15] Huge amounts of American aid underwrote
the reconstruction of war-ravaged Italy, with the two nations'
education and culture industries becoming intertwined through
burgeoning art history programs and study abroad opportunities

("American Girl in Italy"), the cultural cachet of the American Academy in Rome, Peggy Guggenheim's Venetian ventures, and a cosmopolitan film culture linking Rome and Hollywood (*Roman Holiday*, Fellini, Sophia Loren, spaghetti westerns).[16] At the same time, the FBI was bolstering its surveillance of Frank Sinatra, and the Kefauver Committee was earnestly trying to prove the existence of a Sicilian-dominated organized crime conspiracy in the United States.[17]

That blacks and Italians have been seen simultaneously as public enemies, riveting entertainers, cultural degenerates, and—as I have argued throughout this book—maternal protectors of the national soul suggests something about American culture that cannot be readily explained by otherwise powerfully illuminating social scientific indicators such as residency location, education levels, voting patterns, and marriage choices. The mistake—the same one that long ago consigned inflexible and deterministic varieties of Marxism to the dustbin of history—is to imagine that culture exists in a purely symbolic realm with only a secondary, incidental, reflective relation to measurable material reality. As Nick Gillespie observed, the 2000 US Census registered an increase over the previous decade of no fewer than one million Americans claiming Italian ancestry, the only plausible explanation being the colossal impact of the television series *The Sopranos* on American thinking about cultural heritage.[18] Who knows exactly how this "equivalent of a new mass migration," as Simone Cinotto wryly puts it, came to be? Just what combination of blood quantum calculus, heritage identification, and freedom of self-invention governed census-form reporting?[19] I've used *The Sopranos* in my classroom for over a decade, and I can confidently report that at least among a sampling of college students drawn from affluent northeastern suburbia and considerably less affluent rural and small town northern New England, there has most definitely been a strong surge of "feeling Italian" in contemporary America. For the most part these young men and women are not fantasizing about living in households with caches of guns hidden in the eaves; they are hungering for passion, conviviality, intense connectivity, authenticity, and loyalty. American popular media have taught them to take these qualities for granted in black culture, as though they were somehow natural and therefore not to be unduly admired. They *do* duly admire them in Italian American culture, as though they are surprised to see pale people capable of such vitality. They've grown up on hip-hop and neosoul music, and they effortlessly deploy clothing styles and figures of speech drawn from what they have learned to euphemistically call "urban culture." "Feeling black," that is to say, is a familiar part of their cultural repertoire. If "feeling Italian" is yet to be, they're working on it. Regardless of how they might identify themselves by race and ethnicity on a bureaucratic form, they live in an American culture that has been thoroughly imbued with African American and Italian American codes, styles, and aesthetics. Whatever else they also are—most of them call themselves white—they are to some degree aspirants to, if not flat-out embodiments of, a black Italian cultural ethos.

An Even Better *Sopranos*

It seems counterintuitive to think about *The Sopranos* as an expression of a black Italian ethos. After all, Tony Soprano, according to his daughter Meadow, is a "racist retrograde fucking asshole personality." She knows this from, among a much vaster body of evidence, his disgust over her college romance with a multiracial black/Jewish boy he calls a "Hasidic homeboy." She would not be surprised to hear that when her father has a run-in with an African American traffic cop, he maligns the cop as an "affirmative action cocksucker." Tony lives very comfortably in the suburbs, plays golf with local businessmen, and sees a therapist. But he still proudly espouses the worldview he was socialized into growing up in Newark in the late 1960s, its most convulsive period of Italian/black hostility. Notwithstanding an idealistic Ivy League daughter who wants to help the disadvantaged and a wife who goes to a book club and hungers for spiritual nourishment, Anthony Soprano remains an old-school tribal vigilante in the mold of Anthony Imperiale and his own gangster father and uncle.[20]

Indeed, in virtually all the situations in *The Sopranos* in which African Americans are invoked or directly involved, Tony Soprano and his intimates brandish implacable racial attitudes forged in the crucible of the late 1960s Newark race riots and the white ethnic backlash against affirmative action and other racial remediation initiatives launched in the 1970s. Blacks are seen as inescapable but unworthy rivals for neighborhood territory, jobs, college slots, and general socioeconomic positioning who benefit from unfair quota systems concocted by spineless "limousine liberals." Before breathing the progressive air of Columbia University, Meadow herself was a reliable mouthpiece for the tribal code: when she and a high school friend muse over a classmate's acceptance at Wesleyan and the friend labels it an affirmative action travesty, Meadow pleads, "Please, *I'm* blacker than her mother."[21] In one episode, Tony schemes with a Jewish politician and an African American businessman named Maurice on a housing development scam for misappropriating government funds meant to assist inner-city families. The conspirators relax in an elite health club sauna, reminiscing about the explosive summer of 1967. "Were you around for Anthony Imperiale, the White Knight?" Tony asks Maurice. "Around?" Maurice shoots back, "Who do you think he was fighting against? Aspiring Klansmen, some of those boys."[22] The raw cynicism of the housing swindle recalls an earlier episode in which Tony, in the midst of a labor dispute in Newark between a group of black pipe fitters and an Italian American construction company, bribes a local black minister, a preacher in the Martin Luther King Jr. mold, to double-cross and sell out the workers. The minister first urges the pipe fitters to shut down the construction site to protest its discriminatory hiring practices, then lures them to a hidden part of the site where they meet a vicious assault from a posse of Tony's men lying in wait.[23]

Tony's psychopathic violence so saturates the series that we risk becoming inured to it and left to marvel at the sheer naked brio of his acquisitiveness and hunger for power. His malevolence is shrouded in a shrewd business acumen that centers on his mastery of the increasingly multiracial economic landscape leveraged through, rather than in spite of, his atavistic racism. "See," he explains to Meadow's biracial boyfriend, "I've got business associates who are black, and they don't want my son with their daughters and I don't want their sons with mine."[24] For all that, Tony is deeply anguished about his identity, seeing himself as a historical misfit living in an age of decline. He pines romantically for the age of Gary Cooper, the time of a straight-backed "strong and silent" masculinity. But this "cultural fantasy of lost whiteness," as Christopher Kocela terms it, coexists with his contempt for the "medigan" (white Americans) and an even stronger contempt for the "Wonder Bread wop" who "eats his Sunday gravy out of a jar."[25] And this concern about ethnic authenticity is just window dressing for a deeper racial anxiety rooted in his childhood in Baraka- and Imperiale–era Newark. Kocela argues convincingly that Tony's therapist, Jennifer Melfi, misdiagnoses his panic attacks when she fails to recognize the depth of this racial anxiety. The stories Tony tells about his childhood that catch Melfi's attention all involve cruel actions by his Medea mother, leading her to interpret his attacks as the symptom of a classic castration complex. What she misses is that every one of these domestic scenes is framed by references to Newark's racial turmoil. When Tony's mother tells his father she will smother their children if he leaves the Mafia, a television in the background shows images of the race riots smoldering on Newark's streets. Livia is not the only "mother" Tony fears.[26]

If we understand Tony's panic attacks to be caused not just by anxieties generated by the pathological dynamics of his own family, but also by the threat of what an earlier era named "the rising tide of color," we cannot fail to notice how summarily, even blithely, the plotlines of The Sopranos dispense with its characters of color and suppress their agency, desire, and even basic epistemology. The corrupt black Newark businessman and preacher come off as cardboard cutouts, devilishly clever but narratively cheap. Far meatier and more compelling (but also, disappointingly, a single episode one-off) is the character Massive Genius, a young black hip-hop entrepreneur whose talent for a smart, long-game brand of gangsterism cannot help but impress Tony as far outdistancing that of his nephew and putative successor Christopher Moltisanti. In a brilliant episode that plays out as an allegory about national racial reparations, Massive demands $400,000 from Tony and his Jewish associate Heche to compensate for royalties that Heche's company, F Note Records, bilked African American songwriters out of in the 1950s. Massive gets a sit-down and more than holds his own amid the mobster bravado, but in the end he never gets his money. Given this outcome, it is hard not to see *The Sopranos* as aligning itself with a dynamic in which ethnic difference serves as a smokescreen for the maintenance of white power and privilege. Tony can sing the gospel of anti-Italian racism, and Heche, venerable ethnic studies scholar that he is, informs Massive that Jews "were the white man's nigger when yours were still painting their faces and chasing zebras." But when push comes to shove, these are white ethnics who have succeeded, materially if not psychologically, in turning back the forces of racial power realignment.[27]

The Sopranos is a magnificent work of television art, one of the singular cultural achievements of our time.[28] It has spoken not just to Italian Americans but to Americans of all backgrounds (very much including African Americans) not primarily for its gangster trappings but for its thoughtfulness about people of working-class origin dealing with the identity crisis that comes with middle-class prosperity, the travails of family life, and the challenges of mercurial cultural change. Its nuanced attention to microdetails of style, accent, foodways, and general habitus is extraordinary. More than once I was amused to see represented on screen certain behavioral tics—such as Tony's mother Livia's talking in the third person about a friend of his who happens to be standing right in front of her—that I had previously associated only with my mother and my New Jersey relatives. Yet for all its brilliance, the show missed an opportunity to turn its underlying racial subtext toward a fresher, more transformational Italian

FIGURE 12. Hip-hop entrepreneur Massive Genius commands the respect of Tony Soprano and his associates in a much-discussed episode of *The Sopranos* about record royalties bilked from doo-wop era black performers.

American cultural paradigm. Imagine the enthralling possibilities if David Chase had plotted Tony recruiting Massive Genius into the Soprano organization as a replacement for the notoriously unreliable Christopher—Massive's strength as an earner resting on his ability to leverage urban markets and strongarm the entertainment industry, his uneasy presence in the Bada Bing backroom mitigated by his reverence for Frank Sinatra. Imagine a character written expressly for actor Giancarlo Esposito, a mixed-race black Italian from "the other side" who promotes relations with Neapolitan and Sicilian crime families and teaches Paulie to speak serviceable Italian. Imagine flashbacks to the 1960s that include Italian American progressives like civil rights activist Viola Liuzzo and Berkeley free speech icon Mario Savio. Imagine not just a bewitching BMW saleswoman played by Annabella Sciorra but a character based on the actor's brother, the scholar and anti-racist activist Joseph Sciorra.

Just imagine.

Ear, Eye, Hand

The critical race and ethnic studies we will need in order to keep pace with the shifting social landscape of the twenty-first century must be deeply sensitive to the creative imagination, keenly attentive both to the formal arts and to the informal expressive cultures of the eye, the ear, and the hand. As challenging as it is methodologically, this must be a sensuous scholarship attentive to the realm of feeling. And it must recognize that some of the most intensive and clarifying ethnic and racial feeling of our time comes from those who embody multiple ethnicities, transnational identities, and the experience of living on both or several sides of our society's race lines. The concept of race is inherently relational and comparative: "black" makes no sense without a sense of something different from "black," and we can say the same about all other racial categories. Ethnicity, recalling Fredrik Barth's classic formulation, is the drawing of boundaries between groups in a way that perforce defines those groups in relation to each other. In the case of the mixed-raced, transnational, or bicultural subject, these dynamics of relationality and boundary making are written on a single body, imagined in a single mind, felt in a single soul.

Such single subjects are not socially isolated—quite the opposite: they incline more than others toward an intensely social self-consciousness, a sharper awareness of socially constructed boundaries and categories such as race and ethnicity (and class and gender differences within *those* categories). And not infrequently, the feeling of not quite fitting inside conventional boundaries, of occupying only the edges of established categories, is richly conducive to the creative imagination, a spur to making art that challenges the fundamental order of things.

With this in mind, I want to close this book by briefly spotlighting two artists whose bracing challenges to the established order of things black and Italian have been especially meaningful to me.

The Sounds and the Fury

It's Christmas Day 1973, and seven-year-old Kym Ragusa is itching to make some noise. Under the tree is the drum kit she'd been pining for ever since her jazz-loving, beatnik, Italian American father bent her ear to the bebop pulse of Max Roach, the polyrhythmic ecstasies of Elvin Jones, and the multidirectional rhythm tones of Rashied Ali. This father, a bang-around vibraphonist, has taught her to listen into the seams of the sound, where a crisp fill on the snare or a deft kick of the bass drum thickens and seasons the groove. In her precocity she swings seamlessly from free jazz to hard rock, finding her way to Led Zeppelin, to John Bonham's thundering bass pedal and the fattest sonic bottom on vinyl. She is enthralled by the poster in her cousin Mike's bedroom that shows The Who's Keith Moon mauling his kit in a fevered mania. She is ready to thrash and rumble.

"It seems incongruous how that timid, sweet girl . . . could tear so ferociously at my little drum kit, an instrument I had only ever known men and boys to play," Ragusa writes in her memoir, *The Skin between Us: A Memoir of Race, Beauty, and Belonging* (2006), "yet tear and pound at them I did every chance I had."[29] Incongruity linked to willful, gender-bending assertion, resolving in joyous cacophony—these are appropriately fractured tones in a life song marked by cultural, geographic, and color dissonance. This scene takes place in the Bronx, where Kym's father lives with his Puerto Rican girlfriend. Kym's African American mother, meanwhile, pursues her career as a fashion model and actress in Italy; later she will be the one who takes Kym to Milan and Florence and introduces her to Italian high culture. Her light-skinned black grandmother in Harlem, who raises Kym during her early years, blames Kym's kinky hair on her father's Sicilian pedigree. Later, when Kym goes to live with her father's family in Maplewood, New Jersey, she's part of their "white flight" out of the Harlem and Bronx neighborhoods that Italians believe have been ruined by people who look like her.

Ragusa's memoir is exquisitely poignant, lyrical, and–most of all—soundful: it demands a hearing from its readers. Throughout the text, sharply disjunctive experiences carry signature sounds that register precise details of place, time, and feeling. When Kym tears and pounds at her drums in her father's apartment, she's trading fours with the nearby subway clanking its way through Westchester Square. "Whenever a 6 train would rumble by," Ragusa writes, "I would keep time to its rhythm, and see if I could make more noise than it did." This effort to both groove with and outsound the train resonates with earlier passages in which Kym works to establish her sense of self. She describes the experience of walking through the New York streets with her mother, a woman of surpassing beauty: "We would be surrounded by the sensations of the city, stoplights changing from green to red, buses heaving their way up and down 125th Street, steam like hot hangover breath hissing from manhole covers, Albert Ayler's saxophone floating out of an open apartment window, the voice of Celia Cruz flashing like fire from a passing car." Her mother is a figure of auditory power and fascination, her "tiny braids shifting" and her "wild forest sounds" seducing a full symphony out of the cityscape.[30]

Kym knows she will never have this power; she will have to find another way. Her mother is a "poem made of skin," a body that elicits and blends into the desires that surround it. Kym, by contrast, is always running into barriers and needs protection. She finds it—imaginatively—in a trip to the Metropolitan Museum of Art with her father. There, in the arms and armor collection, her mind runs to fantasies of medieval knights in combat: "The horses would leap snorting and whinnying off the platform, the knights' armor would crash and clang as they flew past me, there would be thunderous galloping and the horns blowing." She dreams of being a knight and does so through keen sensory perceptions: "I wanted to feel the weight and heat of metal against my body and hear it clatter as I moved, to close the visor of a great, plumed helmet over my face." These perceptions of touch and sound deliver a feeling of security: "I longed to be that strong, that safe, that untouchable. . . . Armor was skin that protected you from harm."[31]

On her drum kit—a skin of armor turned inside out—Kym is a knight of urban rhythm and locomotive pulse, a clattering, crashing and clanging presence that contrasts sharply with her mother's glamour and liquid elegance. A few years later, still the precociously hip music maven, she fixes her adolescent identity in 1970s punk and glam rock. In the short-lived British punk band X-Ray Spex, Kym finds a sound, look, and attitude that suit her perfectly. Theirs was "the loudest music I ever heard, even louder than when I played my drums to beat the train." The band's lead singer, Poly Styrene, emits a distinctive screech that sounds like a drill tearing through sheet metal. She's also multiracial, with "the same springy corkscrew hair and the same in-between skin" as Kym. She wears go-go boots and silver lamé dresses in wry mockery of high-fashion conventions and sings of "the feeling of freakishness and ugliness that made you want to smash the mirror when you looked into it." Kym, whose unruly hair is an absorbing leitmotif of the memoir, adopts the hot pink and peacock blue plumage, safety pin ornamentation, and combat boot kick-ass defiance of the punk movement. "I had found a new tribe," writes a woman whose story is one of mastering the black and Italian tribal codes of her parents, "and I felt I had nothing left to prove."[32]

Kym Ragusa is a filmmaker, an artist of the eye, and not surprisingly her memoir is organized primarily in visual terms. Her mise-en-scène is keyed to family photographs, starting with the one that appears opposite the title page, of Kym with her two grandmothers, Gilda and Miriam, at Thanksgiving dinner in 1996, a couple of years before both died of cancer. In chapter after chapter, Ragusa takes a photograph and reads it as a narrative, a story of self and family, of the skin that both connects her to and divides her from the people with whom she shares blood. These stories are so rich, so full of texture and detail, that it comes as something of a shock when she tells readers how little visual material she's actually working with and how tenuous she feels in relation to it. She expresses jealousy toward friends "who have reels of Super-8 film of their family, the grandparents, the mothers, and toddlers (the father is always behind the camera), the big family dinners, and the Christmas tree decorating," and whose walls are "full of photographs down through the generations, all framed and arrayed in a neat narrative: this is who we are, this is where we come from." Gilda, her Italian grandmother, has photo albums from the 1950s, a visual record of weddings, christenings, and birthday parties, but Ragusa regards them as "ghost images" that "are really someone else's memories." Still, what Ragusa frequently is doing in this memoir is reading sound into photographs, creating memories of her life experiences through the auditory register. So sensitive is Kym Ragusa's ear, so finely tuned to the acoustic frequencies of the world around her, that finally it seems that sound is the foundational reality Ragusa is trying to get to, sight a mere tool for getting there.[33]

This includes the sound of *silence*, or what Kevin Quashie calls "the sovereignty of quiet."[34] Intriguingly, Ragusa dwells on the "huge silence" that "hung over" her parents after Kym was conceived. "I floated in another kind of silence," she writes in an extraordinary passage imagining her own gestation, "growing blood and bone inside my mother's womb. A mingling of bloodlines, a mutation of genetic codes. Their bodies fused forever in my becoming." Though not yet visible to the world, Ragusa imagines herself biologically as a silence, the very process of her becoming a physical presence marked by an absence of sound. In the memoir's prologue, Ragusa draws on similar imagery to describe her trip on a ferry crossing the Strait of Messina, on her way from Calabria to Sicily, in the Mediterranean crossroads between Europe and Africa. Here, in the geographic womb of her ancestors, the striking detail for Ragusa is "a strange absence of sound." Other than the rumbling of the ship's engine, she hears nothing, "no lapping water, no cries of seabirds, no laughter from the other passengers who stood in clusters around the deck." For the reader, the effect is like watching a movie with the sound turned off. But for Ragusa, the experience is one of *being watched*, of being the object of the gaze of the Sicilian passengers. "What must I have looked like to them?" Ragusa muses. "A woman alone, already an oddity. Already suspect. My dark, corkscrew hair was pulled back, something I had learned to do whenever I went someplace where I didn't want to stand out, which for most of my life had been most of the time. I had the feeling, all too familiar, of wanting to climb out of my skin, to be invisible."[35]

The pattern is clear: Ragusa's vexed visibility—her anxieties about how she is seen, how her skin and hair appear in the eyes of others—correlates with an absence of sound, a denial of the ear. But what if she consciously reverses the pattern, resisting and confounding the eye, foregrounding and trusting the ear? When she does that—perhaps *only* when she does that—Ragusa moves toward at least a tentative sense of belonging that she never fully realizes. As a young girl, Kym visits an east Harlem *salumeria* (deli) with her father; it's one of the places that warms up his memory of a happy childhood in what was then an Italian urban village. But it will work that way for Kym only if she uses sound as a defense against sight: "Holding my father's hand, I closed my eyes and listened to the sound of the voices around me, and I was lulled into a feeling of safety and belonging that my father so often described to me about his own childhood. I didn't notice the suspicious, disapproving looks being cast our way, a woman's voice muttering, *vergogna* [shame]. My father simply ignored them."[36]

Kym is both insider and outsider in this social space, and she must—through her father—filter the sounds in order to feel that she belongs. It is not a comfortably interracial space: there is a "we" and a "they," and Kym has to will herself into the circle of the "we." This is not the case at another east Harlem site Ragusa regularly visits, Mount Carmel Church on 115th Street. There, at the annual Feast of the Madonna, Ragusa finds a kind of tribal kinship, a feeling of unfiltered, unambiguous acceptance. She finds it, typically, in the soundscape—in the "exhalation of breath" she hears as her fellow worshipers (Italians, Puerto Ricans, Mexicans, and Haitians) move in unison; she finds it in the singing, in the "songs of devotion to *La Santissima, La Virgen*, voices filling the air in Spanish and Italian, French and Creole"; and she finds it especially in the Haitian women's songs, songs that rise above the other voices, "a trembling of emotion floating up into the air." Still, Ragusa sounds a note of discord: "I don't know the words of any of the songs, in any language, and I walk with a sense of shame that I can't add my voice to those of the women around me. I feel as though I've lost something I never knew I had, something whose presence I can sense only in its absence."[37]

Here is a silence that resists readers' desire for Kym to find a deep solace and succor that has eluded her throughout her life, something that realizes the full promise hinted at in her adolescent experiences on the drums and as a punk fan. Here, nestled in the bosom of a multiracial tribe, we glimpse the outlines of a soundscape that is also a maternal primal space—a space where bloodline and bone and color mingle and dissolve in a baptism of glorious sound. As a girl, Kym's drum sound was all fury; as a woman, here at the Feast of the Madonna, her silence is a sound of delicate touch and breath, a sound of people inhaling and exhaling each other's spirit. We want to believe in this soundscape as being what Josh Kun calls an "audiotopia." This is the New York of Rudy Giuliani, a city—this is the 1990s—where an Italian American police officer brutalizes a law-abiding Haitian, Abner Louima, and then is loudly defended by the mayor to the whoops and hollers of cops-become-vigilantes massed in the city streets. We want to add our voices instead to the Mount Carmel chorus, to blend with the song of the Haitian women, to float in the air, high above the awful din of racial strife across the metropolis.

Kym Ragusa does and does not join that chorus. She joins it not as a singer but as a listener, a critically aware listener. She is part of the music, but she is also estranged from it. Her life has been full of piercing sounds—the subway train outside her bedroom window, cackling black aunts, screaming Italian grandparents, keening free jazz, thunderous hard rock and punk, and much more. She has struggled mightily to belong to these sounds—to become familiar with and to them, to be part of their family. She *is* family to these sounds, but she is also a stranger among them. So too, at the Feast of the Madonna, among her Italian, Haitian, Puerto Rican, and Mexican sisters, is she both family and stranger; so too is she part of the harmony and also part of the dissonance. Kym Ragusa, an Afro-Italian woman who grew up in a richly soundful world, knows that finally her path to grace is this: to honor the power of silence, and to listen, deeply.

Everythingness

The signature dish was shrimp barka. It started with a simple sauce of chopped fresh tomatoes sautéed in olive oil with onions and garlic. A bunch of finely chopped basil delivered familiar color and accent. Then a surprise: a mound of pitted dates and a hand-ful of unsweetened coconut, bringing a sweet thickness soon aug-mented with a healthy splash of cream. Now the jumbo shrimp, cooked to just-right pink, followed by another curveball: a pile of grated Parmesan stirred in, followed by a second pile of cooked basmati rice. "Women called for it from St. Raphael's and Yale-New Haven Hospitals after they'd delivered their babies," said one of those women, the chef's wife. "People said they literally dreamed of it, a fairy food that tasted like nothing else."[38]

The restaurant was Caffe Adulis in New Haven, Connecticut, a cornerstone of the cultural and economic revival of that struggling city in the 1990s marked by a sudden profusion of nouveau ethnic restaurants: Malaysian, Thai, Japanese, Bolivian, Jamaican, Paki-stani, Turkish, Ethiopian. Caffe Adulis, named for an ancient port city on the Red Sea, was owned and operated by the Ghebreyesus brothers (Ficre, Gideon, and Sahle), sons of a judge in Asmara, Eritrea, who escaped the warfare in that city in the late 1970s but remained staunch Eritrean patriots in the fight for independence from Ethiopia. In the world's longest-running guerrilla war, Eri-trea fought the Ethiopians for thirty years before finally securing independence in 1993, only to find itself back at war with Ethiopia in 1998.

The Eritrean national psyche, much like that of Sicily, remains deeply scarred by the legacy of foreign intervention. Italy had envisioned an Abyssinian empire since the late nineteenth century, when it first occupied the Horn of Africa but managed to gain control only over the territory across the Red Sea from Saudi Arabia and Yemen; this was christened Eritrea, the Greek name for the Red Sea. Italy's defeat in 1896 at the hands of the Ethiopian emperor Menelik II was a source of great shame for Italy and great pride for Ethiopia, the only African nation to retain independent sovereignty in the face of European colonialism. Italy held on to Eritrea, and when Benito Mussolini came to power, a touchstone of his fascist dream was the creation of new Roman Empire anchored in the east by Asmara. Eritrea was to be the industrial center of Italian Africa; thousands of factories sprang up, producing cooking oil, pasta, construction materials, clothing, tobacco, and other commodities. In just five years the population of Italians in Eritrea grew from 5,000 to 75,000. In 1941 the British routed the Italians in the Battle of Keren and began dismantling the factories, selling materials off for scrap. After World War II, Ethiopian emperor Haile Selassie, capitalizing on the feeling against Western imperialism that ran deep in the newly created United Nations, engineered a release of Eritrea into a Greater Ethiopian federation. Selassie became the new imperial master of Eritrea. In 1962 he dissolved its parliament and forcibly annexed its territory, setting off the civil war. At the same time, Eritrea became a hot spot in the global cold war. The Soviet Union used it as a pawn in proxy wars; the United States transformed Kagnew Station in Asmara, built in 1943 by the US Army as a radio station, into an elaborate, state-of-the-art spy station that played a key role in American resistance to Soviet influence in the Middle East and Africa.[39]

Throughout this complicated history, the Italian legacy in the Horn of Africa remained a surrogate for nationalist tensions between Ethiopia and Eritrea. The British journalist Michela Wrong writes, "So central is the Italian experience to both Eritrea and Ethiopia's sense of identity, to how each nation measures itself against the other, that during the war of independence the mere act of eating pasta became a cause of friction between [Eritrea's] rebel fighters and their guerilla allies in northern Ethiopia, a dietary choice laden with politically-incendiary perceptions of superiority and inferiority." Wrong argues that while Eritreans have never forgotten the racism of the Italian colonial regime, they also wear Italianism as a kind of cultural graft (a "new skin") that distinguishes them from Ethiopia, the regional imperial hegemon. Asmara is an Italian modernist architectural museum piece, full of futurist, pastel buildings—"soft apricot, pink, and pistachio tones of melting Neapolitan ice cream"—dating from the Mussolini years. The paint is fading and peeling, and the city emanates a "Toy Town dinkiness." But the education system the Italians left behind, along with the remains of the fascist-era industrial infra structure, helped give Eritrea an edge in the military campaign against Ethiopia.[40]

A generation later, these convulsions in East Africa changed the dining habits of gastro-curious Yale professors and other adventurous New Haven eaters. "If geography has cost Eritrea dear, politically, in the form of long years of foreign domination," the longtime *New York Times* foreign correspondent and gastronome R. W. Apple Jr. wrote after a visit to Caffe Adulis in 1999, "it has conferred great benefits, gastronomically, by opening it to the influences of three continents. Indian spices, the collard greens of sub-Saharan Africa, the hummus of the Middle East and the couscous of North Africa mingle with Greece's feta cheese and the pasta of Italy."[41] Eritrean cuisine overlaps with the Ethiopian in its staples: *injera*, the tart, spongy teff flour crepe used for scooping up various vegetables and meats, and *berbere*, a blend of spices and sun-dried peppers that brings an earthy, smoky richness to chicken, lamb, goat, and beef stews. But Eritrean cooking reflects more of the influences of Italy and the Ottoman Empire: curry and cumin, tomatoes, lighter bases owing to more modest use of seasoned butter, and—because of Eritrea's coastal location—more seafood.

Hence the glorious hybrid swirl that is shrimp barka and its kin on the Caffe Adulis menu, such as seared tuna with fava beans, onions, and a medley of collards, arugula, and spinach. A regular presence at the restaurant was Robert Farris Thompson, the renowned Yale scholar of Afrodiasporic art, music, and dance, connoisseur of mambo, tango, jazz, Jean-Michel Basquiat, and all things Afro/Caribbean/Buenos Aires/New York fabulous. In his eulogy of chef Ficre Ghebreyesus—who died unexpectedly in 2012 of heart failure just days after his fiftieth birthday—Thompson remembered his friend as "the man who brought pasta to Black cuisine." Thompson recalled the night "Ficre was trying out a new dish of pasta dripping gold with sauce and other peppery bites. 'What do you think?' he asked. 'Fabulous,' I replied, 'it's mambo gold.' And damned if he didn't name the dish Mambo Gold right then and there."[42]

Ficre Ghebreyesus was a chef, painter, poet, musician, gardener, linguist, philosopher, athlete, lover—a true Renaissance man for our time. As a child and adolescent in Asmara his teachers were Italian nuns. His first language was Tigrinya, the tongue of the Tigray region of northeastern Ethiopia and bordering Eritrea. In school he studied Latin and used Italian as his first language of learning; later, working in New Haven kitchens, he picked up Spanish on the fly. He was a precocious reader (one of his childhood nicknames was *mangia libro*, "book eater") and a writer with the eye of a painter. One day his teacher read his essay aloud to the class, then announced, "Bambini, this one among you shall become a great writer."[43] This was exactly one day before the terror of the war forced the closing of the school and young Ficre arrived there to find the door padlocked.

Years later, when he took up painting in earnest, his canvases radiated the astonishingly rich and subtle color spectrum of the East African highlands, the Red Sea coast, and the flower-filled compound where his family lived. He studied and worked with a disciple of the color theorist and painter Josef Albers. His mature body of paintings—shown together in a magnificent exhibition at New Haven's Artspace Gallery in the spring of 2013—feature semiabstract landscapes that seem at least in part to be *about* vision, seeing, and pictorial communication. The art critic Anne Higonnet said that Ghebreyesus "saw color the way a poet hears words"; he saw "the greens in the blues, the yellows in the pinks."[44] His polychromatic palette and polyrhythmic shapes seem to wrestle with the subjective perception of color: what we see as a function of how we see, and how we see as a function of spatial location (maps and topographical studies dot the paintings) and the passage of time.

"I have become a conscious synthesizer," Ghebreyesus wrote in his application to the Yale School of Art. It was the end of the 1990s, and he was now married to Elizabeth Alexander, the eminent poet and scholar of African American studies.[45] An aesthetic of cross-cultural fusion marked his work in both kitchen and art studio; indeed, until he moved into a house with his wife and their young boys Solomon and Simon, the kitchen *was* his studio, with color, flavor, and soul passing back and forth between stovetop and canvas. The home library bespoke two lifetimes of deep cultural study—Elizabeth's books of American literature, history, and the visual and performing arts, with special coverage of poetry and African Americana and Ficre's collections on ancient history, geography, world philosophy, religion, architecture, painting, science, and politics. The music collection was anchored by exhaustive holdings of jazz, especially the glory years of Monk, Mingus, and Miles, the bracing post-1960 work of Abbey Lincoln, Betty Carter, Ahmad Jamal, and Randy Weston and the emerging post-millennial canon of Marsalis, Moran, and others.

The family hearth perfectly captured Pellegrino D'Acierno's notion of everyday practices elevated into a total work of art. One might visit the downstairs bathroom not because duty called but to access that room's bookshelf, where certain key volumes of art history were held, or to let one's eyes soak up the color of the walls, a robust, venerable shade of red evoking a row of peppers drying in the sun of the East African highlands. Ficre was known for dressing in the simple, functional garb of the chef/artist/craftsman but was always accenting with a "pop of color," a friend's term for the splash of hot pink or grass green in his socks or scarf.[46] The house teemed with paintings, photographs, objets d'art, and musical instruments. It was a permanent salon where artists, writers, and scholars gathered regularly for festivity, fellowship, and serious, often groundbreaking discourse and debate. Visitors noshed on briny Mediterranean olives, mortadella, buffalo mozzarella, and crusty bread. They left with large mason jars of leftover Eritrean spicy meat stew, fresh garden herbs and vegetables, books, CDs, clothes, personalized haikus, a new dance step in the feet and drum rhythm in the head—a replenishment of flavor and soul to last until the next visit. The domestic ethos was an intensely connective Africanity seasoned with the soulful flavors of African American and Mediterranean sociality. Generosity was just another term for the responsibility of honoring and taking care of one's village of family and friends. Ficre was an *uomo di rispetto* within his extended family and in the greater Eritrean émigré community. Elizabeth, daughter of the mightiest of Harlem-bred parents, high eminences in government, business, and academia, knows that tradition well. In the 1960s, when she was a toddler and her father was a Johnson administration insider, her parents threw a Sinatra party for their Washington, DC, colleagues and friends. Word reached Frank, who sent a note of cheer and a case of Dom Perignon.[47]

In New Haven as in Brooklyn, Newark, Buffalo, Rochester, Philadelphia, Baltimore, and many smaller northeastern cities, recent immigrants from Latin America, Asia, Eastern Europe, and Africa have revamped the ethnic character of the city. Notwithstanding real estate–hungry Yale University, an ever disappearing fringe of the "Elm City" WASP old guard, and a relatively small but robust Jewish community, New Haven through the middle decades of the twentieth century was a black and Italian city, perhaps *the* African American/Italian American city. Its segregated neighborhoods and its thriving manufacturing economy teemed with migrants from two souths—the Italian *mezzogiorno*, and the Piedmont and Atlantic coast areas of Virginia and the Carolinas. From the Italian enclaves on Wooster Street and State Street emerged Frank Pepe's, Sally's, and Modern Apizza, purveyors of New Haven's signature white pie with fresh clams, one of the best flatbreads in the world. In its heyday from the late 1940s to the late

1960s, the pulsing New Haven jazz scene kept up to ten nightclubs humming in the black business district on Dixwell Avenue, including the Playback, launched by French horn player Willie Ruff, and the Monterey, run by former vaudeville star Rufus Greenlee. The upheavals of the late 1960s and a steady loss of manufacturing jobs decimated New Haven's black community, which largely stayed put but saw its neighborhoods and schools fall into a precipitous decline that lasted for decades. Earlier, several large Italian neighborhoods were obliterated by misguided urban renewal projects; liberal technocrats, in their arrogant wisdom, hatched a "model city" plan that forced the closing of over two thousand small businesses, many of them Italian-owned.[48]

Despite constituting a rapidly diminishing share of the city's population, Italian Americans have continued to dominate New Haven public affairs through an entrenched local establishment of politicians, municipal officials, real estate developers, and university administrators. John DeStefano Jr., who served as mayor from 1994 to 2014, presided over the city's downtown redevelopment, a reduction in street crime to a rate that remains high but not astonishingly so, as it was before his tenure, and the launching of police reforms and school renovations. He is a tough and shrewd urban politician apt to be associated with former New York City mayor Rudy Giuliani owing to their shared Italian American heritage. In sharp contrast to Giuliani, however, DeStefano practiced a consensus-building model of leadership and pursued certain progressive policies through alliances with the city's labor unions and with the African American and Latino communities. DeStefano, the son of a New Haven police officer, is no race radical in the tradition of Vito Marcantonio: his most important ally in the black community—an arrangement one might have seen in *The Sopranos*—was with a controversial Baptist minister who was no stranger to writs of indictment. The end of DeStefano's mayorality feels like the beginning of the end of an era, the waning of a certain brand of twentieth-century ethnic and racial urban politics.[49]

But maybe not. Maybe the politics of cities like New Haven and Newark have not seen the last of their long history of black-Italian conflict and collaboration. Maybe these politics will engender new forms that reflect the black-Italian cultural zone I have been tracking throughout this book. It has been fully thirty years, after all, since the "twilight of ethnicity." Just within the past fifteen years, alas, we've seen Frank Sinatra's legend grow through new forms of hip-hop–generation idolatry. We've been brought to tears listening to Dominic Chianese, as Uncle Junior in *The Sopranos*, singing "Core 'ngrato" in a manner worthy of Caruso. We see octogenarian Tony Bennett (Anthony Dominick Benedetto) undertaking concert tours with twenty-something Lady Gaga (Stefani Joanne Angelina Germanotta). We see Mario Batali continuing to imperialize and monetize Italian cuisine in his midtown Manhattan emporium Eataly, while the spirit of Angelo Pellegrini lives on more organically and affordably in new farm-to-fork eateries popping up every week in Bedford-Stuyvesant. With Tom Izzo, John Calipari, and Rick Pitino still high in the saddle, we see one after another "paesan playoff" shaping the championship rounds of college basketball. We suffer through the revival of ethnic minstrelsy in the reality TV shows *Jersey Shore* and *The Real Housewives of New Jersey*.

Amid this bursting *italianità*, I will stake my own Italian American future on this scenario: a man from the highlands of East Africa, Ficre Ghebreyesus, and a woman from the Washington, DC, Afrostocracy, Elizabeth Alexander, host a Feast of the Seven Fishes one Christmas Eve. Elizabeth makes linguine con le vongole and fries fresh flounder to perfect crispness. Ficre sears diver scallops, nestles them back into their shells with a dollop of fresh salsa, then sears tuna and lays it on a bed of arugula and chopped tomatoes anointed with a drizzle of balsamic vinegar reduction. The guests are dear friends, the family of New York art agent Amy Cappellazzo. Ficre brings Amy to tears singing her daughter Marina a lullaby she remembers from her own childhood: "Marina, Marina / Mi sono inamorato di Marina / una ragazza mora ma carina."[50]

Amy has landed on the perfect word to describe Ficre's aesthetic and ethos: *tutti*. "*Tutti*," Elizabeth elaborates, "the unshakable belief in beauty, in overflow, in everythingness, the bursting, indelible beauty in a world where there is so much suffering and wounding and pain, as he well knew."[51]

Tutti: the beauty and suffering, the bursting flavor and soul, the everythingness that sits on the edge—now smooth, now serrated—between Italian America and African America.

Acknowledgments

Only in the past year or so have I been able to work in earnest on this book *as a book*. Its origins, however, lie in a short essay I wrote some twenty years ago, and my head and heart have been deeply immersed in this material ever since. Over these years a number of colleagues, friends, and family members have inspired, challenged, complicated, and nourished my thinking about matters Italian and black. If it takes a village to raise a child, as the well-known African saying goes, it takes many villages to produce a book. This one has come about as I've lingered in the edges and overlaps between several mighty villages. I hope this book honors and exalts each of them. If it does not, the fault is all mine.

It was during a fellowship year at the W. E. B. Du Bois Institute at Harvard that I wrote that original essay ("Passing for Italian: Crooners and Gangsters in Crossover Culture") under the inspiration and encouragement of Gabriel Mendes, Guthrie Ramsey, Daphne Brooks, Michael Vasquez, and Barry Shank (not in Cambridge that year but, as ever, a cherished soul mate and fierce interlocutor). Several readers of the essay helped me see beyond it to a bigger, more intricate story. Tom Ferraro, it turned out, had been reading, watching, and listening to the same stuff I was and was much further along in knowing how to write about it. "I'm more of a romantic than you are," he said when we first met and started trading fours about Sinatra, Spike Lee, and soppressata. A romantic indeed, and also a stunningly original thinker and stylist who's been a lodestar for this work all along. Tom introduced me to people like Pellegrino D'Acierno, whose breathtaking knowledge of Italian / Italian American culture and inimitable high/low voice (find me another semiotician who coins words like *dagotude*) held me in thrall; and Jim Fisher, paragon of Irish soulfulness, who shared with me his deep understanding of New Jersey ethnicity, folk Catholicism, basketball, and the potent intersections thereof. That writers like Gerald Early and Carlo Rotella, two of the best in the business, expressed admiration for "Passing for Italian" first astonished me and then goaded me to work harder to try to catch just a little bit of the magic they routinely harness in their essays on music, literature, boxing, and other topics. Jonathan Rieder, virtuosic ethnographer of Brooklyn ethnicity and fellow enthusiast of the Rascals, engaged me in rich discussions of multiracial issues and commissioned me to write a profile of Giancarlo Esposito for the magazine he was editing. During a subsequent fellowship year at the Carter G. Woodson Institute at the University of Virginia, Eric Lott and Grace Hale embraced the project and breathed into it the power of their super-smart thinking on race and American culture; equally inspiring was their love of music and revelry. Reginald Butler and Scot French helped make my Woodson term both productive and enjoyable, and Reg and I had some great conversations about black and Italian masculinity.

This group of folks baptized my project in the fields of American and African American studies before I knew there was such a thing as Italian American studies. But there it was, alas, thriving in pioneering academic programs at SUNY-Stony Brook and Hofstra, the John D. Calandra Italian American Institute at CUNY, the American Italian Historical Association (recently rechristened the Italian American Studies Association), and fabulous, novelistic dinner parties at the Teaneck home of Edvige Giunta and Joshua Fausty. In such environs I found a community of scholars, writers, and artists that has sustained me with more flavor and soul than I imagined possible. This group includes (in no particular order) Edi and Josh, Louise DeSalvo, Pelle D'Acierno, Kym Ragusa, Maria Laurino, Peter Covino, Laura Ruberto, Circe Sturm, Fred Gardaphé, George Guida, Anthony Tamburri, Stan Pugliese,

Joanna Clapps Herman, Teresa Fiore, Nancy Carnevale, Jennifer Guglielmo, Robert Oppedisano, Peter Vellon, Annie Lanzillotto, Rosette Capotorto, Ronnie Mae Painter, Mary Jo Bona, Mary Anne Trasciatti, LuLu LoLo, Jerome Krase, George De Stefano, James Periconi, Robert Viscusi, Donna Gabaccia, and the late Rudolph Vecoli. I'm indebted above all to Joseph Sciorra, director of academic and cultural programming at Calandra, for the bracing example of his own brilliant work on many of these same issues; for inviting me several times to present my work at the Institute; and for pointing me toward resources that deepened and sharpened my research. At a certain point I noticed I'd labeled my most important research file "Joe." It seemed that every book, article, recording, interview, photograph, and other tangible piece of evidence I was using on this project had come to me on a tip from this remarkable scholar and friend.

In 2008–9, a sabbatical year at Yale, as a visiting research scholar in the American Studies and African American Studies departments, crystallized the project in several crucial ways. First, it placed me in an extraordinary community of scholars—among them Elizabeth Alexander, Alondra Nelson, Daphne Brooks (again), Paige McGinley, Hazel Carby, Michael Denning, Glenda Gilmore, Jonathan Holloway, Matt Jacobson, Mary Lui, Stephen Pitti, Alicia Schmidt Camacho, Robert Stepto, Alan Trachtenberg, Robert Farris Thompson, Laura Wexler, Sarah Lewis, Brandon Terry, and Jeffrey Gonda—who invigorated my thinking and provided an opportunity for several test runs of my material. Special thanks to Vicki Shepard for her deft administrative help and warm friendship that year. Second, it put me in New Haven, a city steeped in a rich history of black-Italian intimacy, collaboration, and conflict—in short, what this book is all about, and something Burlington, Vermont, for all its terrific qualities, simply could not give me. New Haven hosted that year's meeting of the American Italian Historical Association, and Annie Lanzillotto stayed on with my family for a couple of weeks after the conference; our work together during that time seeded many of the ideas about food and music that appear in this book. Third, and most meaningful, the sabbatical year put my family in the home of Elizabeth Alexander and Ficre Ghebreyesus. So much of the feeling of this book channels the flavor and soul of that Livingston Street house: its art, books, music, and something I can only describe as an ineffable African-Mediterranean spirit. Proximity to Nica's Market and Modern Apizza also played its part.

I owe big thanks to Giancarlo Esposito, Annabella Sciorra, Bruce Altman, Tom Fontana, and Carl Capotorto for discussions that helped me better understand not just their own work as film/ television artists but also, on a more basic level, how movies and TV programs actually get made. Annabella and her brother Joe were especially generous in their close readings of the Spike Lee chapter, saving me from embarrassing mistakes about Brooklyn geography and culture. The basketball chapter benefited from similar insider intelligence from my coaching friends Hajj Turner, Gabe Rodriguez, Jesse Cormier, and Josh Meyer, as well as from Julie Byrne, Philly hoops maven and religious studies all-star. That chapter in particular—the book itself, really—is inconceivable to me outside my cherished friendship with Gary Ferrini, whose deep feeling for sport, music, food, and New York *italianità* is unsurpassed. I started reading the work of Simone Cinotto fairly late in the game and was awed by the depth and cogency of his understanding of Italian American culture. Simone's invitation to contribute to his collection *Making Italian America* was a real turning point for my work, as was true a year earlier when Edi Giunta and Nancy Caronia invited me to join their project on the work of Louise De-Salvo, and a decade earlier when Jennifer Guglielmo recruited me into the ranks of those scholars and writers pondering the question "Are Italians white?" Various conversations through the years with Bev and Hal Colston, Jim Hall, Brett Gary, Amy Bentley, Stan Schmidt, Beth Guiffre, Randy and Bunmi Fayote-Matory, Jim and Gerry Hurley, James and Margarita Bernard, Warren Bernard, Doreen Odom, Joan and Peter Tyer, James and Geraldine Gennari, Clifford and Adele Alexander, Robert and Irene Fuster, Lisa and Ron Schwartz, Bernard and Debbie Dal Cortivo, Bobby and Kathy Dal Cortivo, Richie and Chris Annunziato, Barbara Charters, Joel

Dinerstein, Travis Vogan, Ron Radano, Charlie McGovern, Nancy Bernhard, Wilson Valentin, Stephanie Seguino, Todd McGowan, David Jenemann, Hilary Neroni, Major Jackson, Tony Magistrale, Rashad Shabazz, Simon Bronner, Bob Blumenthal, Ben Cawthra, James Pasto, Laura Cook Kenna, Bruce Boyd Raeburn, Bill Tonelli, Frank Lentricchia, Maxine Gordon, Farah Jasmine Griffin, Sabrina Peck, Krin Gabbard, Herman Beavers, Frank Manchel, Robin Kelley, Ethan Iverson, Jason and Alicia Hall Moran, Kevin Gaines, Penny Von Eschen, Frank Couvares, and Brandon Ogbunu have helped generate, clarify, and fine-tune my ideas.

My colleagues and students in the English Department and the Critical Race and Ethnic Studies program (CRES) at the University of Vermont have provided a wonderful environment for doing this work. At my UVM "job talk" way back in 2000, I presented some of my Spike Lee material to a packed house of film and literature students and faculty; with the possible exception of the storied Sinatra conference at Hofstra in 1998, that UVM audience remains the most responsive I've ever enjoyed. Various forms of funding from the English Department, CRES, and the offices of UVM's provost and its dean of the College of Arts and Sciences have been vital to my research and writing. I'm grateful for the unstinting support of successive English Department chairs Robyn Warhol, Tony Bradley, Loka Losambe, Tony Magistrale, and Val Rohy, and CRES directors Brian Gilley, Greg Ramos, Nikki Khanna, and Emily Bernard. I owe special thanks for the administrative support of Stella Moyser, Mary Driscoll, Katherine Layton, Holly Brevant, and Tilza Buschner. And special thanks too to the Tyer, Zeif, and McGrath/Stackpole families and Liza Cohen for child care and other forms of support during crucial junctures, and to David Ferguson for his fine hospitality.

Doug Mitchell, my editor at the University of Chicago Press, grows ever more remarkable in his patience, loyalty, unreconstructed jazz purism (last time I saw him he'd just discovered a '60s pop group called the Beach Boys), and commitment to finding the best food in the cities where the American Studies Association meets. Kyle Wagner has been a mensch in holding my hand through the production process and providing extra help in dealing with artwork permissions and logistics. Alice Bennett's superb copyediting made the book clearer and more elegant. Once again Martin White has furnished my book with a first-rate index. Two readers for the press blew my mind with their perceptive and sensitive critiques of the manuscript.

Portions of this book appeared in preliminary form in previously published work: part of chapter 1 from "Passing for Italian: Crooners and Gangsters in Crossover Culture" and "Mammissimo: Dolly and Frankie Sinatra and the Italian American Mother/Son Thing," in *Frank Sinatra: History, Politics, and Italian American Culture*, ed. Stanislau Pugliese (New York: Palgrave Macmillan, 2004), 127–34 and 147–54; part of chapter 2 from "The Knife and the Bread, the Brutal and the Sacred: Louise DeSalvo at the Family Table," in *Personal Effects: Essays on Memory, Culture, and Women in the Work of Louise DeSalvo*, ed. Nancy Caronia and Edvige Giunta (New York: Fordham University Press, 2014), 233–50; part of chapter 3 from "Giancarlo Giuseppe Alessandro Esposito: Life in the Borderlands," in *Are Italians White? How Race Is Made in America*, ed. Jennifer Guglielmo and Salvatore Salerno (New York: Routledge, 2003), 234–59; and part of chapter 4 from "Sideline Shtick: The Italian American Basketball Coach and Consumable Images of Racial and Ethnic Masculinity," in *Making Italian America: Consumer Culture and the Production of Ethnic Identities*, ed. Simone Cinotto (New York: Fordham University Press, 2014), 2017–24. I am grateful to the publishers of these essays for permission to use certain of their paragraphs in this book.

The writing of *Flavor and Soul* came at a time of major additions and losses in my personal life that are integral to the book's theme. In 2007 my wife Emily and I arrived home from Ethiopia with our adopted twin daughters, Giulia Naima and Isabella Pannonica. Like all names, the ones we chose for the girls (traditional Italian first names with middle names drawn from jazz history) reflect their parents' own values and cultural inclinations. But some nine years on, I'm pleased to report that these hot dog and Taylor Swift–loving fourth graders have also developed a taste for pasta al dente, college basketball, Aretha Franklin, and even what Giulia calls "the kind of jazz with no singing." I count it as a great blessing that my daughters had ample time to bond with my parents, Remo Nicholas Gennari and Clara Maria Dal Cortivo Gennari, who passed away in 2011 and 2015, respectively. Touched by their *nonni* and *nonno*, these girls are full of zest and moxie, and they appreciate a bounteous and congenial dinner table. A few months before leaving us, my mother was the first on the dance floor at a family wedding, dancing with Isabella to Kool and the Gang's "Celebrate." "She's got a lot of rhythm, that one," Mom said, "just like me." Fittingly, my mother's very last social outing (Stage 4 cancer be damned) was to a Tony Bennett/Lady Gaga concert. Similarly, in my father's last weeks, only a completely shot heart valve kept him from turning the soil for that year's vegetable garden. Blessed throughout my life with the example of my parents' courage and resilience in the face of unfathomable loss, my struggle to wrestle this or that chapter into shape while trying to put food on the table equal to my daughters' ever-rising standards has seemed like rather small potatoes.

Giulia and Isabella hail from the mountainous backcountry outside Adigrat, in Ethiopia's northern Tigray region, close to the border with Eritrea. Their birthplace is not far from the childhood home of our beloved friend Ficre Ghebreyesus. It was at Ficre and Elizabeth's apartment in New Haven that Emily and I first met, a matchmaking scene framed by Elizabeth's hyping of my "Passing for Italian" essay (with no fewer than three copies strewn around the apartment) and Ficre's curating of an unforgettable platter of antipasti anchored by paper-thin slices of mortadella and plump balls of scamorza and mozzarella from Liuzzi's in North Haven. When we were in graduate school together, Elizabeth delighted in my interest in "Negro esoterica" (as she later called it in a poem), even as I thrilled to the Italianness she revealed in such gestures as choosing just the right sturdy Barolo to go with my chicken cacciatore and polenta. Ficre, who taught me so much about food, painting, music, history, politics, and fathering, passed away tragically in 2012. We all feel the loss deeply but celebrate the spirit of his goodness that lives on his sons Solomon and Simon.

My wife, Emily Bernard, also lost her parents during the time I've been writing this book and she's been writing her three (or is it four?). Like her late mother, Clara Jean Jefferson Bernard, her mother's people in southern Mississippi, her late father Harold Bernard from Trinidad, and her brothers James and Warren raised in Nashville and now in Brooklyn, Emily is deeply soulful in a black southern way that meshes nicely with my family's Sinatra Belt Italian soulfulness. These families are full of wonderfully loud, passionate, convivial, big-hearted people. Emily, like her mother, is nothing if not a blues woman: downhome, candid, piercingly funny, melancholic and joyous all at once. She is also quiet and bookish, and her strongest passion and fiercest loyalty is to the craft of writing. I hope all these qualities have seeped into these pages. This book is a tribute to Emily's and my families, and to our life together sharing joy in our daughters and working hard to enliven and tune up our sentences.

Notes

Introduction

Note: I'm borrowing this title from Joseph Sciorra's essay "Who Put the Wop in Doo-Wop: Some Thoughts on Italian Americans and Early Rock and Roll," *Voices in Italian Americana* 13, no. 1 (2002): 16–22.

1   Dion DiMucci with David Seay, *The Wanderer: Dion's Story* (New York: Beech Tree Books, 1988), 75; Marvin Gaye quoted by Gerald Early in *One Nation under a Groove: Motown and American Culture* (Hopewell, NJ: Ecco Press, 1995), 9; Amiri Baraka, "The Death of Horatio Alger" (1967), in *Imagining America: Stories from the Promised Land*, ed. Wesley Brown and Amy Ling (New York: Turtleback Books, 1991), 149.

2   This quotation and the foregoing account come from Joseph Sciorra's essay "'Italians against Racism': The Murder of Yusuf Hawkins (R.I.P.) and My March on Bensonhurst," in *Are Italians White? How Race Is Made in America*, ed. Jennifer Guglielmo and Salvatore Salerno (New York: Routledge, 2003), 194.

3   The conference "Frank Sinatra: The Man, the Music, the Legend" took place November 12–14, 1998, on the campus of Hofstra University in Hempstead, New York. Among the deluge of press notices was an advance plug in the *New York Times Magazine* saying "celebs are coming, but the proceedings are basically egghead" (October 4, 1998), 27. My colleagues on the second panel were Pellegrino D'Acierno and Thomas Ferraro, with Stanislao Pugliese, as chair, doing a terrific job moderating the unusually lively Q&A. Singer Jo Thompson and her son Greg Dunmore appeared on a panel on Saturday, November 14.

4   My profile of Giancarlo Esposito was originally published in *Common Quest* 4, no. 2 (Winter 2000): 8–17. It was later included in slightly different form in Guglielmo and Salerno, *Are Italians White?*, 234–49.

5   I do not mean to claim any special authority or to suggest that my experience represents anything like the whole of either Italian American or Afri-

can American culture; rather, I simply hint at why and how I have come to this project. I address some of my personal experience in the interracial spaces of music in my book *Blowin' Hot and Cool: Jazz and Its Critics* (Chicago: University of Chicago Press, 2006), 1–6, and in a specifically black-Italian context in my essay "Nearer, My God, to Thee," in *Some of My Best Friends: Writings on Interracial Friendships*, ed. Emily Bernard (New York: Amistad/HarperCollins, 2004), 32–53.

6 Fredrik Barth, *Ethnic Groups and Boundaries: The Social Organization of Culture Difference* (1969; Long Grove, IL: Waveland Press, 1998).

7 Pellegrino D'Acierno, "Italian American Musical Culture," in *The Italian American Heritage: A Companion to Literature and Arts*, ed. Pellegrino D'Acierno (New York: Garland, 1999), 447.

8 I'm alluding to a vast and still growing literature that includes Eric Lott, *Love and Theft: Blackface Minstrelsy and the American Working Class* (New York: Oxford University Press, 1993); Michael Rogin, *Blackface, White Noise: Jewish Immigrants in the Hollywood Melting Pot* (Berkeley: University of California Press, 1996); Jeffrey Melnick, *A Right to Sing the Blues: African Americans, Jews, and American Popular Song* (Cambridge, MA: Harvard University Press, 1999); Cheryl Lynn Greenburg, *Troubling the Waters: Black-Jewish Relations in the American Century* (Princeton, NJ: Princeton University Press, 2006); Philip Deloria, *Playing Indian* (New Haven, CT: Yale University Press, 1998); Natasha Tamar Sharma, *Hip Hop Desis: South Asian Americans, Blackness, and a Global Race Consciousness* (Durham, NC: Duke University Press, 2010).

9 This sampling of black-Italian collusion streamlines the argument I first advanced in my essay "Passing for Italian: Crooners and Gangsters in Crossover Culture," *Transition* 72 (Fall 1997): 36–48. Nancy Carnevale offers an excellent overview of relations between African Americans and Italian Americans in her essay "Italian American and African American Encounters in the City and in the Suburb," *Journal of Urban History* 40, no. 3 (2014): 536–62. Carnevale notes that in the 1930s Italians represented 75 percent of all bar and cabaret owners in Harlem (558). Commenting on "Italian impresarios" in Harlem, the Harlem Renaissance poet Claude McKay said they were "more engaging, freer, and more intimate in their relationship with the Negroes than were the Irish saloon owners who preceded them" (Carnevale, 543).

10 W. E. B. Du Bois quoted by David Roediger, afterword to *Are Italians White?*, 261–62.

11 Joseph Kerrett Jr., "James Baldwin Imagining Italians and Italian Americans: *Giovanni's Room, Another Country*, and *If Beale Street Could Talk*," *Voices in Italian Americana* 18, no. 2 (Fall 2007): 79–108.

12 James Baldwin, *The Price of the Ticket: Collected Nonfiction, 1948–1985* (New York: St. Martin's Press, 1985), 667.

13 Amiri Baraka, liner notes to Woody Shaw LP *Woody III* (Columbia,

JC35977, 1979); Komozi Woodard, *A Nation within a Nation: Amiri Baraka (LeRoi Jones) and Black Power Politics* (Chapel Hill: University of North Carolina Press, 1999), 75. For more on black-Italian tensions in Newark, see Kevin Mumford, *Newark: A History of Race, Rights, and Riots in America* (New York: New York University Press, 2007), 170–91, and Mark Krasovic, "The Struggle for Newark: Plotting Urban Crisis in the Great Society" (PhD diss., Yale University, 2008). For an interesting discussion of Baraka's interest in Italian immigrant politics, see Matthew Calihman, "'Where Are the Italian Anarchists?' Amiri Baraka and the Usable Pasts of the Immigrant Left," *Voices in Italian Americana* 18, no. 2 (Fall 2007): 64–79.

14 In this I am guided by the stellar example of Yiorgos Anagnostou in *Contours of "White Ethnicity": Popular Ethnography and the Making of Usable Pasts in Greek America* (Athens: Ohio University Press, 2009) and "'White Ethnicity': A Reappraisal," *Italian American Review* 3, no. 2 (Summer 2013): 99–128.

15 Louise DeSalvo, "Color: White/Complexion: Dark," in Guglielmo and Salerno, *Are Italians White?*, 17–28.

16 Anagnostou, "'White Ethnicity,'" 115, 118.

17 Here I allude to Herbert Gans, "Symbolic Ethnicity: The Future of Ethnic Groups and Cultures in America," *Ethnic and Racial Studies* 2 (1979): 1–20, and Richard Alba, *Italian Americans: Into the Twilight of Ethnicity* (Englewood Cliffs, NJ: Prentice Hall, 1985). Still very much worth reading are Nathan Glazer and Daniel Patrick Moynihan, *Beyond the Melting Pot: The Negroes, Puerto Ricans, Jews, Italians and Irish of New York City* (Cambridge, MA: MIT Press, 1963); and Milton Gordon, *Assimilation in American Life: The Role of Race, Religion and National Origins* (New York: Oxford University Press, 1964). A window into the way American historians were thinking about these issues shortly after the Gans essay is the forum "American History and the Changing Meaning of Assimilation," with an essay by Olivier Zunz and responses from John Bodnar and Stephan Thernstrom in *Journal of American Ethnic History* 4, no. 2 (Spring 1985): 53–84. An influential breakthrough came with Mary Waters, *Ethnic Options: Choosing Identities in America* (Berkeley: University of California Press, 1990). For a recent revisiting of the key debates centered on a critique of Gans and Waters, see Yiorgos Anagnoustou, "A Critique of Symbolic Ethnicity: The Ideology of Choice," *Ethnicities* 9, no. 1 (2009): 94–122.

18 Gerald Early, *Tuxedo Junction: Essays on American Culture* (Hopewell, NJ: Ecco Press, 1989), Early, *The Culture of Bruising: Essays on Literature, Prizefighting, and Modern American Culture* (Hopewell, NJ: Ecco Press, 1994), and Early, *One Nation under a Groove: Motown and American Culture* (Hopewell, NJ: Ecco Press, 1995); D'Acierno, *Italian American Heritage*; Guglielmo and Salerno, *Are Italians White?*; Thomas Ferraro,

Feeling Italian: The Art of Ethnicity in America (New York: New York University Press, 2005); Robert Orsi, *The Madonna of 115th Street: Faith and Community in Italian Harlem, 1880–1950* (New Haven, CT: Yale University Press, 2002), and Orsi, "The Religious Boundaries of an In-Between People: Street Feste and the Problem of the Dark-Skinned Other in Italian Harlem, 1920–1990," *American Quarterly* 44, no. 3 (September 1992): 313–47; Joseph Sciorra, "The Mediascape of Hip Wop: Alterity and Authenticity in Italian American Rap," in *Global Media, Culture, and Identity*, ed. Rohit Chopra and Radhika Gajjala (New York: Routledge, 2011), 33–51, and Sciorra, *Built with Faith: Italian American Imagination and Catholic Material Culture in New York City* (Knoxville: University of Tennessee Press, 2015); Simone Cinotto, ed., *Making Italian America: Consumer Culture and the Production of Ethnic Identities* (New York: Fordham University Press, 2014), Cinotto, *The Italian American Table: Food, Family, and Community in New York City* (Urbana: University of Illinois Press, 2013), and Cinotto, "All Things Italian: Italian American Consumers and the Commodification of Difference," *Voices in Italian Americana* 21, no. 1 (2010): 2–44; George De Stefano, *An Offer We Can't Refuse: The Mafia in the Mind of America* (New York: Faber and Faber, 2006); Laura Cook Kenna, "Dangerous Men, Dangerous Media: Constructing Ethnicity, Race, and Media's Impact through the Gangster Image, 1957–2007" (PhD diss., George Washington University, 2008); Fred Gardaphé, *From Wiseguys to Wise Men: The Gangster and Italian American Masculinities* (New York: Routledge, 2006); David Roediger, *Working toward Whiteness: How America's Immigrants Became White* (New York: Basic Books, 2005); Roediger, ed., *Black on White: Black Writers on What It Means to Be White* (New York: Schocken/Random House, 1998); Matthew Frye Jacobson, *Roots Too: White Ethnic Revival in Post–Civil Rights America* (Cambridge, MA: Harvard University Press, 2006), and Jacobson, *Whiteness of a Different Color: European Immigrants and the Alchemy of Race* (Cambridge, MA: Harvard University Press, 1998); George Lipsitz, *The Possessive Investment in Whiteness: How White People Profit from Identity Politics* (Philadelphia: Temple University Press, 1998); Grace Elizabeth Hale, *Making Whiteness: The Culture of Segregation in the South, 1890–1940* (New York: Pantheon, 1998); Hale, *A Nation of Outsiders: How the White Middle Class Fell in Love with Rebellion in Postwar America* (New York: Oxford University Press, 2011).

19 Paul Stoller, *Sensuous Scholarship* (Philadelphia: University of Pennsylvania Press, 1997); Thomas Belmonte, "The Contradictions of Italian American Identity: An Anthropologist's Personal View," in D'Acierno, *Italian American Heritage*, 3.

20 Carlo Rotella, *Good with Their Hands: Boxers, Bluesmen, and Other Characters from the Rust Belt* (Berkeley: University of California Press, 2002). I make clear my high regard for Rotella's work in "Truth and Beauty in the Rust Belt," *American Quarterly* 55, no. 2 (June 2003): 285–93.

21 James Clifford, "Partial Truths," in *Writing Culture: The Poetics and Politics of Ethnography*, ed. James Clifford and George Marcus (Berkeley: University of California Press, 1986), 12.

22 Josh Kun, *Audiotopia: Music, Race, and America* (Berkeley: University of California Press, 2005), 11.

23 Ibid.

24 Richard Gambino, *Blood of My Blood: The Dilemma of the Italian Americans* (New York: Doubleday, 1974); Wallace Terry, *Bloods: Black Veterans of the Vietnam War; An Oral History* (New York: Random House, 1984).

25 Bill Tonelli quoted in De Stefano, *An Offer We Can't Refuse*, 330. Tonelli has served as an editor for *Rolling Stone, Esquire*, and several other magazines. He also is the editor of *The Italian American Reader* (New York: HarperCollins, 2005).

26 D'Acierno, *Italian American Heritage*, xxvi.

27 Albert Murray quoted in Stanley Crouch, *Notes of a Hanging Judge: Essays and Reviews, 1979–1989* (New York: Oxford University Press, 1990), 248–49.

Chapter One

1 Paul Avrich, *Sacco and Vanzetti: The Anarchist Background* (Princeton, NJ: Princeton University Press, 1991); Jerome Delamater and Mary Anne Trasciatti, *Representing Sacco and Vanzetti* (New York: Palgrave Macmillan, 2005). For general surveys of the Italian American experience, see Jerre Mangione and Ben Morreale, *La Storia: Five Centuries of the Italian American Experience* (New York: Harper Perennial, 1993), and Maria Laurino, *The Italian Americans: A History* (New York: W. W. Norton, 2015).

2 Laurino, *Italian Americans*, 44; Donna Gabaccia, *Militants and Migrants: Rural Sicilians Become American Workers* (New Brunswick, NJ: Rutgers University Press, 1988); Thomas Guglielmo, *White on Arrival: Italians, Race, Color, and Power in Chicago, 1890–1945* (New York: Oxford University Press, 2004); Jennifer Gulgliemo, *Living the Revolution: Italian Women's Resistance and Radicalism in New York City, 1880–1945* (Chapel Hill: University of North Carolina Press, 2010).

3 Donna Gabaccia, "Race, Nation, Hyphen: Italian-Americans and Multiculturalism in Comparative Perspective," in *Are Italians White? How Race Is Made in America*, ed. Jennifer Guglielmo and Salvatore Salerno (New York: Routledge, 2003), 44–59.

4 Laurino, *Italian Americans*, 91.

5 Simone Cinotto, "All Things Italian: Italian American Consumers and the Commodification of Difference," *Voices in Italian Americana* 21, no. 1 (2010): 13–14.

6 Simona Frasca, *Italian Birds of Passage: The Diaspora of Neapolitan Musicians in New York* (New York: Palgrave Macmillan, 2014), 39–76; Law-

rence Levine, *Highbrow/Lowbrow: The Emergence of Cultural Hierarchy in America* (Cambridge, MA: Harvard University Press, 1990), 85.

7   Henry Pleasants, *The Great Singers: From Jenny Lind and Caruso to Callas and Pavarotti* (New York: Simon and Schuster, 1981), 296.

8   Pellegrino D'Acierno, "Italian American Musical Culture," in *The Italian American Heritage: A Companion to Literature and Arts*, ed. Pellegrino D'Acierno (New York: Garland, 1999), 447.

9   A. O. Scott, "Soaring from Poverty All the Way to Ecstasy," *New York Times*, June 22, 2011.

10 Pellegrino D'Acierno, "Cultural Lexicon: Italian American Key Terms," in *Italian American Heritage*, 717.

11 For example, Ben Sidran, *Black Talk* (New York: Da Capo, 1983); Olly Wilson, "Black Music as an Art Form," *Black Music Research Journal* 3 (1983): 1–22; Roger Abrahams, *Everyday Life: A Poetics of Everyday Practices* (Philadelphia: University of Pennsylvania Press, 2005); Vorris Nunley, *Keepin' It Hushed: The Barbershop and African American Hush Harbor Rhetoric* (Detroit: Wayne State University Press, 2011).

12 Joseph Sciorra, "The Mediascape of Hip Wop: Alterity and Authenticity in Italian American Rap," in *Global Media, Culture, and Identity*, ed. Rahit Chopra and Radhika Gajjala (New York: Routledge, 2011), 33–51. D'Acierno calls Italy and Italian America "an ear-intense culture in which the voice itself is a sonic spectacle" (*Italian American Heritage*, 419). Certainly the Italian American as a figure of acoustic power and fascination—power and fascination that implicate both mouth and ear—has a long history, from opera singers, organ grinders, and fruit peddlers to crooners and political orators. From Cicero to Cuomo, Mary Anne Trasciatti reminds us, Italians have made a singular mark in the annals of public speaking. Some of the best literary critics and historians in Italian American studies point to the mouth. Notice as much in these titles: Mary Jo Bona, *By the Breath of Their Mouths: Narratives of Resistance in Italian America* (Albany: State University of New York Press, 2010); Edvige Giunta, *Writing With an Accent: Contemporary Italian American Women Authors* (New York: Palgrave Macmillan, 2002); and Nancy Carnevale, *A New Language, a New World: Italian Immigrants in the U.S., 1870–1945* (Urbana-Champaign: University of Illinois Press, 2009). Carnevale's investigation of Italian language in the United States includes discussion of comic songs and Italian language radio, core areas of Italian American sound.

13 D'Acierno, *Italian American Heritage*, xxvi.

14 Joseph Sciorra, "'Core 'Ngrato,' a Wop Song: Mediated Renderings and Diasporic Musings" (paper presented at the annual meeting of the American Studies Association, Washington, DC, November 2013).

15 Joshua Berrett, "Louis Armstrong and Opera," *Musical Quarterly* 76, no. 2 (Summer 1992): 216–41.

16 Ben Ratliff, "Music in Review: Joe Lovano," *New York Times*, May 24, 2000.

17 Bruce Boyd Raeburn, "Italian Americans in New Orleans Jazz: Bel Canto Meets the Funk," *Italian American Review* 4, no. 2 (Summer 2014): 96.

18 Sicilians like trumpeter Nick LaRocca, drummer Tony Sbarbaro, and clarinetist Leon Roppolo were part of the same fertile New Orleans musical environment that produced Buddy Bolden, Freddie Keppard, Joe Oliver, Sidney Bechet, Jelly Roll Morton, Louis Armstrong, Kid Ory, and other great African American figures of early jazz. In 1917, LaRocca's Original Dixieland Jass Band cut the first commercially released jazz record, with "Dixie Jass Band One-Step" on the A-side and "Livery Stable Blues" on the B-side, and went on to tour America and Europe to much renown. Many jazz historians have derided the ODJB as a reactionary, whiteface minstrel outfit that capitalized on the racist bias of the recording industry to eclipse the groundbreaking and ostensibly more authentic jazz of black musicians—a position LaRocca encouraged when he petulantly disparaged black musicians and insisted that jazz was an entirely white invention. Alas, the ODJB records reveal a band with little rhythmic finesse and a penchant for hokum. Still, the ODJB's recordings influenced and abetted the best black jazz bands, such as King Oliver's Creole Jazz Band, by modeling the instrumentation that would become the standard for "real" jazz (a five-piece horn-centered lineup, sans strings), and by enlarging the audience for collectively improvised, ragtime-style music (Bruce Boyd Raeburn, "Jazz and the Italian Connection," *Jazz Archivist* 6, no. 1 [May 1991]: 1–8).

The kind of stylistic hybridizing under discussion here was characteristic of the innovative work of another second-generation New Orleans Sicilian, Cosimo Matassa, the recording engineer and studio owner most responsible for creating the "New Orleans sound" of 1950s and '60s R&B and rock and roll. Matassa grew up in a typically musical Sicilian family, ears full of New Orleans street music as well as the commercial fare that blared from the jukebox in his father's French Quarter grocery store. One of Matassa's first recordings was the ethnic novelty "Pizza Pie Boogie" by New Orleans jazz trumpeter Joe "Sharkey" Bonano and his Kings of Dixieland. Better known to history are the string of hits he later recorded with Fats Domino ("Ain't That a Shame" and "Blueberry Hill" among many others), Big Joe Turner ("Shake, Rattle, and Roll"), Little Richard ("Tutti Frutti," "Good Golly Miss Molly"), Lee Dorsey ("Working in the Coal Mine"), Aaron Neville ("Tell It Like It Is"), and other African American performers (George De Stefano, "Addio, Cosimo," *i-Italy*, September 13, 2014, http://www.i-italy.org/blog/24/archive/2014/9, accessed January 30, 2014).

19 Raeburn, "Italian Americans in New Orleans Jazz," 102–6.

20 George Guida, "Las Vegas Jubilee: Louis Prima's 1950s Stage Act as Multicultural Pageant," *Journal of Popular Culture*, 38, no. 4 (2005): 678–97. Butera's molten sax lines—especially his soloing on the sultry "Fever"—

provided soft-core ambience for Smith and Prima's erotic burlesque of a stoic, icy ingenue deflecting the come-ons of a smitten, lecherous older man. The 1956 Capitol LP *The Wildest*, with "Jump, Jive an' Wail," "Just a Gigolo," "The Lip," and "Buona Sera," beautifully captures this group's innovative synthesis of jazz, jump blues, and rock and roll.

21 Joel Dinerstein, "Lester Young and the Birth of Cool," in *Signifyin(g), Sanctifyin', and Slam Dunking: A Reader in African American Expressive Culture*, ed. Gena Dagel Caponi (Amherst: University of Massachusetts Press, 1999), 239–76.

22 D'Acierno, "Cultural Lexicon," 754.

23 See Bill Dal Cerro and David Anthony Witter, *Bebop, Swing and Bella Musica: Jazz and the Italian American Experience* (Chicago: Bella Musica, 2015), for an overview of Italian Americans and jazz.

24 Robert Farris Thompson, *Flash of the Spirit: African and Afro-American Art and Philosophy* (New York: Random House, 1983); D'Acierno, "Italian American Musical Culture," 447.

25 Henry Pleasants, *The Great American Popular Singers* (New York: Simon and Schuster, 1974), 27.

26 Joe Hyams, "Playboy Interview: Frank Sinatra," *Playboy*, February 1963, reprinted in *The Playboy Interview: Music Men* (Beverly Hills, CA: Playboy Enterprises, 2012), Kindle edition.

27 Bonz Malone, "O.G.: Frank Sinatra Didn't Take Orders; He Took Over," *Vibe*, September 1995.

28 Marvin Gaye quoted by Gerald Early in *One Nation under a Groove: Motown and American Culture* (Hopewell, NJ: Ecco Press, 1995), 9.

29 Bill Coss, "Frank Sinatra: Mr. Personality," *Metronome*, December 1957, 14.

30 Isabella Taves, "The Personal Story of the Tender Tough Guy Who Wouldn't Behave—Frank Sinatra," *Woman's Home Companion*, May 1956, 38.

31 Here I'm indebted to Karen McNally's *When Frankie Went to Hollywood: Frank Sinatra and American Male Identity* (Urbana: University of Illinois Press, 2008), especially 133–70.

32 Ben Sisaro, "Jay Z's Bid for King of the Hill," *New York Times*, November 6, 2009.

33 Christina Tapper, "Frank Sinatra Is One of Diddy's Imaginary Friends," *People*, October 10, 2008, http://www.people.com/people/article/0,,20232 338,00.html, accessed November 7, 2015.

34 James Kaplan, "Straight outta Hoboken," *New York Times*, December 11, 2010.

35 Pete Hamill, *Why Sinatra Matters* (Boston: Little, Brown, 1998), 49.

36 Pellegrino D'Acierno, "Sinatra, the Name Ending in a Vowel, or 'The Voice' as Signifier and Symptom of Italian Americanness," in *Frank Sinatra: History, Identity, and Italian American Culture*, ed. Stanislao G. Pugliese (New York: Palgrave Macmillan, 2004), 160.

37 Hamill, *Why Sinatra Matters*, 38.

38 D'Acierno, "Sinatra, the Name Ending in a Vowel," 159.

39 Tom Kuntz and Phil Koontz, eds., *The Sinatra File: The Life of an American Icon under Government Surveillance* (New York: Three Rivers, 2000).
Widespread suspicion of Sinatra started during World War II. No matter how many USO concerts he performed, Sinatra was still one of the most hated men in the country after earning a 4F exemption (thanks to a punctured eardrum) when millions of Americans were losing their lives in the war against Mussolini, Hitler, and Hirohito. After the war, the haters came to include anti-Communist demagogues for whom Ol' Blue Eyes's liberal politics blazed scarlet red.
James Kaplan covers the government's surveillance of Sinatra well in *Frank: The Voice* (New York: Doubleday, 2010). Kaplan includes discussion of an FBI memo in 1950 showing that Sinatra had volunteered to help the agency in its surveillance in Hollywood and New York, an offer Clyde Tolson and J. Edgar Hoover turned down (445–48). Kaplan argues that Sinatra made the offer to try to clear the way for his upcoming TV show. In 1950, of course, the anti-Communist witch hunts were in full swing, and Sinatra's career was in free fall.

40 Fred Gardaphé, *From Wiseguys to Wise Men: The Gangster and Italian American Masculinities* (New York: Routledge, 2006), 18.

41 David Ruth, *Inventing the Public Enemy: The Gangster in American Culture, 1918–1934* (Chicago: University of Chicago Press, 1996).

42 Rocco Marinaccio, "I Get No Kick from Assimilation," in *Frank Sinatra*, ed. Pugliese, 186.

43 I have drawn here on Laura Cook Kenna's article "The Promise of Gangster Glamour: Sinatra, Vegas, and Alluring, Ethnicized, Excess," UNLV Center for Gaming Research Occasional Paper Series, no. 6, August 2010; quotations on 1, 2, 3. See also Kenna's outstanding "Dangerous Men, Dangerous Media: Constructing Ethnicity, Race, and Media's Impact through the Gangster Image, 1957–2007" (PhD diss., George Washington University, 2008), especially 96–166.

44 Kaplan, *Frank*, 467.

45 Cinotto, "All Things Italian," 18. Sinatra's mastery of the "little guy working the system" persona is crucial to his Italian American iconicity. Let us remember that Monroe Street in Hoboken gave the world not one but two world-class singers. The other one, Jimmy Roselli, ten years Sinatra's junior, was arguably the purer saloon singer and unquestionably the authoritative bard of the Neapolitan romantic ballad. Among the cognoscenti, Roselli was the Italian male singer nonpareil, possessed of more masculine authority than either Sinatra or Tony Bennett, a tonal clarity and pure, classical use of the vowel line, and a surpassing ability to affect just the right calibrations of operatic passion and intimacy needed for such Italian chestnuts as "Malafemmena," "Innamorata," and "Amore e

core." But while the Chairman of the Board was salting the earth with his coin, Rosselli was reduced to hawking records out of the trunk of his car outside Mulberry Street restaurants. Sinatra's life ricocheted from one crisis to another, but those experiences were turned into narratives of plucky resilience carefully honed for presentation in the highest-profile media outlets. Rosselli, David Evanier tells us in *Making the Wiseguys Weep: The Jimmy Rosselli Story* (New York: Farrar, Straus and Giroux, 1998), was too stingy to pay a decent entertainment lawyer and too headstrong to show strategic deference to TV and movie moguls: he turned down Ed Sullivan, Merv Griffin, and Johnny Carson, favoring the schmaltzy, small-cheese environment of the *Joe Franklin Show*, and passed up a part tailor-made for him in *The Godfather II*. Evanier contends that both Sinatra and Rosselli had connections to the underworld that were not always of their own choosing. But Sinatra shrewdly used the connections to his own advantage, showing the wiseguys some appreciation and then enjoying their protection as he swung his way to stardom. He never capitulated to the gangsters or shied away from the oily show business smooth talkers; he out-leveraged both on his way up into the Hollywood stratosphere. Rosselli, by contrast, remained tied down by small-time wiseguys like "Trigger Mike" Cappola, Ruggiero "Richie the Boot" Boiardo, and Anthony "Skinny Skelly" Petrazella. The only reason these goombahs didn't whack Rosselli, Evanier says, is that their mothers loved his singing and wouldn't stand for it.

46 Kaplan, *Frank*, 336.

47 Herbert Gans, *The Urban Villagers: Group and Class in the Life of Italian-Americans* (New York: Free Press of Glencoe, 1962), 192. Thomas J. Ferraro pays tribute to Gans in his splendid essay "Urbane Villager," in *Frank Sinatra*, ed. Pugliese, 135–54.

48 Robert Connolly and Pellegrino D'Acierno, "Italian American Musical Culture and Its Contribution to American Music," in *The Italian American Heritage*, ed. D'Acierno, 426.

49 Thomas J. Ferraro, "Urbane Villager," 135–46, and "Song: A Punch in Everyman's Kisser," in *Feeling Italian: The Art of Ethnicity in America*, by Thomas J. Ferraro (New York: New York University Press, 2005), 100. Ferraro's "boys on the corner" concept recalls a classic sociological study that preceded Gans, William Foote Whyte's *Street Corner Society: The Social Structure of an Italian Slum* (Chicago: University of Chicago Press, 1943).

50 Gay Talese, "Frank Sinatra Has a Cold," in *The Frank Sinatra Reader*, ed. Steven Petkov and Leonard Mustazza (New York: Oxford University Press), 101.

51 Edward Santurri, "Prophet, *Padrone*, Postmodern Prometheus: Moral Images of Sinatra in Contemporary Culture," in *Frank Sinatra*, ed. Pugliese, 205, 206.

52 Ferraro, *Feeling Italian*, 176.

53 Steve Van Zandt's induction speech for the Rascals is available on several videos on YouTube. Van Zandt has been the driving force behind several Rascals reunion events, culminating in his production of a concert performance and theatrical spectacle, *Once upon a Dream*, which debuted on Broadway in the spring of 2013. Van Zandt is an interesting mediating presence, first as an iconic Jersey Shore character (an intimate of Bruce Springsteen and key sideman in the E Street Band), later as an iconic northern Jersey figure (as *The Sopranos* character Silvio Dante, mob consigliere and proprietor of the Bada Bing strip club). By the early 2000s, Van Zandt (born Steven Lento to a Calabrian and Neapolitan family) was perhaps second only to James Gandolfini's Tony Soprano as the leading symbol of Italian New Jersey, the position Frank Sinatra held for more than half a century.

54 Tutored by Joel Dinerstein ("The Soul Roots of Bruce Springsteen's American Dream," *American Music* 25 [Winter 2007]: 441–76), I've come to appreciate Springsteen's deep connections with black music. I just did not hear this in the 1970s.

55 Donald Fagen, *Eminent Hipsters* (New York: Viking, 2013), 39–47.

56 On Sinatra's politics, see Michael Nelson, "Sinatra and Presidential Politics," in *Frank Sinatra*, ed. Pugliese, 47–72. My discussion of Sinatra's becoming a Republican follows Nelson's narrative, 63–66.

57 Talese, "Frank Sinatra Has a Cold," 102.

58 Nelson, "Frank Sinatra and Presidential Politics," 66.

59 John Lahr, "Sinatra's Song," *New Yorker*, November 3, 1997, 94.

60 Nick Tosches, *Dino: Living High in the Dirty Business of Dreams* (New York: Dell, 1992), 267.

61 Talese, "Frank Sinatra Has a Cold," 103.

62 Ibid., 113.

63 *Sinatra*, dir. James Steven Sadwith (Warner Brothers Television, 1992).

64 Donald Clarke, *All or Nothing at All: A Life of Frank Sinatra* (New York: Fromm International, 1997), 208, 223.

65 Kitty Kelley, *His Way: The Unauthorized Biography of Frank Sinatra* (New York: Bantam, 1986).

66 John Lahr, *Sinatra: The Artist and the Man* (New York: Random House, 1997), 7.

67 Lahr, *Sinatra*, 8; Hamill, *Why Sinatra Matters*, 84.

68 Lahr, *Sinatra*, 79; Shirley MacLaine, *My Lucky Stars* (New York: Random House, 1996), 121.

69 On motherhood and mother bashing in American culture, see Shari Thurer, *The Myth of Motherhood: How Culture Reinvents the Good Mother* (New York: Houghton Mifflin, 1994), and Molly Ladd-Taylor and Lauri Umansky, eds., *"Bad" Mothers: The Politics of Blame in Twentieth-Century America* (New York: New York University Press, 1998).

70 *Moonstruck*, dir. Norman Jewison (Metro-Goldwyn-Mayer, 1987).

71 The Moynihan Report was the popular name for Daniel Moynihan's *The Negro Family: The Case for National Action* (Washington, DC: Office of Policy Planning and Research, US Department of Labor, 1965).

72 Athella Knight, "Ads Celebrate Mother's Day," *Washington Post*, June 11, 1995. The NBA players featured in the commercials were Kenny Anderson, Muggsy Bogues, Glenn Robinson, and Nick Van Exel.

73 Alfonse D'Amato, *Power, Pasta, and Politics* (New York: Hyperion, 1995), xv, 97.

74 *Goodfellas*, dir. Martin Scorsese (Warner Brothers, 1990).

75 Suzanne Hamlin, "Remembering an Italian Mother Just as She Would Like," *New York Times*, February 19, 1997, sec. C, 3, 5.

76 Regina Barreca, "Why I Like the Women in '*The Sopranos*,'" in *A Sitdown with "The Sopranos": Watching Italian American Culture on TVs Most Talked-About Series*, ed. Regina Barreca (New York: Palgrave Macmillan, 2002), 35.

77 Dan Greenburg, *How to Be a Jewish Mother: A Very Lovely Training Manual* (1964; Los Angeles: Price Stern Sloan, 1975), 12.

78 Barbara Grizzuti Harrison, "Terrified and Fascinated by His Own Life," *New York Times Book Review*, November 2, 1986, 13.

79 Richard Gambino, *Blood of My Blood: The Dilemma of the Italian Americans* (New York: Doubleday, 1974), 13.

80 Mario Puzo, *The Godfather Papers and Other Confessions* (New York: G. P. Putnam's Sons, 1972). Puzo was familiar with the folklore about Willie Moretti's squeezing Tommy Dorsey to release Sinatra from his onerous service contract. He was widely believed to be drawing on this legend when Michael Corleone tells the story of his father, the Don, making an "offer you can't refuse" to Fontane's bandleader while the Don's enforcer, Luca Brasi, holds a gun to the man's head. When the Don then has his consigliere make the same offer to Hollywood producer Jack Woltz to secure a career-reviving film part for Fontane, Puzo gives us a scenario mighty similar (minus the horse's head) to the often-told legend of how Sinatra ended up playing Maggio in *From Here to Eternity*. One reason it was easy for Puzo to deny the Fontane/Sinatra connection without appearing blatantly disingenuous was that Al Martino, the Italian American singer who played Fontane in Francis Ford Coppola's movie, had had his own well-publicized contretemps in the world of mobbed-up nightclubs and fungible recording contracts, as had many popular singers of the 1940s and '50s.

81 Kaplan, *Voice*, 336.

82 Ibid., 653–58.

83 George Jacobs and William Stadiem, *Mr. S: My Life with Frank Sinatra* (New York: HarperCollins, 2003).

84 Mario Puzo, "Choosing a Dream: Italians in Hell's Kitchen," in *The Immigrant Experience: The Anguish of Becoming an American*, ed. Thomas C. Wheeler (New York: Dial Press, 1971), 39.

85 Luigi Barzini, *The Italians: A Full-Length Portrait Featuring Their Manners and Morals* (1964; New York: Simon and Schuster 1996), 202.

86 See Thomas J. Ferraro, *Feeling Italian*, 72–89.

87 The quotation is from Puzo's preface for the 1997 edition of *The Fortunate Pilgrim* (1964; New York: Ballantine, 1997), xii. On what he calls "the female core of Vito Corleone's masculinity," see Gardaphé, *From Wiseguys to Wise Men*, 31–36.

88 Janny Scott, "Even Scholars Say It's Witchcraft," *New York Times*, May 16, 1998, B9, B11.

89 Lauren Berlant, "Introduction," in *Intimacy*, ed. Lauren Berlant (Chicago: University of Chicago Press, 2000), 2.

Chapter Two

1 Greg Tate, *Everything but the Burden: What White People Are Taking from Black Culture* (New York: Broadway Books/Random House, 2003), 1.

2 Michele Scicolone, *1,000 Italian Recipes* (New York: Wiley, 2004), 1.

3 Charles Hersch, "'Matzo Balls creenic': Ethnic Hybridity in African American Jazz Versions of Jewish Songs," paper presented at the "Jazz Beyond Borders" conference, Amsterdam, Netherlands, September 6, 2014.

4 *Big Night*, dir. Campbell Scott and Stanley Tucci (Samuel Goldwyn Company, 1996).

5 Nat Shapiro and Nat Hentoff, *Hear Me Talkin' to Ya: The Story of Jazz as Told by the Men Who Made It* (New York: Dover, 1955), 354.

6 Annie Rachele Lanzillotto, "Cosa Mangia Oggi," in *Gastropolis: Food and New York City*, ed. Annie Hauck-Lawson and Jonathan Deutsch (New York: Columbia University Press, 2009), 233–51.

7 See http://www.annielanzillotto.com.

8 This Arthur Avenue market performance can be viewed at https://www.youtube.com/watch?v=XqtmfPIn5ug, accessed April 29, 2015.

9 Roland Barthes, "The Grain of the Voice," in *Image/Music/Text* (New York: Hill and Wang, 1977), 179–89.

10 Ralph Ellison, "As the Spirit Moves Mahalia," in *Living with Music: Ralph Ellison's Jazz Writings*, ed. Robert O'Meally (New York: Modern Library, 2002), 87–94.

11 This performance can be viewed at https://www.youtube.com/watch?v=Css07MuQUhY, accessed April 29, 2015.

12 Blake Gopnik, "Fleeting Artworks, Melting Like Sugar: Kara Walker's Sphinx and the Tradition of Ephemeral Art," *New York Times*, July 11, 2014.

13 For a jazz critic's assessment of "Bleed," see Ben Ratliff, "Art, Ancestry, Africa: Letting It All Bleed," *New York Times*, May 14, 2012. For a video sampling of "Bleed," see http://grammarfilm.com/videos/2014/4/13/bleed-breakdown, accessed August 29, 2014.

14 Camille Paglia, "The Italian Way of Death," *Salon*, August 4, 1996, www .salon.com/weekly/paglia960805.html, accessed April 29, 2015.

15 Louise DeSalvo, *Crazy in the Kitchen: Food, Feuds, and Forgiveness in an Italian American Family* (New York: Bloomsbury, 2004). The book's cover was designed by Julie Metz.

16 Ibid., 26.

17 Ibid., 31.

18 Ibid., 30.

19 Ibid., 66.

20 Ibid., 228.

21 Eric Weiner, *Man Seeks God: My Flirtations with the Divine* (New York: Twelve/Hatchett Book Group, 2011), 2–3.

22 William Van Deburg, *New Day in Babylon: The Black Power Movement and American Culture, 1965–1975* (Chicago: University of Chicago Press, 1992), 192–216.

23 Eileen Southern, *The Music of Black Americans: A History* (1997; New York: W. W. Norton, 1997), 52–62, 151–200.

24 Carl Woideck, *Charlie Parker: His Music and Life* (Ann Arbor: University of Michigan Press, 1998), 20–21; Ralph Ellison, *Shadow and Act* (New York: Random House, 1964), 222.

25 LeRoi Jones [Amiri Baraka], *Blues People: Negro Music in White America* (New York: Morrow, 1963), 218–22.

26 Baraka's disdain for this form of theater is noted by Henry Louis Gates Jr. in his essay "The Chitlin Circuit," in *African American Performance and Theater History*, ed. Harry Justin Elam and David Krasner (New York: Oxford University Press, 2001), 140.

27 LeRoi Jones [Amiri Baraka], "Soul Food," in *Home: Social Essays* (New York: Morrow, 1966), 101–4.

28 Doris Witt, *Black Hunger: Food and the Politics of U.S. Identity* (New York: Oxford University Press, 1999), 7.

29 Eldridge Cleaver, *Soul on Ice* (1968; New York: Laurel-Dell, 1992), 40 (quoted by Witt, *Black Hunger*, 47).

30 Ralph Ellison, *Invisible Man* (1952; New York: Vintage/Random House, 1995), 265 (quoted by Witt, *Black Hunger*, 83).

31 Witt, *Black Hunger*, 83.

32 Ibid., 90.

33 Angelo Pellegrini, *The Unprejudiced Palate: Classic Thoughts on Food and the Good Life* (1948; New York: Modern Library/Random House, 2005), 100.

34 Jones, *Blues People*, 219–20.

35 Witt, *Black Hunger*, 21–53.

36 Anthony Slide, *The Encyclopedia of Vaudeville* (Westport, CT: Greenwood, 1994), 16; Middleton Harris, with Morris Levett, Roger Furman, and Ernest Smith, *The Black Book* (New York: Random House, 1974), 41 (quoted by Witt, *Black Hunger*, 34). Current scholarly consensus—see, for

example, M. M. Manning, *Brands, Trademarks, and Good Will: The Story of the Quaker Oats Company* (Charlottesville, University of Virginia Press, 1998)—is that the original Aunt Jemima was Nancy Green, a former slave who was hired by the R. T. Davis Milling Company in 1890. The Quaker Oats Company bought the Aunt Jemima brand in 1928.

37 *Ethnic Notions*, dir. Marlon Riggs (California Newsreel, 1987).

38 Patricia Turner, *Ceramic Uncles and Celluloid Mammies: Black Images and Their Influence on Culture* (Charlottesville: University of Virginia Press, 2002).

39 John Mariani, *How Italian Food Conquered the World* (New York: Palgrave Macmillan, 2011), 45.

40 Ibid., 55–56.

41 Ibid., 3.

42 *Molto Mario*, exec. prod. John Parry (Food Network, 1996–2006). This section on Batali is informed by my viewing of *Molto Mario* and by my reading of Bill Buford, *Heat: An Amateur's Adventures as Kitchen Slave, Line Cook, Pasta-Maker, and Apprentice to a Dante-Quoting Butcher in Tuscany* (New York: Knopf, 2006), and David Kamp, *The United States of Arugula: The Sun-Dried, Cold-Pressed, Dark-Roasted, Extra-Virgin Story of the American Food Revolution* (New York: Broadway/Random House, 2006).

43 Buford, *Heat*, 6.

44 Ibid., 139–40.

45 Fred Pfeil, *White Guys: Studies in Postmodern Domination* (New York: Verso, 1995), 79.

46 Buford, *Heat*, 59.

47 Ibid., 33.

48 Bastianich has had a succession of cooking shows on PBS since 1998: *Lidia's Italian-American Kitchen*, *Lidia's Family Table*, *Lidia's Italy in America*, *Lidia's Kitchen*, and *Lidia's Italy*.

49 DeSalvo, *Crazy in the Kitchen*, 38, 123.

50 Ibid., 4–5.

51 Ibid., 166.

52 Louise DeSalvo and Edvige Giunta, eds., *The Milk of Almonds: Italian American Women Writers on Food and Culture* (New York: Feminist Press, 2002), 12.

53 Quoted by DeSalvo and Giunta, *Milk of Almonds*, 8.

54 DeSalvo, *Crazy in the Kitchen*, 137.

55 DeSalvo and Giunta, *Milk of Almonds*, 5.

56 Simone Cinotto, *The Italian American Table: Food, Family, and Community in New York City* (Champaign-Urbana: University of Illinois Press, 2013); Carol Helstosky, *Garlic and Oil: Food and Politics in Italy* (Oxford: Berg, 2004); Mariani, *How Italian Food Conquered the World*.

57 Donna Gabaccia, *We Are What We Eat: Ethnic Food and the Making of Americans* (Cambridge, MA: Harvard University Press, 1998), 231–32.

58 Maria Laurino, *Old World Daughter, New World Mother: An Education in Love and Freedom* (New York: W. W. Norton, 2009), 32.

59 Ibid., 36, 202.

60 Ibid., 55, 154–55.

61 DeSalvo, *Crazy in the Kitchen*, 173.

62 Ibid., 188.

63 Joanna Clapps Herman, *The Anarchist Bastard: Growing Up Italian in America* (Albany: SUNY Press, 2011), 9.

64 DeSalvo, *Crazy in the Kitchen*, 187, 140.

65 Ibid., 190.

66 Craig Claiborne, A *Feast Made for Laughter: A Memoir with Recipes* (New York: Doubleday, 1982), 109 (quoted by Witt, *Black Hunger*, 71).

67 Witt, *Black Hunger*, 74.

68 Craig Claiborne, *Craig Claiborne's Southern Cooking* (New York: Times/Random House, 1987), xvi.

69 Witt, *Black Hunger*, 66–68.

70 Claiborne, *Southern Cooking*, xvii (quoted by Witt, *Black Hunger*, 68).

71 Hortense Spiller, "Mama's Baby, Papa's Maybe: An American Grammar Book," *Diacritics* 17, no. 2 (Summer 1987): 65.

72 Calvin Trillin, *The Tummy Trilogy* (New York: Farrar, Straus and Giroux, 1994), 259–67.

Chapter Three

1 Royko is cited by David Roediger in his introduction to the anthology *Black on White: Black Writers on What It Means to Be White* (New York: Random House, 1998), 7.

2 See Jim Sleeper, *The Closest of Strangers: Liberalism and the Politics of Race in New York* (New York: W. W. Norton, 1990), 184–85. Though I consider the general polemic in this book overwrought, on the Howard Beach and Yusuf Hawkins incidents I find Sleeper illuminating and fair-minded.

3 David Denby, "Jungle Fever," *New Yorker*, November 6, 1995, 118–20.

4 Kaleem Aftab and Spike Lee, *Spike Lee: That's My Story and I'm Sticking to It* (New York: W. W. Norton, 2005), 130–31.

5 Robert Orsi, "The Religious Boundaries of an In-Between People: Street *Feste* and the Problem of the Dark-Skinned Other in Italian Harlem, 1920–1990," *American Quarterly* 44, no. 3 (September 1992): 313.

6 For reasons of space and cogency, I've chosen not to look closely in this chapter at *Summer of Sam* or at *Miracle at St. Anna* (2008), which centers on African American soldiers in Italy during World War II. For a provocative interpretation of *Summer of Sam*, see Dan Flory, "Race and Black American *Film Noir*: *Summer of Sam* as Lynching Parable," in *The Spike Lee Reader*, ed. Paula Massood (Philadelphia: Temple University Press, 2008), 196–211.

7   Peter Biskind, *Easy Riders, Raging Bulls: How the Sex-Drugs-and-Rock 'n' Roll Generation Saved Hollywood* (New York: Simon and Schuster, 1998); Stanley Corkin, *Starring New York: Filming the Grime and the Glamour of the Long 1970s* (New York: Oxford University Press, 2011).

8   In the growing literature on this history, I've been especially informed by Rick Perlstein's *Nixonland: The Rise of a President and the Fracturing of America* (New York: Simon and Schuster, 2008), and his *The Invisible Bridge: The Fall of Nixon and the Rise of Reagan* (New York: Simon and Schuster, 2014). For a superb and concise treatment of how these national dynamics affected the New York City borough of the Bronx, see Jeff Chang, *Can't Stop Won't Stop: A History of the Hip-Hop Generation* (New York: St. Martin's Press, 2005), 7–20. For an account of the devastating effects of the "war on drugs," see Michelle Alexander, *The New Jim Crow: Mass Incarceration in the Age of Colorblindness* (New York: New Press, 2010).

9   The term *underclass* generally is credited to Gunnar Myrdal in his analysis of urban poverty in *Challenge to Affluence* (New York: Random House, 1963). Sociologist William Julius Wilson adopted the term for his studies of the black urban poor in *The Declining Significance of Race: Blacks and Changing American Institutions* (Chicago: University of Chicago Press, 1978) and his *The Truly Disadvantaged: The Inner City, the Underclass, and Public Policy* (Chicago: University of Chicago Press, 1987). See also Ken Auletta, *The Underclass* (New York: Random House, 1983).

10 The story I briefly sketch here involving Italians and other ethnic groups in New York City is part of a larger national history of housing and race that George Lipsitz synopsizes brilliantly in *How Racism Takes Place* (Philadelphia: Temple University Press, 2014), 1–24, and his *The Possessive Investment in Whiteness: How White People Profit from Identity Politics* (Philadelphia: Temple University Press, 1998), 1–23.

11 Jonathan Rieder, *Canarsie: The Jews and Italians of Brooklyn against Liberalism* (Cambridge, MA: Harvard University Press, 1985); Jerome Krase, "Bensonhurst, Brooklyn: Italian-American Victimizers and Victims," *Voices in Italian Americana* 5, no. 2 (1994): 48, 49; Simone Cinotto, "Italian Doo-Wop: Sense of Place, Politics of Style, and Racial Crossover in Postwar New York City," in *Making Italian America: Consumer Culture and the Production of Ethnic Identities*, ed. Simone Cinotto (New York: Fordham University Press, 2014), 166–67; Donna Gabaccia, "Inventing Little Italy," *Journal of the Gilded Age and Progressive Era* 6, no. 1 (January 2007): 7–41; Donald Tricarico, "Consuming Italian Americans: Invoking Ethnicity in the Buying and Selling of Guido," in *Making Italian America*, ed. Simone Cinotto, 181–82.

12 Rieder, *Canarsie*, 2–3, 7.

13 Corkin, *Starring New York*, 48–73.

14 Ibid., 72.

15 Jacobson, *Roots Too: White Ethnic Revival in Post-Civil Rights America* (Cambridge, MA: Harvard University Press, 2006), 148.

16 Mario Puzo, *The Godfather* (1969; New York: Signet, 1978), 288.

17 Corkin, *Starring New York*, 74–102.

18 Victoria Johnson, "Polyphony and Cultural Expression: Interpreting Musical Traditions in *Do the Right Thing*," in *Spike Lee's "Do the Right Thing*," ed. Mark Reid (Cambridge: Cambridge University Press, 1997), 55.

19 Kaleem Aftab and Spike Lee, *Spike Lee: That's My Story and I'm Sticking to It* (New York: W. W. Norton, 2005), 1–26.

20 Reid speaks these lines in *Brooklyn Boheme*, a documentary film by Diane Paragas and Nelson George (Blackapino Productions, 2011).

21 Ibid.

22 Trey Ellis, "The New Black Aesthetic," *Calaloo* 38 (Winter 1989): 133–43.

23 My characterizations of *Welcome Back, Kotter* and *Saturday Night Fever* draw on comments by Maria Laurino in *Were You Always an Italian? Ancestors and Other Icons of Italian America* (New York: W. W. Norton, 2000), 136–37. Laurino points out that the concept for *Saturday Night Fever* came from a *New York* magazine article called "Tribal Rites of the New Saturday Night," written by London-based rock critic Nik Cohn, a piece Cohn later said was a gross exaggeration fabricated to meet his editors' demands for a "raw cut" (Laurino's words) of Italian American life.

24 Tricarico, "Consuming Italian Americans," 182, 188.

25 Marianna De Marco Torgovnick, *Crossing Ocean Parkway* (Chicago: University of Chicago Press, 1997), 3–18.

26 Laurino, *Were You Always an Italian?*, 123, 142, 153.

27 Sciorra's extensive body of work includes *Built with Faith: Italian American Imagination and Catholic Material Culture in New York City* (Knoxville: University of Tennessee Press, 2015); *Italian Folk: Vernacular Culture in Italian American Lives* (New York: Fordham University Press, 2011); and *Embroidered Stories: Interpreting Women's Domestic Needlework from the Italian Diaspora* (Oxford: University of Mississippi Press, 2014).

28 Joseph Sciorra, "'Italians against Racism': The Murder of Yusuf Hawkins (R.I.P.) and My March on Bensonhurst," in *Are Italians White? How Race Is Made in America*, ed. Jennifer Guglielmo and Salvatore Salerno (New York: Routledge, 2003), 193, 194, 196, 200, 201.

29 See, for example, Mark Reid, ed., *Spike Lee's "Do the Right Thing"* (Cambridge: Cambridge University Press, 1997).

30 Gene Siskel, "This Picture's as Good as *The Godfather*," *Chicago Tribune*, June 25, 1989.

31 Peter Bonadella, *Hollywood Italians: Dagos, Palookas, Romeos, Wise Guys, and Sopranos* (New York: Continuum, 2006), 86–88, and De Stefano, *An Offer We Can't Refuse: The Mafia in the Mind of America* (New York: Faber and Faber, 2006), 245.

32 Giancarlo Esposito quoted in Aftab and Lee, *That's My Story*, 77.

33 Danny Aiello quoted in Aftab and Lee, *That's My Story*, 80.

34 Spike Lee (with Lisa Jones), *Do the Right Thing: A Spike Lee Joint* (New York: Simon and Schuster, 1999), 83, 99.

35 Lee and Jones, *Do the Right Thing*, 82.

36 John Turtutto quoted in Aftab and Lee, *That's My Story*, 81, 118.

37 This section focusing on Giancarlo Esposito is adapted from my essay "Giancarlo Giuseppe Alessandro Esposito: Life in the Borderlands," in *Are Italians White?*, 234–49, originally published in *Common Quest* 4, no. 2 (Winter 2000): 8–17. All quotations from Esposito in this section are from my interview with him on October 12, 1999.

38 Esposito plays Julian, the sadistic fraternity president in *School Daze* (1988); Buggin' Out, the amateur political agitator in *Do the Right Thing* (1989); Left Hand Lacey, the dandyish jazz pianist in *Mo' Better Blues* (1990); and Thomas Hayer, one of the assassins in *Malcolm X* (1992).

39 I'm quoting here from an unpublished manuscript of Ferraro's essay "Giancarlo and the Border Police." His chapter of that same title, in *Feeling Italian*, 162–81, offers an extraordinarily rich reading of *Do the Right Thing*. I'm indebted to Ferraro for our many discussions about that film and Giancarlo Esposito.

40 Sciorra, "'Italians against Racism,'" 202.

41 "Spiking a Fever," *Newsweek*, June 9, 1991.

42 Gennari, "Giancarlo Giuseppe Alessandro Esposito," 244.

43 Annabella Sciorra quoted in Aftab and Lee, *That's My Story*, 128.

44 John Turturro quoted in Aftab and Lee, *That's My Story*, 124.

45 Gennari, "Giancarlo Giuseppe Alessandro Esposito," 245.

46 Spike Lee quoted in Aftab and Lee, *That's My Story*, 123.

47 Annabella Sciorra, interview with author, January 4, 2011.

48 Annabella Sciorra quoted in De Stefano, *An Offer We Can't Refuse*, 252.

49 Ibid.

50 Ed Guerrero, "Spike Lee and the Fever in the Racial Jungle," in Massood, *Spike Lee Reader*, 87.

51 Douglas Kellner, "Aesthetics, Ethics, and Politics in the Films of Spike Lee," in Reid, *Spike Lee's "Do the Right Thing,"* 75.

52 Writer bell hooks initiated this line of criticism with her withering analysis of *She's Gotta Have It* in her essay "Whose Pussy Is This? A Feminist Comment," in *Talking Back: Thinking Feminist, Thinking Black*, ed. bell hooks (Boston: South End Press, 1989), 131–41. She places Lee's gender politics in a larger framework in her book *Reel to Real: Race, Sex, and Class at the Movies* (New York: Routledge, 2008), 10–26.

53 Gerald Early, *One Nation under a Groove: Motown and American Culture* (Hopewell, NJ: Ecco Press, 1995), 10.

54 Simone Cinotto, "Italian Doo-Wop: Sense of Place, Politics of Style, and Racial Crossovers in Postwar New York City," in her *Making Italian America*, 163–77.

55 Cinotto, "Italian Doo Wop," 175–76. See also Joseph Sciorra, "Who Put the Wop in Doo-Wop? Some Thoughts on Italian Americans and Early Rock

and Roll," *Voices in Italian Americana* 13, no. 1 (2002): 16–22. Sciorra notes that the term doo-wop was not used exclusively for the Italian American groups.

56 Rieder, *Canarsie*, 1.

57 Peter Shapiro, *Turn the Beat Around: The Secret History of Disco* (New York: Faber and Faber, 2005), 205.

58 Sciorra's extensive work in this area includes a conference he organized, "Eye-talian Flava: The Italian American Experience in Hip Hop," Calandra Institute, October 2002; a website he produced, www.italianrap.com, from 1998 to 2012; and his article "The Mediascape of Hip Wop: Alterity and Authenticity in Italian American Rap," in *Global Media, Culture, and Identity*, ed. Rohit Chopra and Radhika Gajjala (New York: Routledge, 2011), 33–51.

59 Nelson George, "Brothers in Arms: The Borough's Warring Tribes Are Closer Than We Think," *Village Voice*, May 29, 1990, 27–28.

60 Joseph Sciorra reports that in his fifteen years as an employee in the CUNY system, he has seen no evidence that the 1992 antidiscrimination suit has resulted in policies or programs that have substantively benefited Italian American students, faculty, and staff. Further, he doubts that most Italian American families in neighborhoods such as Bensonhurst have ever been aware of the suit or of the idea that Italians are a protected class in the CUNY system (Joseph Sciorra, e-mail message to the author, May 17, 2015).

61 Laurino, *Were You Always an Italian?*, 130–35.

62 Stephen Hall, "Italians Coming into Their Own," *New York Times Sunday Magazine*, May 15, 1983.

Chapter Four

1 Frank Deford, "Geno Auriemma + Diana Taurasi = Love, Italian Style," *Sports Illustrated*, November 24, 2003, 124–33. See also Geno Auriemma (with Jackie MacMullan), *Geno: In Pursuit of Perfection* (New York: Warner Books, 2006).

2 *Hoop Dreams*, dir. Steve James (Kartemquin Films, 1994).

3 I was introduced to D'Acierno's term dagotude at the symposium "For a Dangerous Pedagogy: A Manifesto for Italian and Italian American Studies," Hofstra University, April 15, 2010.

4 The relevant portion of Vitale's appearance in *Hoop Dreams* is conveniently accessible on YouTube at http://www.youtube.com/watch?v=LW d5odFHW2A, accessed April 2, 2013.

5 This background information on Vaccaro is gleaned from the ESPN "30 for 30" documentary *Sole Man*, directed by Jon Weinbach and Dan Marks, which had its premier viewing on April 16, 2015.

6   Quoted in Marty Dobrow, *Going Bigtime: The Spectacular Rise of UMass Basketball* (Northampton, MA: Summerset Press, 1996), 48–49.

7   Among the voluminous writings about Vaccaro, I especially recommend Ric Bucher, "The Last Don," *espnmag.com*, available at http://espn.go.com/magazine/vol5no23vaccaro.html, accessed August 2, 2011, and Jason Zengerle, "The Pivot," *New Republic*, July 9, 2008, 24–26, 31–32. For a powerful critique of Vaccaro and the whole business of college recruiting, see Alexander Wolff and Armen Keteyian, *Raw Recruits: The High Stakes Game Colleges Play to Get Their Stars—and What It Costs to Win* (New York: Pocket Books, 1991).

8   Bucher, "Last Don."

9   For a smart discussion of the racial and gender politics of Bobby Knight's approach, see Jeffrey Lane, *Under the Boards: The Cultural Revolution in Basketball* (Lincoln: University of Nebraska Press, 2007), 147–96.

10   Curry Kirkpatrick, "A New Mr. Bones Has a Winner," *Sports Illustrated*, January 27, 1969, 48–49.

11   Rick Reilly, "I've Gotta Be Me," *Sports Illustrated*, March 7, 1994, 72–82.

12   Mark Asher of the *Washington Post* introduced the phrase "Hoya paranoia"—"Hoya" comes from the early Greek-Latin cheer "Hoya saxa," roughly "What rocks"—in 1980. Asher was referring to the insecurity of Georgetown fans, their sense that local media were slighting the Hoyas in favor of the University of Maryland. This original meaning was soon lost, however, as the term came to refer (not quite logically) to the fear Georgetown induced in its opponents. *Sports Illustrated* reporter Curry Kirkpatrick put a different spin on the term when he used it to voice his grievance about coach John Thompson's adversarial stance toward the media and tight control over access to his players. See Kirkpatrick, "Hang on to Your Hats . . . and Heads," *Sports Illustrated*, March 19, 1984, 20–25.

13   James Fisher, "Clearing the Streets of the Catholic Lost Generation," in *Catholic Lives, Contemporary America*, ed. Thomas Ferraro (Durham, NC: Duke University Press, 1997), 95.

14   Writing about Catholic high school basketball in the 1990s in *The Last Shot: City Streets, Basketball Dreams* (New York: Simon and Schuster, 1996), Darcy Frey observes that in New York and many other cities the Catholic leagues "siphon off the best public school players by offering a safer environment, better academic preparation, and travel budgets for out-of-town tournaments" (40–41). In a project similar to *Hoop Dreams*, Frey tracked the lives of African American high school players in the Coney Island section of Brooklyn.

15   David Maraniss's *When Pride Still Mattered: A Life of Vince Lombardi* (New York: Simon and Schuster, 1999) provides a wonderful history of mid-twentieth-century Catholic high school and college football. Maraniss advances an interesting argument connecting football's ethic of pain and suffering with southern Italian religious beliefs and practices.

16 Frank Deford, "A Heavenly Game?" *Sports Illustrated*, March 3, 1985.

17 Frank Deford, "Guess Who's Not Coming to Dinner?" *Sports Illustrated*, February 1, 1999. Deford's profile was occasioned by the cause célèbre in which Carlesimo, while coaching the NBA's Golden State Warriors, was viciously choked by his player Latrell Sprewell. Deford was sympathetic to Carlesimo. *New York Times* sports columnist William Rhoden was not, arguing that Carlesimo's "incessantly grating style" did not suit the NBA, where, unlike the college game, the players can refuse to be treated like "field hands" (William C. Rhoden, "Just Ranting and Raving Doesn't Win," *New York Times*, December 30, 1999). In another column (cited by Deford), Rhoden added P.J.'s father to his indictment: "Carlesimo, whose father, Peter Sr., is an important figure in college basketball . . . learned how to maneuver early in his career. He could disrespect players and get away with it because his daddy, or some facsimile thereof (athletic director, team president) was standing by to bail him out." In *Under the Boards*, Jeffrey Lane discusses the Carlesimo/Sprewell incident in the context of the racial politics of NBA labor/management relations (69–112). Unlike Deford, neither Lane nor Rhoden addresses Carlesimo's Irish/Italian Catholic background.

18 Lou Carnesecca quoted in Kirkpatrick, "Hang on to Your Hats . . . and Heads."

19 Rick Pitino and Bill Reynolds, *Born to Coach: A Season with the New York Knicks* (New York: NAL, 1988), 191.

20 Kirkpatrick, "Hang on to Your Hats."

21 Tim Layden, "The Upset," *Sports Illustrated*, March 29, 2004, 70–80.

22 *Perfect Upset: The 1985 Villanova vs. Georgetown NCAA Championship* (Home Box Office, 2005). Written by Brian Hyland.

23 Ed Pinckney with Bob Gordon, *Ed Pinckney's Tales from the Villanova Hardwood* (Champaign, IL: Sports Publishing LLC, 2004), 142.

24 Layden, "Upset."

25 Pinckney and Gordon, *Tales from the Villanova Hardwood*, 16.

26 Deford, "Heavenly Game?"

27 Ibid.

28 Bill Gilbert, "The Gospel according to John," *Sports Illustrated*, December 1, 1980.

29 Thompson worked for several years as director of the District of Columbia's 4-H program while moonlighting as basketball coach at St. Anthony's, a small Catholic high school he quickly turned into a city power. When the Georgetown job opened up in 1972, Thompson, lacking college experience, was a long-shot candidate. But his proven track record in the local community, his strong commitment to education, and, not least, his proud and assertive blackness, recommended him to the hiring committee and the Georgetown president, the Reverend Timothy S. Healy, S.J. "After the 1968 riots," Healy later said, "it became obvious that the university's position [vis-à-vis DC] wasn't very smart or defensible—socially, intellectually, morally or empirically. We began making some changes, some statements to the local community that we were going to try to at least be more responsible and useful. I think it's fair to say that hiring John Thompson was one of those statements" (Gilbert, "Gospel according to John").

30 Ibid.

31 Ibid.

32 Deford, "Heavenly Game?"

33 Timothy Healy quoted in Frank Fitzpatrick, *The Perfect Game: How Villanova's Shocking 1985 Upset of Mighty Georgetown Changed the Landscape of College Hoops Forever* (New York: Thomas Dunne/St. Martin's Press, 2013), 136. Fitzpatrick's superb book was published after I had written most of this chapter. I highly recommend it as a journalistic account of the 1985 championship game, the season that preceded it, and the social issues it brought to the surface.

34 Pinckney and Gordon, *Tales from the Villanova Hardwood*, 146. The Villanova athletic department person was Jim DeLorenzo.

35 Ibid., 91.

36 *Perfect Upset.*

37 I am thinking here about Matthew Frye Jacobson's discussion, in *Roots Too: White Ethnic Revival in Post-Civil Rights America* (Cambridge, MA: Harvard University Press, 2006), of how the ethnoracial tensions of the *Rocky* films relate to the white backlash against the civil rights movement (98–110). But I don't mean to suggest that Massimino was in any way an adherent of white ethnic backlash ideology; indeed, I know nothing about his politics. Like other basketball coaches of his time, he worked on the front lines of the new world that was created by the civil rights revolution, interacting with African Americans much more closely than other leaders at his own university. Such coaches are among the occupational groups that deserve much more study for their roles in shaping America's post–civil rights social order.

38 Gary McLain (as told to Jeffrey Marx), "A Bad Trip: The Downfall of a Champion," *Sports Illustrated*, March 16, 1987, cover, 42–64.

39 Pinckney and Gordon, *Tales from the Villanova Hardwood*, 186.

40 *Perfect Upset.*

41 Michael Freeman, *ESPN: The Uncensored History* (Lanham, MD: Rowman and Littlefield, 2000), 167.

42 On Italian Americans and sports talk radio, see Alan Eisenstock, *Sports Talk: A Journey inside the World of Sports Talk Radio* (New York: Pocket Books, 2001), 109–66; and Nick Paumgarten, "The Boys," *New Yorker*, August 30, 2004, 75–83.

43 Reilly, "I've Gotta Be Me," 76.

44 Steve Rushin, "Your Choice, Babeee!," *Sports Illustrated*, April 1, 1996, 120.

45 Feinstein, *March to Madness*, 50.

46 Ibid., 50–51.

47 Curry Kirkpatrick, "How King Rat Became the Big Cheese," *Sports Illustrated*, December 5, 1983.

48 Ibid. See also Gary Smith, "As Time Runs Out," *Sports Illustrated*, January 11, 1993.

49 The book was Peter Golenbock's *Personal Fouls: The Broken Promises and Shattered Dreams of Big Money Basketball at Jim Valvano's North Carolina State* (New York: Simon and Schuster, 1989). Simon and Schuster dropped the book after some of its allegations didn't prove out. Carroll and Graf publishers picked it up and put out an edition in 1991.

50 Kirkpatrick, "How King Rat Became the Big Cheese," and Smith, "As Time Runs Out."

51 Kirkpatrick, "How King Rat Became the Big Cheese."

52 Feinstein, *March to Madness*, 52.

53 Dobrow, *Going Bigtime*, 42–43.

54 Pitino and Reynolds, *Born to Coach*, 189 ("more organized than crime," attributed to John Marinatto); 11 ("boyish enthusiasm"); and 9 ("superior-conditioned team").

55 Ibid., 86.

56 Ibid., 67 ("Phoenix tan") and 33 ("sauna"). A running theme throughout *Born to Coach* is Pitino's deep anguish about how his coaching career is affecting his family.

57 Ibid., 168. *Sports Illustrated* has published several lengthy articles on Pitino, including Curry Kirkpatrick, "The Bluegrass Isn't So Blue," *SI*, December 11, 1989; Alexander Wolff, "Bluegrass Revival," *SI*, November 23, 1992; and William Nack, "Full-Court Pressure," *SI*, February 28, 1996.

58 Harvey Araton, "Calipari a Good Fit to Coach Kentucky," *New York Times*, April 1, 2009, B11–12.

59 Dobrow, *Going Bigtime*, 61–63.

60 Ibid., 56–58, xiii.

61 Ibid., xi.

62 Ibid, 218.

63 Derrick Rose turned out to have paid someone to take his SAT test and to have blown off classes the second semester of his freshmen year, knowing he'd be drafted into the NBA the following spring.

64 For a discussion of the NBA dress code, see Lane, *Under the Boards*, 27–68.

65 Press reports in the summer of 2009 revealed that Pitino had paid hush money to a woman with whom he'd had consensual sex in a Louisville restaurant earlier in the decade. The woman later was convicted of extortion.

66 Lane, *Under the Boards*, xvi.

Chapter Five

1 Wilbur Zelinsky, *The Enigma of Ethnicity: Another American Dilemma* (Iowa City: University of Iowa Press, 2001), 44–53; David Roediger, *Work-*

ing toward Whiteness: How America's Immigrants Became White (New York: Basic Books, 2005), 3–34; Matthew Frye Jacobson, *Whiteness of a Different Color: European Immigrants and the Alchemy of Race* (Cambridge, MA: Harvard University Press, 1998), 7–14.

2 Perry Weed, *The White Ethnic Movement and Ethnic Politics* (New York: Praeger, 1973).

3 Michael Novak, *The Rise of the Unmeltable Ethnics: Politics and Culture in the Seventies* (New York: Macmillan, 1971).

4 Jon Wiener, "When Old Blue Eyes Was Red: The Poignant Story of Frank Sinatra's Politics," *New Republic*, March 31, 1986, 21–23; Wiener, *Professors, Politics, and Pop* (New York: Verso, 1991), 263–69.

5 Lisa Lowe, *Immigrant Acts: On Asian American Cultural Politics* (Durham, NC: Duke University Press, 1996), 30.

6 Richard Alba, *Italian Americans: Into the Twilight of Ethnicity* (Englewood Cliffs, NJ: Prentice Hall, 1985). See Christa Wirth, *Memories of Belonging: Descendants of Italian Migrants to the U.S., 1884–Present* (Leiden: Brill Academic, 2015), for an overview of debates about Italian Americans and assimilation. To track the debates within Italian American studies, see Rudolph Vecoli, "The Search for an Italian American Identity: Continuity and Change," in *Italian Americans: New Perspectives in Italian Immigration and Ethnicity*, ed. Lydia Tomasi (Staten Island, NY: American Italian Historical Association, 1985); Rudolph Vecoli, "Are Italians Just White Folks?," *Italian Americana* 13 (1995): 149–61; Richard Gambino, "Are Italians in the 'Twilight of Ethnicity' or a New Dawn?" in *Industry, Technology, Labor, and Italian American Communities*, ed. Mario Aste et al. (Staten Island, NY: American Italian Historical Association, 1997), 161–74; Patricia Boscia-Mulé, *Authentic Ethnicities: The Interactions of Ideology, Gender Power, and Class in Italian American Experience* (Westport, CT: Praeger, 1999); and Jordan Stanger-Ross, *Staying Italian: Urban Change and Ethnic Life in Postwar Toronto and Philadelphia* (Chicago: University of Chicago Press, 2009). Donna Gabaccia reframes the issue in *Italy's Many Diasporas* (Seattle: University of Washington Press, 2000), conceptualizing Italian Americans not as immigrants but as transnational migrants.

7 Mary Waters, *Ethnic Options: Choosing Identities in America* (Berkeley: University of California Press, 1990).

8 Richard Hollinger, *Postethnic America: Beyond Multiculturalism* (New York: Basic Books, 1995).

9 Waters, *Ethnic Options*, 150.

10 Herbert Gans, "Symbolic Ethnicity: The Future of Ethnic Groups and Cultures in America," *Ethnic and Racial Studies* 2 (1979): 1–20.

11 Simone Cinotto, "All Things Italian: Italian American Consumers and the Commodification of Difference," *Voices in Italian Americana* 21, no. 1 (2010): 23–24; Arjun Appadurai, *Modernity at Large: Cultural Dimensions of Globalization* (Minneapolis: University of Minnesota Press,

1996); Homi Bhabha, *The Location of Culture* (New York: Routledge, 1994); Dick Hebdige, *Subculture: The Meaning of Style* (New York: Routledge, 1981); Werner Sollors, ed., *The Invention of Ethnicity* (New York: Oxford University Press, 1991).

12 Jennifer Guglielmo and Salvatore Salerno, eds., *Are Italians White? How Race Is Made in America* (New York: Routledge, 2003), 4.

13 Neil Leonard, *Jazz and the White Americans: The Acceptance of a New Art Form* (Chicago: University of Chicago Press, 1962); Kathy Ogren, *The Jazz Revolution: Twenties America and the Meaning of Jazz* (New York: Oxford University Press, 1987); McDonald Smith Moore, *Yankee Blues: Musical Culture and American Identity* (Bloomington: Indiana University Press, 1985).

14 Robert Foerster, *The Italian Emigration of Our Time* (New York: Russell and Russell, 1919); Donna Gabaccia, *Italy's Many Diasporas* (London: UCL Press, 2000).

15 Penny Von Eschen, *Race against Empire: Black Americans and Anticolonialism, 1937–1957* (Ithaca, NY: Cornell University Press, 1997); Brenda Gayle Plummer, *Rising Wind: Black Americans and U.S. Foreign Affairs, 1935–1960* (Chapel Hill: University of North Carolina Press, 1996).

16 Benjamin Cawthra, "Under the Volcano: Gordon Parks, the Bergman-Rossellini Romance, and Postwar US-Italian Relations," paper presented at the annual meeting of the American Studies Association, Washington, DC, November 2013.

17 Lee Bernstein, *The Greatest Menace: Organized Crime in Cold War America* (Amherst: University of Massachusetts Press, 2009).

18 Nick Gillespie, "The Census and *The Sopranos*: Adventures in a Post-racial America," *Reason*, May 2001, http://reason.com/archives/2001/05/01/the-cenus-and-the-sopranos, accessed June 4, 2015.

19 Cinotto, "All Things Italian," 25.

20 Christopher Kocela, "Unmade Men: The Sopranos after Whiteness," *Postmodern Culture*, 2005, http://pmc.iath.virginia.edu/text-only/issue.105/15.2kocela.txt, accessed June 5, 2015. The dialogue quotations come from *The Sopranos* (Home Box Office—Time-Warner; David Chase, Creator and Executive Producer), season 3, episode 4, and season 3, episode 5.

21 *The Sopranos*, season 2, episode 6.

22 *The Sopranos*, season 4, episode 7.

23 *The Sopranos*, season 2, episode 2.

24 *The Sopranos*, season 3, episode 2.

25 *The Sopranos*, season 1, episode 10.

26 Kocela, "Unmade Men."

27 *The Sopranos*, season 1, episode 10.

28 As such, *The Sopranos* has generated a large and impressive scholarly literature, including Regina Barreca, ed., *A Sitdown with "The Sopranos": Watching Italian American Culture on T.V.'s Most Talked-About Series*

(New York: Palgrave Macmillan, 2002); Glen Gabbard, *The Psychology of "The Sopranos": Love, Death, Desire, and Betrayal in America's Favorite Gangster Family* (New York: Basic, 2002); David Lavery, ed., *This Thing of Ours: Investigating "The Sopranos"* (New York: Columbia University Press, 2002); Dana Polan, *The Sopranos* (Durham, NC: Duke University Press, 2009); and Maurice Yacowar, *"The Sopranos" on the Couch: Analyzing Television's Greatest Series* (New York: Continuum, 2002).

29 Kym Ragusa, *The Skin between Us: A Memoir of Race, Beauty, and Belonging* (New York: W. W. Norton, 2006), 177.

30 Ibid., 177, 76.

31 Ibid., 108–9.

32 Ibid., 221.

33 Ibid., 136–37.

34 Kevin Quashie, *The Sovereignty of Quiet: Beyond Resistance in Black Culture* (Brunswick, NJ: Rutgers University Press, 2012).

35 Ragusa, *Skin between Us*, 17–19, 30.

36 Ibid., 132–33.

37 Ibid., 144.

38 Elizabeth Alexander, *The Light of the World: A Memoir* (New York: Grand Central, 2015), 9.

39 Michela Wrong, *I Didn't Do It for You: How the World Betrayed a Small African Nation* (New York: Harper Perennial, 2005); Donald Levine, *Greater Ethiopia: The Evolution of a Multiethnic Society* (1974; Chicago: University of Chicago Press, 2000); John Sorenson, *Imagining Ethiopia: Struggles for History and Identity in the Horn of Africa* (New Brunswick, NJ: Rutgers University Press, 1993).

40 Wrong, *I Didn't Do It for You*, 5–6, 9.

41 R. W. Apple Jr., "A Culinary Journey out of Africa into New Haven," *New York Times*, February 24, 1999, http://www.nytimes.com/1999/02/24/dining/a-culinary-journey, accessed June 7, 2015.

42 Robert Farris Thompson, "Remember Ficre," in *Polychromasia: Selected Paintings by Ficre Ghebreyesus* (printed on the occasion of the exhibition, *Ficre Ghebreyesus, Polychromasia*, March 30–April 24, 2013, Artspace, New Haven, CT), 47.

43 Alexander, *Light of the World*, 56.

44 Anne Higonnet, "On Paintings by Ficre Ghebreyesus," in *Polychromasia*, 19.

45 Ficre Ghebreyesus, "Artistic Statement," in *Polychromasia*, 4. After fifteen years at Yale, most recently as the first Frederick Iseman Professor of Poetry and as chair of the African American Studies Department from 2009 to 2013, Elizabeth Alexander in 2015 became the Wun Tsun Tam Mellon Professor in the Humanities at Columbia University and the director of creativity and free expression at the Ford Foundation. Her books include *The Venus Hottentot* (Minneapolis, MN: Graywolf Press, 1990),

Body of Life (Chicago: Tia Chucha Press, 1997), *The Black Interior* (Minneapolis, MN: Graywolf Press, 2003), and *American Sublime* (Minneapolis, MN: Graywolf Press, 2005). In January 2009 Alexander delivered her poem, "Praise Song for the Day," at the inauguration of President Barack Obama.

46 Alexander, *Light of the World*, 55.

47 Elizabeth Alexander, personal e-mail communication with the author, June 8, 2015. Elizabeth's father, Clifford Alexander Jr., a lawyer by training, served as chairman of the Equal Employment Opportunity Commission under President Lyndon Johnson and later as Secretary of the Army under President Jimmy Carter. Her mother, Adele Logan Alexander, is an adjunct professor of history at George Washington University and a former board member of the National Endowment for the Humanities. See "Husband and Wife Team Paved Way for Blacks in Diplomacy," National Public Radio, February 10, 2010, http://www.npr.org/templates /story/story.php?storyId=123565407, accessed June 14, 2015.

48 Anthony Riccio, *The Italian American Experience in New Haven* (Albany: State University of New York Press, 2006); Mandi Isaacs Jackson, *Model City Blues: Urban Space and Organized Resistance in New Haven* (Philadelphia: Temple University Press, 2008); Paul Bass, "New Hope for New Haven, Connecticut," *Nation*, January 25, 2012; Philip Lutz, "Making a Comeback Where Jazz Was Jumping," *New York Times*, September 5, 2008; *Unsung Heroes: The Music of Jazz in New Haven* (Rebecca Abbott, producer and director, 2001).

49 Josef Goodman, "Master of the City: How John DeStefano, Jr. Ruled New Haven," *Politic*, reprinted in *HuffPost Blog*, August 27, 2013, http:// www.huffingtonpost.com/josef-goodman/new-haven-john-destefano_b _3825089.html, accessed June 14, 2015. The minister in question, Boise Kimber, canvassed votes for DeStefano in New Haven's black wards in several elections. The mayor testified on Kimber's behalf when the minister was indicted—he later was convicted—of stealing a parishioner's funeral money. Later DeStefano appointed Kimber chairman of the city's Board of Fire Commissioners. In that capacity Kimber received wide media attention in connection with the 2009 US Supreme Court case *Ricci v. DeStefano*. In that case the court ruled unconstitutional a program in which African American firefighters were advanced into higher-level positions despite scoring lower on a promotion exam than a group of their white and Latino colleagues.

50 Alexander, *Light of the World*, 77–78.

51 Elizabeth Alexander, "Light of the World," in *Polychromasia*, 12.

Index

Corchiani, Chris, 198
"Core 'ngrato" (Caruso), 29, 31, 240
Corkin, Stanley, 123, 127
Corner, The (television series), 130
Cornish, Gene, 55
"Cosa Mangia Oggi" (Lanzillotto), 79, 82
Cosby, Bill, 197
Coss, Bill, 40, 41
Costello, Frank, 46
Cotton Comes to Harlem (film), 127
crack cocaine, 119, 129, 131, 157, 158
Craig Claiborne's Southern Cooking, 112
Crazy in the Kitchen (DeSalvo), 85–87, 103–11,
    114, 213
Crests, 159
crime: anxiety about, 119; black masculinity
    associated with, 129; in Brooklyn, 131;
    gun violence, 120, 131; in Harlem, 158; in
    New Haven, 239; Rockefeller's "tough on
    crime" policies, 120. *See also* gangsters
critical race studies, 14–15, 17, 226, 247
Crooklyn (Lee), 130
crooning, 35, 37, 67, 70
Crosby, Bing, 35–36
Crossing Ocean Parkway (Torgovnick), 134
cross-racialism, 129, 159, 172–73, 202
Crouch, Stanley, 138
Cruising (Friedkin), 119
Cuomo, Mario, 118, 163
Curtis, King, 90

D'Acierno, Pellegrino: author's indebted-
    ness to, 17; on *dagotude*, 14, 167, 175; at
    "Frank Sinatra: The Man, The Music, The
    Legend" conference, 251n3; on Italian
    America as ear-intensive, 256n12; on
    Italian American feeling for scenes and
    spectacles, 30; on Italian Americans as
    hottest of white ethnics, 9, 35; on Nea-
    politan song, 29; on Rat Pack's game of
    improper name, 43; on Sinatra's grandi-
    ose self, 48; on using everyday practices to
    enact work of total art, 22, 237; on wound
    of ethnicity, 43
dagotude: as charismatic ethnicity, 14; of
    Italian American college basketball
    coaches, 173–80, 211; of Izzo, 209; Pitino
    as incarnation of, 203, 213; in stylistic
    innovations in basketball, 195; of Vitale,
    167, 213
Dal Cortivo, Celeste ("Bunny"), 53, *53*
Dal Cortivo, Everesto ("Abby"), 52–53, *53*,
    54, 59, 76
D'Alea, Angelo, 159
Daly, Chuck, 200
D'Amato, Alfonse, 64
D'Amato, Cus, 210
Damone, Vic, 3, 34–35, 158

Danelli, Dino, 55
Dantley, Adrian, 186
Dapper Dan Roundball Classic, 169
Darin, Bobby, 34–35, 158
Davis, Miles, 71, 78, 90, 237
Davis, Ossie, 138, 145, 150
Davis, Sammy, Jr., 10, 49–50
death, 84–87
Dee, Ruby, 145
Deford, Frank, 178, 179, 185, 272n17
DeFranco, Buddy (Boniface), 34
De Laurentiis, Giada, 75
DeLillo, Don, 118
Del Negro, Vinny, 198
Denby, David, 116, 117
De Niro, Robert, 116, 118, 125, 129–30, 141
De Palma, Brian, 118, 125, 171
Departed, The (Scorsese), 216
DeSalvo, Louise: "Color: White/Complexion:
    Dark," 16; *Crazy in the Kitchen*, 85–87,
    103–11, 114, 213; *The Milk of Almonds*,
    106, 107–8
De Stefano, George, 18, 139–40, 159
DeStefano, John, Jr., 239, 278n49
Diamond, Neil, 56
Dickerson, Ernest, 130, 155
DiMaggio, Joe, 115, 144, 163, 210
DiMucci, Dion, 10, 22, 158, 159
Dinerstein, Joel, 261n54
Dinkins, David, 135
Dion and the Belmonts, 22, 158, 159
disco movement, 45, 54, 133, 160
diversity, 216
Dobrow, Marty, 206
Dog Day Afternoon (Lumet), 119
Domino, Fats, 17, 257n18
Donaldson, Lou, 90
Donnie Brasco (film), 135
doo-wop: Afro-Italian intersection in, 30;
    golden age of, 159–60; lyricism and rhyth-
    mic groove in, 32; as neighborhood, 160;
    Valli influenced by, 54; "Who put the wop
    in doo-wop?," 10
Dorsey, Lee, 257n18
Dorsey, Tommy, 36, 262n80
"Do the Funky Chicken" (Thomas), 91
Do the Right Thing (Lee), 137–49; Aiello in,
    139, 141, *147*, 149; Denby on, 116, 117; doo-
    wop culture and, 160; economic colonial-
    ism in, 144; Esposito in, 5, 144–45, 146,
    148–49, 269n38; historical trajectories
    captured in, 14, 118; incident that it was
    based on, 115–16; as "Italian American"
    film, 13; Italian American masculinity in,
    162; Italian Americans on, 139–40; Klein
    on, 145, 147; Lee-Aiello tension reported,
    141; maternal paternalism in, 213; pivotal
    showdown in, 146, 148–49; underclass in,